Withdrawn

THE TRUE CRIME FILES OF SIR ARTHUR CONAN DOYLE

THE TRUE CRIME FILES OF SIR ARTHUR CONAN DOYLE

By Sir Arthur Conan Doyle

Rediscovered by
Stephen Hines

With an Introduction by Edgar Award–winning author
Steven Womack

BERKLEY PRIME CRIME, NEW YORK

THE TRUE CRIME FILES OF SIR ARTHUR CONAN DOYLE

A Berkley Prime Crime Book
Published by The Berkley Publishing Group,
a division of Penguin Putnam Inc.,
375 Hudson Street, New York, New York 10014

Visit our website at
www.penguinputnam.com

First edition: October 2001

Library of Congress Cataloging-in-Publication Data

Doyle, Arthur Conan, Sir, 1859–1930.
The true crime files of Sir Arthur Conan Doyle / by Sir Arthur Conan Doyle ; rediscovered by
Stephen Hines ; with an introduction by Steven Womack.—1st ed.
p. cm.
Includes bibliographical references (p.).
Contents: The case of George Ernest Thompson Edalji — The case of Oscar Slater.
ISBN 0-425-17952-4 (alk. paper)
1. Crime—Great Britain—History—Case studies. 2. Doyle, Arthur Conan, Sir, 1859–1930. Case of
Oscar Slater. I. Hines, Stephen. II. Doyle, Arthur Conan, Sir, 1859–1930. Case of Oscar Slater. III.
Title.

HV6943 .D69 2001
364.941—dc21
2001037517

Printed in the United States of America

10 9 8 7 6 5 4 3 2 1

My thanks to the ones I love—Gwen, my wife, and daughters Megan, Laura, and Amy. And special thanks to researcher James P. Derriman.

—S.H.

My thanks to Stephen Hines for offering me the chance to get involved with such an exciting literary project, to Michael Sims for his invaluable help in researching the life of Conan Doyle, and to my wife, Alana, and daughter, Isabel, for their love and support.

—S.W.

And we both wish to thank Gail Fortune, our superb editor at Berkley Books, and Nancy Yost of the Lowenstein Agency, who brought this all together.

CONTENTS

Introduction by Steven Womack   1

PART ONE
The Case of George Ernest Thompson Edalji

CHAPTER ONE:
Sir Arthur Conan Doyle to the Rescue   29

CHAPTER TWO:
The Readers Reply: The Public Fray Begins   68

CHAPTER THREE:
Mr. A. H. Henderson-Livesey Stirs the Waters: 87
The Public Fray Escalates

CHAPTER FOUR:
Public Interest Continues to Grow: 132
The *Daily Telegraph* Publishes a Report on the
Trial as the Public Debate Rages On

CHAPTER FIVE:
The Home Office Responds; Sir Arthur Fires Back;   176
the Controversy Continues; Edalji Is Pardoned
(but With a Catch)

Contents

CHAPTER SIX:
Sir Arthur Tackles the Problem of the   190
Anonymous Letters

POSTSCRIPT:
Some Mysteries Are Never Solved   218

PART TWO
The Case of Oscar Slater

CHAPTER ONE:
"A Disreputable, Rolling-Stone of a Man"   223

CHAPTER TWO:
A Desperate Plea Gets Mixed Results   263

POSTSCRIPT:
Slater Finally Gets His Say   277

Selected Bibliography   289

The True Crime Files of Sir Arthur Conan Doyle

If you walk up to any ten random, reasonably well-read people on the street and speak the words "Arthur Conan Doyle," you'll likely get one of two reactions: "Oh, yes, the man who created Sherlock Holmes," or "Didn't he go a bit dotty in his old age—all that stuff about fairies and ghosts?"

Both these comments would be equally true and yet, curiously, equally misleading. Sir Arthur Conan Doyle did create Sherlock Holmes, thereby essentially inventing the modern detective story and giving birth to a literary phenomenon that can best be described as an industry. And it is widely accepted that Conan Doyle's obsession with spiritualism through the latter part of his adult life defied both logic and the deductive reasoning that his most well-known creation employed so well.

Yet to assume that these two statements are in any way a complete portrait of one of the most intriguing literary minds in human history makes about as much sense as describing Abraham Lincoln as that poor president who got shot in the head.

Sir Arthur Conan Doyle was, in fact, one of the most fascinating and complex people of his age. He was an adventurer, a scientist and physician, a crusader for an eclectic and often unpopular set of causes, a deeply spiritual lapsed Catholic, a loyal and faithful husband who waited until after his wife's death to marry the woman he really loved, and an incredibly versatile writer not only of detective fiction but also of science fiction and fantasy, horror, historical fiction, political tomes, and polemics. He was haunted, troubled, and frustrated by the very thing that made him rich and famous. In many ways he was a man of contradictions, although in all likelihood he would have denied this vehemently.

Even today, over seven decades after his passing out of this world and into a world he believed was every bit as real as this one, Conan Doyle continues to intrigue us, so much so that since 1997, two major, superb accounts of his life have been published (Martin Booth's *The Doctor and the Detective: A Biography of Arthur Conan Doyle* and Daniel Stashower's Edgar Award–winning *Teller of Tales: The Life of Arthur Conan Doyle*).

Conan Doyle had a thirst for life and for experience. He was restless and curious. Once he believed something, he committed himself, his energies, his intellect, and his resources to that belief. He was a man who risked his reputation, his fortune, and even his honor standing up for causes in which he believed. And in doing so, he lived a life that was infinitely more fascinating and full than any page he ever wrote.

"I have had a life which, for variety and romance, could, I think, hardly be exceeded," Doyle once wrote, in a masterful piece of understatement.

So who was this complex and driven man?

*

Arthur Ignatius Conan Doyle was the grandson of the man who many believe invented the modern political cartoon, John Doyle. Trained at the Dublin Society Drawing School, John Doyle eventually moved to London, where he established both an artistic and social reputation. He moved among the very elite of London society, including Queen Victoria and the Prince of Wales. He also traveled in the same circles as Disraeli, Thackeray, Sir Walter Scott, and Charles Dickens. What his contemporaries did not know—and the world was not to know for over thirty years—was that John Doyle had a secret identity: "HB," arguably the most famous political caricaturist of his day. "HB" skewered his subjects (perhaps *targets* would be a better word) with a subtle and dry wit. Other political cartoonists of the day beat their subjects to death with a bludgeon; John Doyle preferred the rapier.

Doyle and his wife, Mariana, had seven children: two girls and five boys. Of the boys, only four survived to adulthood. Of John Doyle's four adult sons, three achieved considerable success in the art world. The fourth, Charles Altamont, did not. Charles had a difficult and unsuccessful life; he was certainly an alcoholic and probably suffered from what contemporary psychiatrists would label bipolar disorder. At the age of nineteen, Charles moved to Edinburgh to seek his fortune. He managed to obtain a post—probably with his father's help—as an assistant surveyor in Scotland's Board of Works. However, his emotional problems combined with his alcoholism ultimately kept him from advancing in his career.

He did, however, father Arthur Ignatius.

At the age of twenty-two, Charles Doyle married eighteen-year-old Mary Foley, a bright, enthusiastic young girl. It was by most accounts a marriage founded on the principal of opposites attracting. Charles and Mary were to have nine children, seven of whom survived into adulthood. Arthur Ignatius was the firstborn son, and he came into a family that was already troubled and in dire financial straits. The family moved often, usually to cheaper lodgings each time, as little by little, Charles Doyle began to lose his lifelong battle with the bottle and his own demons. By the time young Arthur was ten, the family had moved at least seven times. On at least one occasion, Mary sent the boy to stay with relatives to get him away from the family difficulties.

As Charles spiraled ever deeper into melancholia and alcoholism, young Arthur grew closer and closer to his mother. She taught him to read at an early age and guided his early education. Conan Doyle became steeped in Arthurian legend and lore, myth and story. Mary was a compulsive reader—perhaps to escape her difficult marriage and genteel poverty—and she inculcated the habit into her son at a very early age.

Throughout Conan Doyle's life, his attachment to his mother was one of the strongest relationships in his life. As he grew older, she became more than a parent to him; she became his best friend and confidante. He called her "the Ma'am," and whenever apart from her, wrote to her almost constantly.

At the age of nine, young Arthur was to experience his first separation from the Ma'am. His wealthy uncles offered to foot the bill for boarding school; the catch was that the boarding school they had in mind was run by the Jesuits. Arthur boarded a train by himself in Edinburgh—crying most of the way—and left home. For the next seven years, he would see his family only during summer holidays.

For two years, Arthur attended Hodder, the Jesuit preparatory school for Stonyhurst College near Whalley in Lancashire. After that, he graduated to Stonyhurst and spent five years there. While there is some indication that Conan Doyle's first two years at Hodder were less austere than his later time at Stonyhurst, there can be no doubt that life with the Jesuits was harsh at best and downright cruel at its worst.

The dorm rooms were cold and drafty. The food was lousy, and there was damn little of it. Corporal punishment was still widely practiced and accepted; the most common form had the miscreant being beaten across the palm with a thick slab of India rubber about the size of a boot sole. Conan Doyle was to write later that "corporal punishment was severe, and I can speak with feeling as I think few, if any, boys of my time endured more of it."

While the Jesuits attempted to beat an education into Conan Doyle, they never quite succeeded in beating the spirit out of him. He rebelled against the harsh discipline and the petty rules. He smoked, he sneaked extra food into the dorms, he was stubborn and untidy. As he grew more and more unpopular with the Stonyhurst faculty, he—not surprisingly—grew more and more popular with the students. In a prescient demonstration of his later work and talent, he loved to tell stories. He regaled his fellow students with tales of danger and adventure, often taking the story all the way up to the climax, then forcing a bribe out of his audience to reveal the ending.

He devoted most of his energies to sport, and it was here that he began to excel. All his life, Conan Doyle was to believe in the benefits of physical exercise and sport. He grew into a stout, robust young man of great energy and physical courage.

Stonyhurst, however, had a much greater influence on Arthur Conan Doyle, one that would ultimately become a much larger part of his makeup. It was at Stonyhurst that Conan Doyle began to doubt his faith.

Conan Doyle was descended from a long line of devout Catholics who had migrated all over England and Ireland in an attempt to escape religious persecution. At Stonyhurst, though, young Arthur began to view the tenets of the Catholic faith with skepticism. He first voiced doubt over the doctrine of transubstantiation—the literal changing of bread and wine, when consecrated in the Eucharist, into the body and blood of Christ. As his questions and doubts grew, Conan Doyle began to turn more and more toward science as a belief system.

"Never will I accept anything which cannot be proved to me," he said. "The evils of religion have all come from accepting things which cannot be proved."

Ultimately, he would reject religion altogether. However, his rejection of Christianity left him with an empty place in his soul, a place that he would in later life fill with a committed, passionate, even blind belief in spiritualism.

Conan Doyle was sixteen when he graduated from Stonyhurst. The Jesuits had educated him, but they had also instilled in him a sense of personal rebellion, spiritual emptiness, and extreme discipline and drive. These qualities, for better or worse, defined him as a man and as a writer. His sense of intellectual order and discipline, in particular, would serve him well throughout his life.

*

Still too young for university, Conan Doyle chose to spend a year at Feldkirch, a larger Jesuit school in the Austrian Alps. Feldkirch was a much more relaxed school than Stonyhurst, and Conan Doyle enjoyed his time there. He polished his already proficient German, so much so that the Ma'am—apparently concerned that young Arthur might be becoming just a bit too Germanic—asked him to write her in French. He skated and tobogganed, played football, and joined the school band. He played the bombardon, an enormous brass-valved tuba, mainly because he was one of the only students who could lift the massive instrument and get wind through it. It was an enjoyable time for young Arthur, and it accomplished two important objectives: It got him away from home and allowed him to recover from his years at Stony-hurst.

Almost by accident, Conan Doyle's year at Feldkirch proved a pivotal one in the young man's development as a writer as well; it introduced him to Edgar Allan Poe.

Conan Doyle connected with Poe immediately. He first read "The Gold Bug," followed by "The Murders in the Rue Morgue." He was astonished by Poe's inventiveness, and he identified with Poe's obsession with the dark side, the macabre. And he probably felt a personal kinship with Poe as well. Both had experienced difficult early childhoods, had been raised without fathers, and retreated into a rich and complex fantasy life as solace.

Conan Doyle's year at Feldkirch was his first taste of travel as well, and it gave him a sense of restlessness and adventure that would only grow larger in the years to come.

*

One of the myths that has surrounded Conan Doyle's life is that he was a mediocre student at medical school, and afterward, a mediocre doctor. The truth is considerably more complicated than that. While it's true that Conan Doyle's marks at the University of Edinburgh weren't stellar, it's equally true that for most students of Conan Doyle's background and circumstances, simply surviving the rigors of medical school was an accomplishment.

For one thing, the University of Edinburgh was then and still is today one of the finest and most demanding medical schools in the world. For another, university life was considerably different in 1876 than it is today. The modern financial aid system for university education didn't exist then, resulting in Conan Doyle's never-ending scramble for money. There seems to have been little of the social and academic support systems that mark most universities today. As always, though, the young Conan Doyle devoted considerable energy to sports. He played rugby, cricket, and boxed. In every sport he attempted, he seemed a natural.

Still, he found the curriculum demanding and tedious. Teaching was largely done in huge lecture classes, and students paid their teacher directly to attend lectures. Studies were a grind as well, primarily theoretical with little hands-on work. Because of Conan Doyle's difficult financial circumstances, he often took on extra course work in an attempt to get through school as quickly as possible. Conan Doyle would not remember his university years with much fondness. Years later, in a novel entitled *The Firm of Girdlestone*, he would describe the university as "a great unsympathetic machine."

However, there was one event in his university career that would change Conan Doyle's life forever: He met Professor Joseph Bell.

Much has been written of Conan Doyle's encounter with Bell, to the extent that the episode has taken on mythical status. Although Bell was modest to the point of self-effacement, he was a figure of great historical importance in the field of medicine. He was an outstanding teacher, scientist, and doctor, and his methods of diagnosis had a profound impact on Conan Doyle.

Bell demonstrated to his students a technique whereby from close observation of specific characteristics, symptoms, and the appearance of his patients, he could infer or deduce a staggering amount of information about the subject. In 1878, Bell appointed Conan Doyle the clerk for his clinic, and Arthur had the opportunity to study Bell's methods close up. In his autobiography, Conan Doyle described what became a famous case of a patient who gave no information to Bell before meeting him. Simply by examining the patient, Bell deduced that he was a recently discharged army veteran, a member of the Highland regiment, a noncommissioned officer who had been stationed in Barbados, and that he was suffering from elephantiasis.

Conan Doyle was to learn his lessons well from Professor Bell, and years later would put them to use not in the arena of medicine but in the fiction that would make him a legend.

*

Conan Doyle struggled through medical school, juggling schoolwork and outside jobs in a sometimes desperate attempt to make ends meet. Between his workload, his financial straits, and his ever-deteriorating family situation, his life was in turmoil. In 1880, though, he got the chance to get away for a few months on what he would later consider the first real adventure of his life.

A fellow student, Claude Currie, accepted a job as ship's doctor aboard an arctic whaling ship. At the last minute, he reversed his decision and offered the job to Arthur. The fact that neither of them had actually graduated from medical school was irrelevant; most ship's doctors of the era were barely qualified at best.

Conan Doyle jumped at the chance, despite the meager pay (two pounds a month plus a cut of the take) and the danger. In late February 1880, Conan Doyle shipped out on the *Hope*, a steam-powered whaler. From the beginning, the robust and hearty young Conan Doyle fit right in with the crew. The first day out, he was challenged to a boxing match by the ship's steward. Conan Doyle blacked his eye, and the two men began a friendship that would last for years.

The work, however, was hard and dangerous. The *Hope* sailed north, beginning the season by hunting seals. Conan Doyle, bored and always on the lookout for adventure, joined the hunters in the brutal, bloody work of clubbing seals to death. On one occasion, Conan Doyle was nearly killed when he slipped off an ice floe into the frigid sea and barely managed to haul himself back up by grabbing the flipper of a dead seal. Several other times, he fell into water so cold survival time is measured in minutes.

Then the ship headed north to hunt whales. Whaling is bloody, violent, hard work, but as always, Conan Doyle joined in with his shipmates. Never lacking physical courage, Conan Doyle began a lifelong practice of putting himself in harm's way.

The seven months he spent on board the *Hope* gave him his first real taste of danger and adventure. It also gave him enough money to ease his financial worries, at least for a while. Most of it he gave to the Ma'am, which meant for the first time he was helping support his family.

Conan Doyle passed his twenty-first birthday on the *Hope*, and he had turned into a rugged, strong, fully grown man. He was held in such high regard by his captain and shipmates that he was offered a slot on the next voyage as a harpooner, a job that would have paid some serious money for those times. Conan Doyle, though, decided to finish his studies at Edinburgh. In August 1881, he received his bachelor of medicine and master of surgery qualifications. He was a year late in graduating, thanks to his adventure on the *Hope*, and he graduated without distinction. Given his workload, his compressed studies, and the drain on his energies presented by all aspects of his family circumstance, this is hardly surprising.

Still, he finished, and now Dr. Arthur Conan Doyle could go out into the world.

*

As any doctor living and working today in our era of managed care and health care "reform" will confess, being a doctor is not all it's cracked up to be. The same was true, perhaps even more so, in Conan Doyle's day. Doctors were then, as now, expected to present a certain image. They were expected to maintain a certain lifestyle. Both the image and the lifestyle can best be described in one word: expensive.

With no patron backing him, and with his family's still-declining circumstances, there was little help available to Conan Doyle in establishing a practice. Conan Doyle was young and confident, however. As luck would have it, he got an offer to become ship's doctor aboard the *Mayumba*, a steamer that ran a regular route from Liverpool down the west coast of Africa and back. The job paid twelve pounds a month, a better salary than Conan Doyle had ever seen before.

Almost immediately, though, Conan Doyle's hopes of exotic adventure were dashed. To begin with, the tired, old *Mayumba* was little more than a tramp steamer. His cabin flooded as the ship ran into rough seas, and for a solid week Conan Doyle was soaked to the bone as he treated seasick passengers while quite ill himself. Once far enough south, the seas calmed, but as they approached tropical Africa, the ship's company suffered from both malaria and blackwater fever. Conan Doyle became ill with what was probably malaria and was delirious for several days.

Still, there was some adventure. Conan Doyle was exposed to people, places, and cultures the likes of which he'd never seen. Already a budding photographer, he greatly improved his skills with a camera and in the lab. He wrote about his travels for the *British Journal of Photography*. He swam in both shark- and crocodile-infested waters, several times taking chances that can best be described as imprudent.

The young Conan Doyle also faced a somewhat more insidious danger. The climate and conditions in Africa were, by European standards, dismal, and many whites—both travelers and those who lived in Africa—medicated their pain with liberal doses of alcohol. Conan Doyle, with his robust constitution and hail-fellow-well-met personality, had never been concerned about his drinking before.

In Africa, though, Conan Doyle found himself drinking heavily, and it scared him. He swore off alcohol for the remainder of the trip, and for the rest of his life, he was careful. No doubt the sight of so many of his countrymen drowning their sorrows reminded him of his own father. In any case, as he was to write later, ". . . my reason told me the unbounded cocktails of West Africa were a danger, and with an effort I cut them out."

*

Conan Doyle realized after his experience on the *Mayumba* that shipboard life was not for him. He returned home and began a struggle to establish his medical practice that would go on for years. While still an undergraduate, he had published his first short story, entitled "The Mystery of Sasassa Valley" in *Chamber's Journal*, a weekly magazine in Edinburgh. He soon began to see writing as a way to supplement his meager income as a young, unestablished doctor. After several false starts, he moved to Portsmouth, where he slowly yet surely began to build a career. He continued writing and joined the Portsmouth Literary and Scientific Society. He became involved in the literary community and began what for him was the long process of becoming a confident public speaker.

In 1885, Conan Doyle was asked to provide a second opinion on a patient named Jack Hawkins, who was suffering from a severe case of cerebral meningitis. Conan Doyle actually took the patient into his own house in an attempt to save him, but it was too late. Jack died within a few days. But in the course of taking care of him, Conan Doyle met Jack's twenty-seven-year-old sister, Louise. A few months later, they were married.

Louise would never be described as a great beauty, and the marriage of Arthur and Louise would, to put it kindly, never be earmarked by great passion. But Louise was pleasant, sweet tempered, and supportive, with just the kind of personality to be a successful doctor's wife. She was quiet, even submissive, as over the years Conan Doyle would pack up the family and move with little notice. Louise always obediently tagged along. The Ma'am approved of her. Arthur called her "Touie," and of her he said, "No man could have had a more gentle or amiable life's companion."

Helped by the annual income of £100 from her late father's estate, Touie and Arthur settled into a respectable, middle-class life. Marriage suited Conan Doyle well. For once, the wolves were away from the door. His practice improved, his professional relationships grew, and his writing output increased.

"After my marriage," he would write years later, "my brain seems to have quickened and both my imagination and my range of expression were greatly improved."

Still only twenty-six-years old, Conan Doyle also began having some commercial success as a writer. He wrote quickly, scribbling his stories in longhand between patients and at night. One of the myths surrounding Conan Doyle's early days as a writer is that he wrote during the day because he had no patients; the truth is quite the opposite. As Conan Doyle the doctor became more and more busy, Conan Doyle the writer got more and more prolific. He wrote thrillers and adventure stories, fantasy and horror. Not every story sold, and most sold for only a few guineas each, but Conan Doyle was seeing his work in print with some regularity, and the experience drove him on to write even more.

Martin Booth, in his *The Doctor and the Detective: A Biography of Sir Arthur Conan Doyle*, maintains that Conan Doyle's early work is so fine that he deserves a place in literary history outside the Sherlock Holmes stories: "It may be argued, although Conan Doyle himself insistently refuted it, that he was the father of the modern short story, for he approached the genre with a taut control and disciplined structure that have been the basis for short fiction ever since."

Unfortunately for Conan Doyle, though, it was common practice in nineteenth-century magazine publishing to not include the author's name with the publication of the short story. Conan Doyle knew he had to sell a novel with his name on the cover in order to finally break out as a writer. He'd written a novel early on, *The Narrative of John Smith*, but it had never sold, and the manuscript was lost. In 1884, Conan Doyle began *The Firm of Girdlestone*, which actually turned out to be a pretty good early novel. And in keeping with most novelists' early efforts, the book was rejected unanimously.

Conan Doyle began another manuscript, this one an almost knee-jerk reaction to the bad stories about crime and detection that he was reading. His main complaints with contemporary mysteries were that the plots were nonsensical or illogical and that the protagonist solved the mystery at the end by pulling a clue or a revelation more or less "out of his hat" that had been hidden from the reader. In modern crime-writing terms, this is what's known as cheating the reader. Then, as now, it tended to rile them a great deal.

So Conan Doyle decided to write a story in which everything is laid out before the reader. The reader will see and hear everything the detective protagonist does. Through wit and observation, the detective will observe things that are there but the reader misses. In other words, Conan Doyle had not only grasped the dramatic concept of setups and payoffs, he had used them to redefine an entire genre.

The result, which Conan Doyle completed in only three weeks in March of 1886, was *A Study in Scarlet*.

The rest, as the saying goes, is history.

*

A Study in Scarlet was rejected nearly as unanimously as much of Conan Doyle's other early work. Finally, the editor of the publishing firm of Ward, Lock & Co., Professor G. T. Bettany, at the insistence of his wife, offered twenty-five pounds for the entire copyright to the novella. Conan Doyle asked for royalties and was refused. Ultimately, he took the deal and never received a penny more for the story for the rest of his life.

It was a rare case, from then on, of Conan Doyle being underpaid. In a very short time, Arthur Ignatius Conan Doyle was to become the richest and most famous writer of his era. At a time in history when a middle-class British professional might make £150 a year, Conan Doyle earned £100 per *thousand words*. The American magazine *Collier's Weekly* would eventually offer $25,000 for six Sherlock Holmes short stories, roughly a decade's income or more for most Americans of the time. To describe it in today's terms, Conan Doyle was the Stephen King of his time, and Sherlock Holmes was the Harry Potter.

Conan Doyle also brought the business of writing into the modern era. He was the first author in history to have a representative, A. P. Watt, the man who coined the term "literary agent." With Sherlock Holmes, Conan Doyle invented the series character. Conan Doyle, always restless and inventive, pioneered the concept of moving a fictional character from one medium to another. Sherlock Holmes lived in the short story, the novella, and the novel, as well as the stage play, the radio play, film, and today, television.

Arthur Conan Doyle was also the first modern celebrity author. He dabbled in politics, running for Parliament twice and losing both times. He engaged in public debates, even battles, over political and literary issues. He became a media celebrity, jousting with George Bernard Shaw over the causes of the *Titanic* disaster and Harry Houdini over the existence of the spirit world. He moved in the most elite circles of his time, counting everyone from Winston Churchill to Oscar Wilde as friends. He went to war as a medical officer, volunteering during the Boer War and seeing firsthand the horrors of combat. He was a British patriot who risked his own neck in service to his country when he was far too rich, famous, and old for anyone to have expected such behavior. He was a war correspondent during World War I and wrote a huge, six-volume account of the war that survives even today as an important historical document. Throughout his life, almost up until his death at the age of seventy-one on July 7, 1930, he remained an active and robust sportsman. And while Arthur Conan Doyle did not—as is often said—invent snow skiing, he was an early and enthusiastic proponent of the sport. In fact, he was one of the first skiers ever to climb and ski down an Alpine mountain.

And when he believed something, he went all out for it. When he saw what he perceived to be injustice, then the rest of the world be damned, he was going to fight it. He had quite a temper and wasn't afraid to display it.

As two men—George Edalji and Oscar Slater—would learn, when Arthur Conan Doyle was on your side, the odds could suddenly and drastically change.

*

The two volumes contained herein—"The Case of Mr. George Edalji: Special Investigation" and "The Case of Oscar Slater"—both stand as a testament to Conan Doyle's willingness to enter the fray whenever he felt wrongs had been committed. They also stand as evidence of Conan Doyle's keen mind and powers of observation. He had an exceptional memory and could process and draw connections between apparently random pieces of information. In short, one reason Arthur Conan Doyle was able to create a detective like Sherlock Holmes was because he was a fine detective himself.

The two cases, though, are entirely different. Each took place at a different time in Conan Doyle's life, and each had a different impact on him personally.

The Edalji case occurred first, and there are many who speculate that one of the reasons Conan Doyle became so passionate about helping Edalji was because it allowed him to stop grieving over the death of Louise. The truth, however, is considerably more complicated than that.

As mentioned earlier, Arthur and Louise were happily married, but their marriage was staid and comfortable. Louise obediently followed him throughout his demanding travels that often took them through harsh climates and on physically demanding—even dangerous—treks. Louise, being made of less sterner stuff, began to weaken, and in 1893 was diagnosed with a particularly virulent form of TB. As a medical man, Conan Doyle knew what this meant; it was a death sentence. Louise was expected to live only a few months.

A guilt-ridden Conan Doyle threw himself passionately into caring for her. His efforts were successful; Louise lived thirteen more years. But she was never completely well, and the disease eventually took a toll on both of them and on their marriage.

Unlike our contemporary obsession with airing the most intimate details of our lives in public, the subject of sex during the Victorian era was rarely discussed, even among and between married people. But it was generally accepted medical reasoning that marital relations were simply too much exertion for sick people, especially women. So the robust and manly Arthur Conan Doyle spent the years of his wife's illness as a celibate. Perhaps more than anything else, Conan Doyle was an English gentlemen, and the thought of straying or seeking release elsewhere simply wasn't considered.

In time, this began to wear on him. As one might expect, he became irritable and sullen. His children and family tiptoed around him. His already restless nature grew even more so, and whenever he perceived Louise as being at least stable for the time being, he took any excuse available to head out on another trip.

Then, on March 15, 1897 (an anniversary he would celebrate for the rest of his life), lightning struck thirty-seven-year-old Conan Doyle: He met Jean Leckie.

Jean was beautiful, headstrong, and thirteen years his junior. The two fell in love immediately. They were to become the center of each other's lives for the rest of their days. Again, however, Conan Doyle was an English gentlemen; he informed Jean that he was not going to leave or divorce Louise. He would take care of his wife for as long as she lived. Furthermore, while he made no bones about his love for Jean—even confessing to the Ma'am and ultimately receiving her approval—he wasn't going to be unfaithful to Louise. Even among writers who were English gentlemen, this was astonishing behavior. (H. G. Wells and Charles Dickens, two other acclaimed English gentlemen of letters, had both mistresses and illegitimate children.)

One could surmise that it was a measure of her affection and devotion to Arthur that Jean accepted this. In any case, the two carried on a public relationship that was acknowledged by all concerned as both loving and physically, at least, platonic. If the by now largely bedridden Louise knew or objected to this arrangement, she gave no notice of it. On her deathbed, she was to give her blessing to Arthur remarrying.

In the spring of 1906, Louise's health took a turn for the worse. On July 4, she died at the age of forty-nine.

Conan Doyle's reaction to his wife's death was surprising, given the circumstances: he grew seriously depressed. Perhaps it was guilt at his own relief at her passing. Perhaps he still shouldered some of the responsibility for her becoming ill in the first place. Maybe he just missed her. In any case, his health and his work began to suffer. For months, his family and friends watched helplessly as the stalwart, vigorous Arthur Conan Doyle seemed to deteriorate before their eyes. They must have wondered what it would take to bring him out of it.

Their questions were soon answered: what it took was George Edalji.

*

Conan Doyle had been peppered with requests for help about true crimes for years. The cases often involved missing persons, and occasionally Conan Doyle would put forth a little effort to make a few suggestions. He had even begun to take an interest in real-life crime as a subject but had yet to get personally involved in anything of note.

That changed in late 1906 when Conan Doyle, still in a depressed funk over the death of Louise, read a news article about George Edalji headlined "Edalji Protests His Innocence." As Conan Doyle read the article, his interest was piqued by what was surely one of the weirdest stories he'd ever read.

George Edalji was a thirty-year-old solicitor who not only still lived at home but actually slept in the same bedroom with his father, the Reverend Shapurji Edalji. He was shy, anxious, and physically quite frail; not exactly your hardened criminal type. He was homely, and his eyesight was terrible; he wore thick glasses that gave him an even less appealing physical appearance. Although he'd excelled in law school and was successful in his profession, he had few friends.

Of course, for Edalji, making friends in an English village would have been difficult under the best of circumstances: Edalji's father was a Parsee convert to Anglicanism. Parsees—Indian Zoroastrians descended from the

Persian Zoroastrians who fled to India in the seventh and eighth centuries to escape Muslim persecution—were an oddity in the first place. To have a Parsee convert as the local vicar was even more bizarre. To make matters worse, the Reverend Edalji had married an Englishwoman and had three children by her, one of whom was George.

Even in this allegedly more enlightened age of tolerance toward racial intermarriage, the Edaljis would no doubt be targets of considerable abuse. In the English town of Great Wyrley, near the city of Birmingham, their lives were made miserable. They were taunted on the streets—the locals freely using the word "nigger" in reference to them—and were the subject of threatening and abusive anonymous letters, cruel practical jokes, and other forms of what is often referred to in the American South as "just plain meanness."

The anonymous threatening letters were the most frightening of all. The Edaljis complained to the local police, but they took little note. With absolutely nothing whatsoever upon which to base his accusations, Captain George Anson, the chief constable in Great Wryley, decided that young George—then sixteen—had written them.

The Reverend Edalji protested mightily, but the captain's mind was made up, despite the fact that George was an honor student of apparently impeccable character and that there was no evidence to tie him to the letters. Eventually, for a while, the letters stopped.

Now the story gets really strange: In 1903, there occurred an outbreak of animal maiming. Sheep, cows, and horses were found horribly mutilated, disemboweled, and left to die. Obviously, a very sick hand was at work. Furthermore, the threatening and abusive letters started up again, one warning police that while farm animals were the target today, innocent young girls were next.

One August evening, George, now grown and a successful solicitor, came home from work late and decided to take a stroll before dinner was ready. He was gone for a short while, went home, ate, went to bed and, as was their custom, he and his father locked the bedroom door tightly and neither emerged until the next morning.

That night, in a field less than a mile from his home, someone disemboweled a small pony and left it to die. The police arrested George and charged him with the crime.

Ridiculous though it seems, and as Conan Doyle so eloquently pointed out, Edalji was prosecuted. A calligraphy "expert" testified it was George's handwriting that wrote the letters. This same expert's testimony had already sent one innocent man to prison, thus qualifying him to testify in the Edalji case as a reliable specialist.

Hopelessly framed by the police, poor George was found guilty and sentenced to seven years hard labor. He was shipped off to prison where he was saved from breaking rocks in a quarry solely by his terrible eyesight.

Curiously, the animal attacks continued. The Great Wyrley police blamed them on other members of George's cult. One is tempted to ask, "What cult?" since there had never been any evidence presented of such an organization. This, however, seemed an irrelevant detail to the constables.

This was not the end of the story. Despite the racism of the Great Wyrley locals and the frame-up by the police, there was an immense public outcry at this clear injustice. Young Edalji may have been a weird-looking little foreigner of mixed parentage, but he was a *lawyer*, by God, and you just can't do that to a man of the law. Judge R. D. Yelverton led the charge and got up a petition in support of Edalji with over 10,000 signatures, a large portion of which came from solicitors and barristers.

It took three years, but George's supporters finally won. He was released from prison in October 1906, although no reason was given for his release. He was not pardoned, and there was no official overturning of the verdict. He'd lost his reputation and his livelihood and suffered terribly, all without even an apology, let alone compensation.

George went on a public campaign to clear his name, and this is where Conan Doyle came in. After several months of investigation, Conan Doyle decided a horrible miscarriage of justice had occurred. He published a series of in-depth articles in the *Daily Telegraph*, without copyright so that they could be reprinted all over the world freely. Then he began a letter-writing campaign that kept the story before the public. He later republished the articles as a short, 18,000-word book.

Conan Doyle's handling of this situation was brilliant, and "The Case of Mr. George Edalji: Special Investigation" contains some of the most pointed and acerbic writing of Conan Doyle's career. In describing the police seizure of Reverend Edalji's set of razors as evidence, Conan Doyle wrote: "Some were said to be wet—a not uncommon condition for razors in the morning."

Later, Doyle questioned the findings of a doctor who drew some conclusions about hair found on Edalji's coat when the police had not been very attentive to the rules regarding the chain of evidence.

"With all desire to be charitable," he wrote, "the incident leaves a most unpleasant impression on the mind."

Conan Doyle is clearly accusing the police of tampering with evidence here. This is strong stuff. And when an investigation into the verdict was essentially turned back over to the very police who'd framed Edalji in the first place, Conan Doyle got really hot.

"It would be a vicious circle if a police prosecution, when doubted, is referred back again to the police for report. I cannot imagine," he maintained, "anything more absurd and unjust in an Oriental despotism than this."

After establishing to his own satisfaction that Edalji was innocent, Conan Doyle then went on a search for the real perpetrator. He soon encountered two brothers, Royden and Wallace Sharp. These two were apparently bad news, especially Royden, who'd been a classmate of Edalji's before being kicked out of school. Royden had a reputation for lying, forgery, and was quick with a knife. He'd been a butcher's apprentice before going to sea on a cattle boat, a trip that just happened to coincide with a mysterious cessation of the letter-writing campaign. The letters and the maimings began after Royden's return to Great Wyrley. Conan Doyle eventually wrote a pamphlet, *The Case Against Royden Sharp*, but the local police ignored his evidence and warned him he'd be prosecuted for libel if he published the piece. Conan Doyle took the warning seriously; *The Case Against Royden Sharp* was not published in full until 1985.

In the end, largely through the efforts of Conan Doyle, the writer Jerome K. Jerome, and others who made up the "Edalji Committee," poor George got his pardon and was able to return to his law practice. However, he never received any compensation for his suffering, which caused a furious Conan Doyle to write: "The sad fact is that officialdom in England stands solid together, and that when you are forced to attack it, you need not expect justice."

Again, strong words from a rich, famous, English gentlemen who mingled with the elite of society and politics. But Conan Doyle was never afraid to speak his mind. In this case, the power of Conan Doyle's voice and name had an effect that far surpassed its impact on the outcome of the Edalji case. Conan Doyle's efforts on behalf of Edalji directly led to the establishment of England's first Court of Criminal Appeals in 1907. Prior to the Edalji case, if you were found guilty of a crime under English law, the only recourse was to appeal directly to the king for a pardon (and one can only surmise the chances of that happening very often).

And Conan Doyle always stuck by his friends. When Arthur and Jean Leckie finally married on September 18, 1907, George Edalji was an invited and honored guest.

Years later, the story of Oscar Slater was to have a considerably less warm and fuzzy ending.

*

Oscar Slater was a pimp, a hustler, and a draft-dodging German Jew. He had several aliases, had abandoned his wife, run off with his mistress—herself a hooker—and called himself a dentist when he'd never set foot inside a dental school. None of this would endear him to the Glasgow police or the Scottish legal system.

Oscar Slater's world swirled down the toilet on a gray December evening in 1908. It was four days before Christmas, and Oscar was planning to move to America. He and his mistress, Andrée Antoine, had fallen on hard times, and Oscar's wife was after him for money he owed her. It seemed a good time to relocate. He had a friend in San Francisco who was going to help him get a fresh start. Oscar had even been forced to hock some things, a few pieces of jewelry and some other items, and he was scurrying all over Glasgow trying to either retrieve the items or sell the pawn tickets to his cronies. He played billiards with a few friends, wrapped up the last of his meager financial affairs, then went home, discharged his maid, and began packing.

Oscar had originally planned to leave without Antoine. Whether he was tired of her or couldn't afford to take her isn't really known, but she raised so much hell that Oscar finally gave in and bought her a companion second-class ticket on the *Lusitania*.

On the night of December 21—as Oscar and Antoine were spending one of their last nights in Glasgow—in a large flat a few blocks away, an elderly, rich, fearfully paranoid spinster named Marion Gilchrist sent her maid, Helen Lambie, to the corner to buy a newspaper. Helen returned a short time later and, as she opened the door, a man walked past her into the street. Strangely (or perhaps suspiciously), this didn't alarm young Helen. She wandered around the flat, searching for her mistress.

She found Marion Gilchrist in the dining room, faceup on the floor, partially covered in a rug. She was still breathing, but barely, and died a few minutes later. The elderly lady had been horribly beaten to death, her face caved in, one eyeball driven into her brain. In the autopsy photographs, her face is barely recognizable as human. The apartment had been ransacked, papers strewn all about, but nothing had been taken except a small diamond brooch.

Apparently, Marion Gilchrist's paranoia was well-founded.

The police began an investigation that Conan Doyle and many others were to later claim was incredibly botched. Desperate to nail anyone for this horrible crime that had precipitated the early twentieth-century equivalent of a media circus, the police soon got wind of Oscar's trip to America. They began digging into Oscar's past, and the more they dug, the less they liked what they found. They wired the New York police, who took Oscar and Antoine into custody as they left the ship and held them for questioning.

Over a month later, homicide investigators would travel with Helen Lambie and another supposed witness to New York City, where they questioned Slater about the murder. Oscar Slater had never heard of Marion Gilchrist and had nothing to do with her murder. However, the police had found a pawn ticket for a diamond brooch in his pocket, and the two witnesses made halfhearted identifications that the police would later beef up by coaching them. Ultimately, Slater was able to prove the diamond brooch belonged to his mistress but that didn't faze the police.

In addition to being unlucky, Oscar Slater also was afflicted with what can only diplomatically be described as bad judgment. His English wasn't all that great, and he must have known how he looked to the police, yet he agreed to talk to them without a lawyer. Even after questioning, though, the case against Slater was circumstantial at best. At least one writer familiar with the case would later claim that if Slater had fought extradition from America, he probably would have won.

Then, as if any further evidence was needed of Slater's bad thinking skills, he agreed to accompany the Glasgow police back to prove himself innocent. He had nothing to hide, he felt, so he had nothing to fear.

Needless to say, this was the wrong answer. In short order, Oscar Slater was tried, found guilty, and sentenced to hang in one of the most outrageous kangaroo court trials in English history. Slater was not allowed to take the stand in his own defense. The prosecution's case was full of holes but was helped immeasurably by the judge's instruction to the jury that since Slater was a debauched pimp, he was not entitled to the same presumption of innocence as an English gentleman. Even then, the jury couldn't come up with a unanimous verdict.

Everyone agreed Oscar Slater was not an English gentleman, but this was going too far. There was a great public outcry. Slater's lawyers organized a petition, and three weeks later, only two days before his scheduled execution, were able to get his sentence reduced to life without parole at hard labor.

Conan Doyle was drawn in after the commutation of the sentence. He began an investigation that resulted in his writing *The Case Of Oscar Slater*, which was published in the summer of 1912. Conan Doyle argued persuasively that the police investigation was incompetent and the trial unfair. However, Conan Doyle's sentiments were far different this time from those he experienced in the Edalji case. Edalji was an educated, middle-class English-born lawyer. Slater was a foreigner and a petty criminal who lived off the proceeds of a woman's fallen honor; in short, as Conan Doyle would describe him, "a worthless fellow," an "unsatisfactory Bohemian," and most harshly, a "disreputable, rolling-stone of a man." Later, he compares Slater unfavorably to George Edalji, referring to him as a "blackguard."

But as always with Arthur Conan Doyle, his sense of honor and his moral code superseded all other concerns. Injustice was injustice, even if it was meted out to a rascal, and it was up to men of honor to correct it.

Meanwhile, another man of honor was at work, and he would emerge as the other tragic figure in the Oscar Slater case. Lieutenant John Trench, a Glasgow police detective, was a peripheral investigator in the Marion Gilchrist murder. He was not the first detective on the scene, and he wasn't the lead in the case, but he was privy to the details of the crime. The more he studied the case, the fishier it all got. He began asking questions and battling his conscience; finally, he came forth with new evidence, among which was the startling revelation that on the night of the murder, Helen Lambie had named the man whom she saw running from Marion Gilchrist's flat.

And it wasn't Oscar Slater.

Incredibly, this new evidence did not gain Slater a new trial. For his efforts, John Trench was sacked from the police force, lost his pension, and was disgraced. He spent the rest of his life trying to salvage his reputation and never really recovered.

Conan Doyle was incensed. He wrote in a letter to the editor of the *Spectator*: "The whole case will, in my opinion, remain immortal in the classics of crime as the supreme example of official incompetence and obstinacy."

For decades now, that has been the take on the Glasgow police performance in the Marion Gilchrist homicide; that an incompetent police force under great public pressure to arrest anyone, somehow nailed an innocent man. Yet in the late 1980s, Thomas Toughill, a British historian who was once a police officer and, of all things, Henry Kissinger's bodyguard, began researching the case with access to government files that had been under lock and key until 1989. Toughill came to some startling conclusions as a result of his investigation, which he revealed in his book *Oscar Slater: The Mystery Solved* (Edinburgh: Canongate Press Ltd., 1993).

It is beyond the scope of this narrative to even begin to summarize the complexities of this twisted, bizarre case, but Toughill makes a very persuasive argument—based on two anonymous letters to the police that named the real killer—that the Glasgow police deliberately and criminally framed Oscar Slater in order to protect the identity of the real murderer. Toughill theorizes that when the Glasgow police went to New York City to question Slater, they deliberately put forth a shoddy case in hopes that they would lose the extradition appeal. Then they could go home, throw up their hands, and say, "Well, he got away with it. That's the end of it." The last thing the police wanted was for Slater to agree to return to Scotland, and when he did, it threw them into a panic. It was a case of a conspiracy gone awry that then had to become an even greater, more criminal conspiracy in order to avoid exposure.

Oscar Slater would have rotted in prison for the rest of his miserable life, except once again, Sir Arthur Conan Doyle quite literally came to the rescue. Sixteen years after his imprisonment, Slater (who had been a real pain in the neck as a prisoner and thus denied mail privileges as well as newspapers) sneaked out a message to Conan Doyle with a paroled prisoner, who stuffed the letter into his mouth to avoid detection.

Slater, who didn't know that Conan Doyle had from time to time tried to reopen his case, appealed once again for help and protested his innocence. Conan Doyle responded to Slater's desperate plea with renewed energy. He began a letter-writing campaign and appealed to politicians and judges. Meanwhile, a Glasgow journalist named William Park, who had devoted his whole career to the Oscar Slater case (ultimately burning himself out in the process), came to Conan Doyle with all his information, much of which he had discovered during the John Trench affair. Conan Doyle helped Park put the book together, wrote a strong foreword to it, and published it himself under his Psychic Press imprint.

The press got hold of the story, and all hell broke loose. One newspaper claimed to have tracked down Helen Lambie in America, who said she told the police the man she saw wasn't Slater. A rival newspaper had a woman who claimed the police bribed her to identify Slater as the killer.

A few days later, on November 14, 1927, Oscar walked out of prison a free man. He carried everything he owned in the world in a small brown parcel. As one might expect, he was overwhelmed. A huge crowd met him at the railway station, but he was unable to speak to them. It was said that when he walked into the bedroom that had been offered to him in a private home and saw clean sheets and a hot water bottle, he burst into tears.

Conan Doyle, however, still wasn't satisfied. Slater was free, but he hadn't been pardoned or had his conviction overturned. His reputation, such as it was, was still besmirched, and this was intolerable. Conan Doyle led the fight for Slater's appeal. He updated and republished *The Case of Oscar Slater*. He even personally guaranteed the money for his defense costs, which was ultimately granted. The Scottish appeals court, in an apparent bid to save face, overturned the conviction on a technicality. The original judge, the court ruled, should not have told the jury Slater was undeserving of the presumption of innocence.

It was a bitter pill for Slater to swallow. The British government granted a relatively miserly £6,000 compensation for his years of imprisonment. (As an aside, Thomas Toughill in his book noted that Slater took the first offer of compensation without seeking advice or counsel. Toughill speculates that if Slater had held out, he could have gotten at least £10,000. This seems yet another example of Slater's less-than-stellar judgment.) Slater was so embittered he refused to compensate Conan Doyle or anyone else for the money they spent on his behalf. This infuriated Conan Doyle; it wasn't the money, it was the principle of the thing. Ultimately, Slater agreed to pay back the small sum of £250. He then retired to the country, eventually married again, and died a reasonably happy old man of seventy-eight in 1949.

As a token of gratitude after his release, Oscar Slater sent Conan Doyle a silver cigar cutter. Sir Arthur promptly sent it back.

*

Sir Arthur Conan Doyle spent the rest of his life fighting for causes. Despite his devotion to the institution of marriage and his loyalty to both his wives, he fought for divorce reform. He fought for the right of women to vote (although he had no patience with the suffragettes and their policy of violent protest). Most of all, he fought for the cause of spiritualism, which was the belief that the dead could communicate with the living through earthly conduits called mediums. He devoted his energies, his bank account, and his considerable powers of persuasion and intellect to a losing battle to convince the rest of the world he was right. He died peacefully, at home, on July 7, 1930. A few days later, his beloved wife Jean, now Lady Conan Doyle, crowded into London's Royal Albert Hall with a throng estimated at upwards of 6,000 people for a mass séance to contact her husband's spirit. The spirit medium on duty that night leaned down and whispered a hushed message to Lady Doyle, who by all accounts smiled serenely.

For the rest of her life, she refused to disclose the contents of that message. But she was sure, Lady Doyle maintained, that it had come from Arthur.

PART ONE

THE CASE OF
GEORGE ERNEST THOMPSON EDALJI

CHAPTER ONE

SIR ARTHUR CONAN DOYLE
TO THE RESCUE

On the morning of Friday, January 11, 1907, the *Daily Telegraph* of London commenced the publication of a series of articles by famous detective writer Sir Arthur Conan Doyle that was to change forever the face of the English judicial system.

In a series of articles, interviews, news stories, and letters, Sir Arthur used the platform of the *London Daily Telegraph* to wage a campaign of vindication on behalf of the Anglo-Indian solicitor George Ernest Thompson Edalji, convicted in 1903 of maiming cattle and horses in the vicinity of the Village of Great Wyrley, where his father was the vicar. Edalji served three years of a seven-year sentence before an outcry from other legal men secured his release, which was without explanation or exonerating pardon.

The hue and cry that Conan Doyle stirred on behalf of Edalji cannot be overstated. For most of a whole year, the *Daily Telegraph* continued to run stories and letters on the case. The popular imagination was aroused because that linchpin of British justice, trial by jury, was shown to have serious defects when it came to overturning the results of incompetently run trials. No Court of Criminal Appeals existed because British officialdom refused to believe an occasional miscarriage of justice warranted such a radical solution.

Of such a system, Sir Arthur wrote bitterly: "The sad fact is that officialdom in England stands solid together, and that when you are forced to attack it, you need not expect justice, but rather that you are up against an avowed Trade Union, the members of which are not going to act the blackleg to each other, and which subordinates the public interest to a false idea of loyalty."

Here then is the story of George Edalji, convicted of maiming animals at the Staffordshire Quarter Session, as presented in the pages of the *Daily Telegraph* in chronological order.

First, Conan Doyle presents his statement in favor of George Edalji's innocence, which appeared on two consecutive days early in January of 1907.

Second, there is presented but a sampling of the numerous letters and articles generated in response to Conan Doyle's feature, then there are further articles either by the *Daily Telegraph* or excerpted from other papers interested in the case.

Third, various observers comment on the trial or on their knowledge of the Edaljis and offer observations pro and con on what they knew and saw.

Fourth, there is a newspaper account of Edalji's trial and continuing letters either criticizing or exculpating the solicitor's behavior during both the investigation and the trial.

Fifth, the Home Office finally responds by initiating a limited investigation.

Finally, the Home Office grants Edalji a free pardon but refuses him compensation because they hold him guilty of having written some of the anonymous letters. An outraged Conan Doyle attempts to show that scurrilous letters against the whole Edalji family had a long history and could not have been the work of the defamed solicitor.

The Home Office remains firm, and Edalji never receives compensation for his three years in jail.

JANUARY 11, 1907

THE CASE OF MR. GEORGE EDALJI
SPECIAL INVESTIGATION BY
SIR A. CONAN DOYLE

The first sight which I ever had of Mr. George Edalji was enough in itself to convince me both of the extreme improbability of his being guilty of the crime for which he was condemned, and to suggest some at least of the reasons which had led for his being suspected. He had come to my hotel by appointment, but I had been delayed, and he was passing the time by reading the paper. I recognised my man by his dark face, so I stood and observed him. He held the paper close to his eyes and rather sideways, proving not only a high degree of myopia, but marked astigmatism. The idea of such a man scouring fields at night and assaulting cattle while avoiding the watching police was ludicrous to anyone who can imagine what the world looks like to eyes with myopia of eight diopters—the exact value of Mr. Edalji's myopia according to Mr. Kenneth Scott of Manchester-square. But such a condition, so hopelessly bad that no glasses availed in the open air, gave the sufferer a vacant, bulge-eyed staring appearance, which, when taken with his dark skin, must assuredly have made him seem a very queer man to the eyes of an English village, and therefore to be naturally associated with any queer event. There, in a single physical defect, lay the moral certainty of his innocence, and the reason why he should become the scapegoat.

Before seeing him I had read the considerable literature which had been sent to me about his case. After seeing him I read still more, saw or wrote to everyone who could in any way throw light upon the matter, and finally visited Wyrley and had a useful day's work upon the spot. The upshot of my whole research has been to introduce me to a chain of circumstances which seem so extraordinary that they are far beyond the invention of the writer of fiction. At all times in my inquiries I have kept before my mind the supreme necessity of following truth rather than any preconceived theory, and I was

always prepared to examine any point against the accused with as much care as if it made for his innocence, but I have felt at last that it was an insult to my intelligence to hold out any longer against the certainty that there had been an inconceivable miscarriage of justice.

Let me now tell the strange story from the beginning. I hope that the effect of my narrative will be to raise such a wave of feeling in this country as will make some public reconsideration of his case inevitable, for I am convinced that such reconsideration can only end in his complete acquittal and to his restoration to the ranks of that honourable profession from which he has been most unjustly removed.

The story begins as far back as the year 1874, when the Rev. S. [Shapurji] Edalji, a Church of England clergyman of Parsee origin, was married to Miss C. [Charlotte] Stoneham. An uncle of the bride, as I understand it, held the gift of the living of Great Wyrley, which was a parish, half agricultural and half mining, about six miles from Walsall, in Staffordshire. Through this uncle's influence Mr. Edalji became vicar of Great Wyrley, a cure which he has now held for thirty-one years, living a blameless life in the sight of all men. Placed in the exceedingly difficult position of a coloured clergyman in an English parish, he seems to have conducted himself with dignity and discretion. The only time that I can ever find that any local feeling was raised against him was during elections, for he was a strong Liberal in politics, and had been known to lend the church school-room for meetings. Some bitterness was aroused among the baser local politicians by this action.

There were three surviving children from this union—George, who was born in 1876, Horace in 1879, and Maud in 1882. Of these Horace received a Government post, and was absent at the time when the long persecution to which the family had been subjected culminated in the tragedy which overwhelmed his brother.

In the year 1888, George Edalji being at that time twelve years of age, a number of threatening anonymous letters were received at the vicarage. The aid of the police was called in, and an arrest was made. This was of the servant-maid at the vicarage, one Elizabeth Foster, who was accused, among

other things, of writing up ribald sentences about her employers on out-houses and buildings. She was tried at Cannock in 1889, but her solicitor pleaded that it was all a foolish joke, and she was bound over to keep the peace. An attempt has been made since to contend that she was not guilty, but I take it that no barrister could make such an admission without his client's consent. She and her friends were animated afterwards by bitter feelings of revenge; and there is good reason to believe that in this incident of 1888 is to be found the seed which led to the trouble of 1892–95 and the subsequent trouble of 1903. The 1892–95 letters openly championed Elizabeth Foster; the 1903 ones had no direct allusion to her, but a scurrilous postcard on Aug. 4 contained the words, "Why not go on with your old game of writing things on walls?" this being the very offence Elizabeth Foster was charged with. The reader must remember that in 1888 George Edalji was a schoolboy of twelve, and that the letters received at that date were in a formed handwriting, which could not possibly have been his.

In 1892 the second singular outbreak of anonymous letters began, some of which were published in the Staffordshire papers at the time by Mr. [Shapurji] Edalji, in the hope that their style or contents might discover the writer. Many were directed to the vicarage, but many others were sent to different people in the vicinity, so malevolent and so ingenious that it seemed as if a very demon of mischief were endeavouring to set the parish by the ears. They were posted at Walsall, Cannock, and various other towns, but bore internal evidence of a common origin, and were all tainted with the Elizabeth Foster incident. They lasted for three years, and as they were accompanied by a long series of most ingenious and elaborate hoaxes, it is really wonderful that they did not accomplish their proclaimed purpose, which was to drive their victim off his head.

On examination of such of these letters as I have been able to see their prevailing characteristics are:

1. A malignant, diabolical hatred of the whole Edalji family, the 16-17-18-year old George coming in for his fair share of the gross abuse. This hatred is insane in its intensity, and yet is so coldly resolute that three years of

constant persecution caused no mitigation. Here are extracts to illustrate the point: "I swear by God that I will murder George Edalji soon. The only thing I care about in this world is revenge, revenge, revenge, sweet revenge, I long for, then I shall be happy in hell." "Every day, every hour, my hatred is growing against George Edalji." "Do you think, you Pharisee, that because you are a parson God will absolve you from your iniquities?" "May the Lord strike me dead if I don't murder George Edalji." "Your damned wife." "Your horrid little girl." "I will descend into the infernal regions showering curses upon you all." Such are a few of the phrases in which maniacal hatred of the Edalji family is shown.

2. The second characteristic of the letters is a frantic admiration, real or feigned, for the local police. There was a Sergeant Upton on duty in Cannock, who is eulogized in this way: "Ha, ha, hurrah for Upton! Good old Upton! Blessed Upton. Good old Upton! Upton is blessed! Dear old Upton!

> *Stand up, stand up for Upton,*
> *Ye soldiers of the Cross.*
> *Lift high your Royal banner,*
> *It must not suffer loss."*

"The following in this district we love truly—the police of Cannock in general." Again: "I love Upton. I love him better then life, because for my sake he lost promotion."

3. The third characteristic of these letters, besides hatred of Edalji and eulogy of the police, is real or simulated religious mania, taking the form, in some portions of the same letter, that the writer claims to be God, and in others that he is eternally lost in hell. So consistent is this that it is hard to doubt that there was a real streak of madness in the writer.

4. A fourth remarkable characteristic of the letters is the intimacy of the writer with the names and affairs of the people in the district. As many as

twenty names will sometimes be given, most of them with opprobrious epithets attached. No one can read them and doubt that the writer lived in the immediate neighborhood, and was intimately acquainted with the people of whom he spoke.

One would imagine that under these circumstances there would be little difficulty in tracing the letters to their source, but, as a matter of fact, the handwriting was never recognized, nor was the culprit discovered. The opinion was strongly held, however, by those who were most concerned, that there was a connection with the former incident, and that the letters were done by some male ally or allies of the discharged maid.

Whilst these letters had been circulating the life of the Edaljis had, as I have already said, been made miserable by a series of most ingenious and daring hoaxes, many of which might have seemed comic had it not been for the tragedy of such a persecution. In all sorts of papers the curious wants of the Rev. S. Edalji, of Great Wyrley, broke out by letter and by advertisement. Forgery caused no qualms to the hidden conspirator. Mr. Edalji became in these effusions an enterprising matrimonial agent, with a number of ladies, their charms and fortunes most realistically catalogued, whom he was ready to dispose of to any eligible bachelor. His house was advertised to be let for the most extraordinary purposes. His servant-girl was summoned over to Wolverhampton to view the dead body of a non-existent sister supposed to be lying at a public-house. Tradespeople brought cartloads of unordered goods to the vicarage. An unfortunate parson from Norwich flew across to Great Wyrley on the urgent summons of the Rev. Shapurji Edalji, only to find himself the victim of a forgery. Finally, to the confusion of anyone who imagines that the youth George Edalji was annoying himself and playing heartless tricks upon his own people, there came a forged apology in the public press, beginning with the words: "We, the undersigned, G. E. T. Edalji and Fredk. Brookes, both residing in the parish of Great Wyrley, do hereby declare that we were the sole authors and writers of certain offensive and anonymous letters received by various persons during the last twelve months." The apology then goes on to express regret for utterances against the favourite protégé of the unknown, Upton, the sergeant of police at Cannock, and also against Elizabeth Foster. This pretended apology was, of course, at once disowned by the Edaljis, and must, I think, convince any reasonable man, if there were already any room for doubt, that the Edaljis were not persecuting themselves in this maddening fashion.

Before leaving this subject of the anonymous letters of 1893, which breathe revenge against the Edalji family, I should like to quote and strongly emphasize two expressions which have a lurid meaning when taken with the actual outcome of the future.

On March 17, 1893, this real or pretended maniac says in a letter to the father: "Before the end of this year your kid will be either in the graveyard or disgraced for life." Later, in the same letter, he says: "Do you think that when we want we cannot copy your kid's writing?" Within ten years of the receipt of that letter the "kid," or George Edalji, had indeed been disgraced for life, and anonymous letters which imitated his handwriting had played a part in his downfall. It is difficult after this to doubt that the schemer of 1893 was identical with the writer of the letters in 1903.

Among the many hoaxes and annoyances practiced during these years was the continual laying of objects within the vicarage grounds and on the window-sills, or under the doors, done with such audacity that the culprit was more than once nearly caught in the act. There was one of these incidents which I must allude to at some length, for though it was trivial in itself, it has considerable importance as forming a link between the outrages of 1893 and of 1903, and also because it shows for the first time the very strong suspicion which Captain the Honourable G. A. Anson, Chief Constable of Staffordshire—influenced no doubt by those reports of his subordinates, which he may or may not have too readily believed—has shown towards George Edalji. Personally I have met with nothing but frankness and courtesy from Captain the Hon. G. A. Anson during the course of my investigation, and if in the search after truth I have to criticise any word or action of his, I can assure him that it is with regret and only in pursuit of what seems to me to be a clear duty.

On Dec. 12, 1892, at the very beginning of the series of hoaxes, a large key was discovered lying upon the vicarage doorstep. This key was handed to the police, and was discovered in a few days to be a key which had been taken from Walsall Grammar School. The reason why I say that this incident has an important bearing upon the connection between the outrages of 1893 and those of 1903 is that the very first letter in the latter series proclaimed the writer to be a scholar at Walsall Grammar School. Granting that he could no longer be a scholar there if he were concerned in the hoaxes of 1893, it is still an argument that the same motive power lay behind each, since we find Walsall Grammar School obtruding itself in each case.

The incident of the key was brought before the chief constable of the county, who seems at once to have concluded that young George Edalji was the culprit. George Edalji was not a scholar at the Walsall School, having been brought up at Rugeley, and there does not appear to have been the slightest reason to suppose that he had procured a key from this six miles distant school and laid it on his own doorstep. However, here is a queer-looking boy, and here are queer doings, and here is a zealous constable, the very Upton whose praises were later to be so enthusiastically voiced by the writer of the letters. Some report was made, and the chief constable believed it. He took the course of writing in his own hand, over his own name, in an attempt to bluff the boy into a confession. Under date Jan. 23, 1893, he says to the father, in a letter which now lies before me: "Will you please ask your son George from whom the key was obtained which was found on your doorstep on Dec. 12? The key was stolen, but if it can be shown that the whole thing was due to some idle freak or practical joke, I should not be inclined to allow any police proceedings to be taken in regard to it. If, however, the persons concerned in the removal of the key refuse to make any explanation of the subject, I must necessarily treat the matter in all seriousness as a theft. I may say at once that I shall not pretend to believe any protestations of ignorance which your son may make about this key. My information on the subject does not come from the police."

Considering the diabolical ingenuity of the hoaxer, it would seem probable that the information came directly or indirectly from him. In any case, it seems to have been false, or, at least, incapable of proof, as is shown by the fact that after these threats from the chief constable no action was taken. But the point to be noted is that as early as 1893, when Edalji was only seventeen, we have the police force of Staffordshire, through the mouth of their chief, making charges against him, and declaring in advance that they will not believe any protestation of innocence. Two years later, on July 25, 1895, the chief constable goes even further. Still writing to the father he says: "I did not tell Mr. Perry that I know the name of the offender (the writer of the letters and author of the hoaxes), though I told him that I had my suspicions. I prefer to keep my suspicions to myself until I am able to prove them, and I trust to be able to obtain a dose of penal servitude for the offender; as although great care has apparently been exercised to avoid, as far as possible, anything which would constitute any serious offence in law, the person who writes the letters has overreached himself in two or three instances, in such a manner as to render him liable to the most serious punishment. I have no doubt that the offender will be detected."

Now, it must be admitted that this is a rather sinister letter. It follows after eighteen months upon the previous one in which he accuses George Edalji by name. The letter was drawn from him by the father's complaint of gossip in the neighourhood, and the allusion to the skill of the offender in keeping within the law has a special meaning, in view of the fact that young Edalji was already a law student. Without mentioning a name, he assures Edalji's father that the culprit may get a dose of penal servitude. No doubt the chief constable honestly meant every word he said, and thought that he had excellent reasons for his conclusions; but the point is that if the Staffordshire police took this attitude towards young Edalji in 1895, what chance of impartiality had he in 1903, when a culprit was wanted for an entirely new set of crimes? It is evident that their minds were steeped in prejudice against him, and that they were in the mood to view his actions in the darkest light.

At the end of 1895 this persecution ceased. Letters and hoaxes were suddenly switched off. From that date till 1903 peace reigned in Wyrley. But George Edalji was resident at the vicarage all the time. Had he been the culprit there was no reason for change. But in 1903 the troubles broke out in a far more dangerous form than ever.

It was on Feb. 2, 1903, that the first serious outrage occurred at Wyrley. On that date a valuable horse belonging to Mr. Joseph Holmes was found to have been ripped up during the night. Two months later, on April 2, a cob belonging to Mr. Thomas was treated in a similar fashion, and a month after that a cow of Mrs. Bungay's was killed in the same way. Within a fortnight a horse of Mr. Badger's was terribly mutilated, and on the same day some sheep were killed. On June 6 two cows suffered the same fate, and three weeks later two valuable horses belonging to the Quinton Colliery Company were also destroyed. Next in order in this monstrous series of barbarities was the killing of a pony at Great Wyrley Colliery, for which George Edalji was arrested and convicted. His disappearance from the scene made no difference at all to the sequence of outrages, for on Sept. 21, betwixt his arrest and his trial, another horse was disembowelled, and, as if expressly to confute the views of those who might say that this outrage was committed by confederates in order to affect the trial, the most diabolical deed of all was committed, after Edalji's conviction upon Nov. 3, when a horse and mare were found mutilated in the same field, an additional touch of horror being added by the discovery of a newly-born foal some little distance from the mare. Three months later, on Feb. 8, 1904, another horse was found to be injured, and finally, on March 24, two sheep and a lamb were found mutilated, and a rough miner named Farrington was convicted, upon entirely circumstantial evidence, and condemned to three years.

Now here the results of the police are absolutely illogical and incompatible. Their theory was that of a moonlighting gang. Edalji is condemned as one member of it, Farrington as another. But no possible connection can be proved or was ever suggested between Edalji and Farrington; the one a rude, illiterate miner, the other the son of the vicar and a rising professional man; the one a loafer at public-houses, the other a total abstainer. It is certainly suggestive, presuming that Farrington did do the deed for which he was convicted, that he was employed at the Wyrley Colliery, and may have had to pass in going to his work that very pony which Edalji was supposed to have injured. It is also, it must be admitted, suggestive that while Edalji's imprisonment had no effect upon the outrages, Farrington's was at once followed by their complete cessation. How monstrous, then, to contend, as the Home Office has done, that no new facts have arisen to justify a revision of Edalji's case. At the same time, I do not mean to imply Farrington's guilt, of which I have grave doubts, but merely that, as compared with Edalji, a strong case could be made out against him.

Now let me, before examining the outrage of Aug. 17, 1903, which proved so fatal to Edalji, give some account of the fresh epidemic of letters which broke out in the district. They were synchronous with the actual outrages, and there were details in them which made it possible, though by no means certain, that they were written by someone who was actually concerned in the crime.

It cannot be said that there is absolute proof that the letters of 1903 were by the same hand as those of 1895, but there are points about their phrasing, about their audacity and violence of language, finally, about the attentions which they bestow upon the Edalji family, which seem to point to a common origin. Only in this case the Rev. Edalji escapes, and it is the son—the same son who has been menaced in the first series with disgrace for life—who receives some of the communications, and is referred to in the others. I may say that this series of letters present various handwritings, all of which differ from the 1895 letters, but as the original persecutor was fond of boasting that he could change his handwriting, and even that he could imitate that of George Edalji, the variance need not be taken too seriously.

And now for the letters. They were signed by various names, but the more important purported to come from a young schoolboy, named Greatorex. This youth denied all knowledge of them, and was actually away in the Isle of Man when some of them were written, as well as on Aug. 17, the date of the Wyrley outrage. It is a curious fact that this youth, in going up to Walsall every day to school, travelled with a certain number of schoolfellows upon the same errand, and that the names of some of these schoolfellows do find their way into these letters. In the same carriage travelled young Edalji upon some few occasions. "I have known accused by sight for three or four years," said Greatorex at the trial, "he has travelled in the same compartment with me and my schoolmates, going to Walsall.

This has not occurred many times during the last twelve months—about a dozen times, in fact."

Now, at first sight, one would think this a point for the police, as on the presumption that Edalji wrote these anonymous letters it would account for the familiarity with these youths displayed in them. But since Edalji always went to business by the 7.30 train in the morning, and the boys took the same train everyday, to find himself in their company twelve times in one year was really rather more seldom than one would expect. He drifted into their compartment as into any other, and he seems to have been in their company but not of it. Yet the anonymous writer knew that group of boys well, and the police, by proving that George Edalji might have known them, seemed to make a distinct point against him.

The "Greatorex" letters to the police are all to the effect that the writer is a member of the gang for maiming cattle, that George Edalji is another member, and that he (Greatorex) is prepared to give away the gang if certain conditions are complied with. "I have got a dare-devil face and can run well, and when they formed that gang at Wyrley they got me to join. I know all about horses and beasts and how to catch them best . . . they said they would do me in if I funked it, so I did, and caught them both lying down at ten minutes to three, and they roused up; and then I caught each under the belly, but they didn't spurt much blood, and one ran away but the other fell. . . . Now I'll tell you who are in the gang, but you can't prove it without me. There is one named ———, from Wyrley, and a porter who they call ———, and he's had to stay away, and there's Edalji, the lawyer . . . Now I have not told you who is at the back of them all, and I shan't unless you promise to do nothing at me. It is not true we always do it when the moon is young, and the one Edalji killed on April 11 was full moon." (It is worthy mentioning here that there was no outrage at all within a week of that date). "I've never been locked up yet, and I don't think any of the others have, except the Captain, so I guess they'll get off light."

I would draw attention in passing to the artistic touch of "ten minutes to three." This is realism overdone, as no mutilator on a dark night could readily consult his watch nor care to remember the exact hour to a minute. But it corresponds closely to the remarkable power of imaginative detail—a rather rare gift—shown in the hoaxes of 1893–95.

In the next letter, also to the police, the unknown refers to his previous communication, but is a good deal more truculent and abusive than before. "There will be merry times at Wyrley in November," he says, "when they start on little girls, for they will do twenty wenches like the horses before next March. Don't think you are likely to catch them cutting the beasts; they go too quiet, and lie low for hours, till your men have gone. . . . Mr. Edalji, him they said was locked up, is going to Brum on Sunday night to see the Captain, near Northfield, about how it's to be carried on with so many detectives about, and I believe they are going to do some cows in the daytime instead of at night. . . . I think they are going to kill beasts nearer here soon, and I know Cross Keys Farm and West Cannock Farm are the two first on the list. . . . You bloated blackguard, I will shoot you with father's gun through your thick head if you come in my way or go sneaking to any of my pals."

This letter was addressed, like the last, to:

The Sergeant,
Police Station, Hednesford,
Staffordshire

bearing a Walsall postmark of July 10, 1903. Edalji is openly accused of the crimes in the letters, and yet the police put forward the theory that he himself wrote them, and founded upon the last sentence of them, which I have quoted, that second charge, which sounded so formidable in his indictment, viz., of threatening to murder Sergeant-Robinson.

A few days previously a second police officer, Mr. Rowley, of Bridgetown, had received another letter, evidently from the same hand. Here the detail as to the method of the crime is more realistic than ever, though no accusations against others are made. I quote this letter in extenso:

"Sir—A party whose initials you'll guess will be bringing a new hook home by the train from Walsall on Wednesday night, and he will have it in his special long pocket under his coat, and if you or your pals can get this coat pulled aside a bit you'll get sight of it, as it's an inch and a half longer than the one he threw out of sight when he heard someone a slopin it after him this morning. He will come by that after five or six, or if he don't come home tomorrow he is sure on Thursday, and you have made a mistake not keeping all the plain clothes men at hand. You sent them away too soon. Why, just think, he did it close where two of them were hiding only a few days gone by. But, sir, he has got eagle eyes, and his ears is as sharp as a razor, and he is as fleet of foot as a fox, and as noiseless, and he crawls on all fours up to the poor beasts, an fondles them a bit, and then pulls the hook smart across 'em, and out their entrails fly, before they guess they are hurt. You want 100 detectives to run him in red-handed, because he is so fly, and knows every nook and corner. You know who it is, and I can prove it; but until £100 reward is offered for a conviction, I shan't spilt no more."

There is, it must be admitted, striking realism in this account also, but a hook—unless it were a billhook or horticultural hook—could not under any circumstances have inflicted the injuries.

It seems absurd enough that these letters incriminating himself in such violent terms should be attributed to young Edalji, but the climax is reached when a most offensive postcard, handed in at Edalji's own business office, is also sworn to by the expert employed by the police as being in Edalji's own writing. This vile effusion, which cannot be reproduced in full, accuses Edalji of guilty relations with a certain lady, ending up with the words, "Rather go back to your old game of writing anonymous letters and killing cows and writing on walls."

Now this postcard was posted at Wolverhampton upon Aug. 4, 1903. As luck would have it, Edalji and his sister had gone upon an excursion to Aberystwith that day, and were absent from very early morning till late at night. Here is the declaration of the station official upon the point: On the night of 4th of August, 1903, and early morning of the 5th I was on duty at Rugeley Town Station, and spoke to Mr. George Edalji and his sister, who were in the train on their return from Aberystwith—William Bullock, Porter-Signalman, Rugeley Town Station.

The station-master at Wyrley has made a similar declaration.

It is certain, then, that this postcard could not have been by him, even had the insulting contents not made the supposition absurd. And yet it is included in that list of anonymous letters which the police maintained, and the expert declared, to be in Edalji's own handwriting. If this incident is not enough in itself to break down the whole case, so far as the authorship of the letters goes, then I ask, what in this world would be sufficient to demonstrate its absurdity?

Before leaving this postcard, let me say that it was advanced for the prosecution that if a card were posted at certain country boxes to be found within two and a half miles of Wyrley they would not be cleared till evening, and so would have the Wolverhampton mark of next day. Thus the card might have been posted in one of these out-of-the-way boxes on the 3rd, and yet bear the mark of the 4th. This, however, will not do. The card has the Wolverhampton mark of the evening of the 4th, and was actually delivered in Birmingham on the morning of the 5th. Even granting that one day was Bank Holiday, you cannot stretch the dislocation of the postal service to the point that what was posted on the 3rd took two days to go twenty miles.

Now, during these six months, while Edalji was receiving these scurrilous letters, and while the police were receiving others accusing the young lawyer, you will naturally ask why did he not take some steps himself to prove his innocence and to find out the writer? He did, as a matter of fact, everything in his power. He offered a reward of £25 in the public Press—a reward, according to the police theory, for his own apprehension. He showed the police the letters which he received, and he took a keen interest in the capture of the criminals, making the very sensible suggestion that bloodhounds should be used. It seems hardly conceivable that the prejudice of the police had risen to such a point that both these facts were alleged as suspicious circumstances against him, as though he were endeavouring to worm himself into their confidence, and so find out what measures they were taking for the capture of the offender. I am quite prepared to find that in these dialogues the quick-witted youth showed some impatience at their constant blunders, and that the result was to increase the very great malevolence with which they appear to have regarded him, ever since their chief declared, in 1895, "I shall not pretend to believe any protestations of ignorance which your son may make."

And now, having dealt with the letters of 1903, let me, before I proceed to the particular outrage for which Edalji was arrested and convicted, say a few words as to the personality of this unfortunate young man, who was, according to the police theory, an active member, if not the leading spirit, of a gang of village ruffians. Anyone more absurdly constructed to play the role could not be imagined. In the first place, he is a total abstainer, which in itself hardly seems to commend him to such a gang. He does not smoke. He is very shy and nervous. He is a most distinguished student, having won the highest legal prizes within his reach, and written, at his early age, a handbook of railway law. Finally, he is as blind as the proverbial bat, but the bat has the advantage of finding its way in the dark, which would be very difficult for him. To find a pony in a dark field, or, indeed, to find the field itself, unless it were easily approached, would be a hard task, while to avoid a lurking watcher would be absolutely impossible. I have myself practiced as an oculist, but I can never remember correcting so high a degree of astigmatic myopia as that which afflicts Mr. Edalji. **[Conan Doyle badly overstates his expertise in ophthalmology throughout his campaign to clear Edalji. It is true that he did intend to specialize in ophthalmology at one time, but when he took up his studies in Vienna, he soon learned that his German was not up to the course of study. Writing his detective stories and novels soon became his sole employment. See Martin Booth, *The Doctor and the Detective: A Biography of Sir Arthur Conan Doyle* (New York: St. Martin's Minotaur, 1997), p. 138.]** "Like all myopics, Mr. Edalji," says an expert, "must find it at all times difficult to see clearly any objects more than a few inches off, and in dusk it would be practically impossible for him to find his way about any place with which he was not perfectly familiar." Fearing lest it might be thought that he was feigning blindness, I asked Mr. Kenneth Scott, of Manchester-square, to paralyse the accommodation by atropine, and then to take the result by means which were independent of the patient. Here is his report:

Right eye   −8.75 Diop Spher.
            −1.75 Diop cylindaxis 90 deg.
Left eye   −8.25 Diop Spher.

"I am prepared to testify as to the accuracy of the above under oath," says Mr. Kenneth Scott.

As to what such figures mean, I will bring it home to the uninitiated by saying that a glass made up to that prescription would cause the normal healthy eye to see the world as Edalji's eyes always see it. I am prepared to have such a glass made up, and if any defender of the police will put it on at night, and will make his way over the route the accused is alleged to have taken inside of an hour, I will admit that what seems to me absolutely impossible could be done. I may add that this blindness is a permanent structural condition, the same in 1903 as in 1906.

I appeal to the practicing oculists of this country, and I ask whether there is one of them who would not admit that such a condition of the eyes would make such a performance practically impossible, and that the circumstance must add enormously to a defence which is already overwhelmingly strong. And yet this all-important point was never made at the trial.

It is this studious youth who touches neither alcohol nor tobacco, and is so blind that he gropes his way in the dusk, who is the dangerous barbarian who scours the country at night, ripping up horses. Is it not perfectly clear, looking at his strange, swarthy face and bulging eyes, that it is not the village ruffian, but rather the unfortunate village scapegoat, who stands before you?

I have brought the narrative down to the Aug. 17 outrage. At this period twenty constables and detectives had been brought into the district, and several, acting, I presume, upon orders from higher quarters, watched the vicarage at night. On Aug. 17, Edalji, following his own account, returned from his day's work at Birmingham—he had started in practice there as a lawyer—and reached his home about 6.30. He transacted some business, put on a blue serge coat, and then walked down to the bootmaker's in the village, where he arrived about 8.35, according to the independent evidence of John Hands, the tradesman in question. His supper would not be ready before 9.30, and until that hour he took a walk round, being seen by various people. His household depose to his return before suppertime, and their testimony is confirmed by the statement of Walter Whitehouse, who saw the accused enter the vicarage at 9.25.

After supper Edalji retired to bed in the same room as his father, the pair having shared an apartment for seventeen years. The old vicar was a light sleeper, his son was within a few feet of him, the whole house was locked up, and the outside was watched by constables, who saw no one leave it. To show how close the inspection was, I may quote the words of Sergeant Robinson, who said, "I saw four men observing it when I was there. . . . I could see the front door and side door. I should say no one could get out on the side I was watching without my seeing." This was before the night of the outrage, but it is inconceivable that if there was so close a watch then, there was none on the 17th. By the police evidence there were no less than twenty men scattered about waiting for the offender.

I may add at this point some surprise has been expressed that the vicar should sleep in the same room as his son with the door locked. They slept thus, and had done for many years, so that the daughter, whose health was precarious, might sleep with the mother, and the service of the house, there being only the one maid, should be minimized. Absurd emphasis has been placed by the police upon the door being locked at night. I can only suppose that the innuendo is that the vicar locked the door to keep his son from roving. Do we not all know that it is the commonest thing for nervous people to lock their doors whether alone or not, and Mr. Edalji has been in the habit of doing so all his long life. I have evidence that Mr. Edalji always locked his door before he slept with his son, and that he has continued to lock his door after his son left him. If, then—to revert to the evidence—it is possible for a person in this world to establish an alibi, it was successfully established by Edalji that night from 9.30 onwards. Granting the perfectly absurd supposition that the old vicar connived at his son slipping out at night and ripping up cattle, you have still the outside police to deal with. On no possible sup-position can George Edalji have gone out after 9.30.

And yet upon that night a pony had been destroyed at the Great Wyrley Colliery. Sergeant Parsons gave evidence that he saw the pony, apparently all right, at eleven o'clock at night. It was very dark, but he was not far off it. It was a wild night, with rain coming in squalls. The rain began about twelve, and cleared about dawn, being very heavy at times. On the 18th, at 6.20, a lad, named Henry Garrett, going to his work at the colliery, observed that the pony was injured. "It had a cut on the side," he said. "The blood was trickling from the wound. It was dropping pretty quickly." The alarm was at once given. Con-stables appeared upon the scene. By half-past eight Mr. Lewis, a veterinary surgeon, was on the spot. "The wound," he deposed, "was quite fresh, and could not have been done further than six hours from the time he saw it." The least learned of laymen might be sure that if the pony was standing bleeding freely at six it could not have been so all night, as the drain must have exhausted it. And here, on the top of this obvious consideration, is the opinion of the surgeon, that the injury was inflicted within six hours. Where George Edalji was during those six hours has already been shown beyond all possible question or dispute. So already the whole bottom has dropped out of the case; but, none the less, the indefatigable police went on with their pre-arranged campaign.

That it was pre-arranged is evident, since it was not on account of evi-dence, but in search of evidence, that the constables raided the vicarage. The young lawyer had already started for his day's work in Birmingham. The star-tled parents were ordered to produce all the young man's clothing. The mother was asked for his dagger, but could produce nothing more formidable than a botany spud. A hunt was made for weapons, and a set of razors belonging to the vicar were seized. Some were said to be wet—a not uncom-mon condition for razors in the morning. Dark spots were perceived upon the back of one, but they proved upon chemical examination to be rust stains. Twelve men quartered the small garden, but nothing was found.

The clothes, however, were a more serious matter. One coat was seized by the police and declared to be damp. This is vigorously denied by the vicar, who handled the coat before it was removed. Damp is, of course, a relative term, and all garments may give some feeling of dampness after a rainy night, when the whole atmosphere is humid; but if the condition had been caused by being out in the wild weather which prevailed that night, it is certain that the coat would have been not damp, but sopping wet.

The coat, however, was not one which Edalji used outside, and the evidence of Mr. Hands was called to show that he had not worn it the night before. It was an old house-coat, so stained and worn that it is not likely that an ambitious young professional man would, even in the lamplight, walk in the streets and show himself to his neighbours in such a garment. But it was these very stains which naturally attracted the attention of the police. There were some whitish stains—surely these must be the saliva of the unfortunate animal. They were duly tested, and proved to be starch stains, probably from fish sauce or bread and milk. But there was something still more ominous upon this unhappy coat. There were, according to Inspector Campbell, "dark red or brown stains, right cuff much more stained than the left. There were other stains on each sleeve, further up, reddish brown or white. The coat was damp. . . . There are other spots and stains upon it."

Now the police try to make two points here! That the coat was damp, and that there were stains which might have been the traces of the crime upon it. Each point is good in itself; but, unfortunately, they are incompatible and mutually destructive. If the coat were damp, and if those marks were blood-stains contracted during the night, then those stains were damp also, and the inspector had only to touch them and then to raise his crimson finger in the air to silence all criticism. But since he could not do so it is clear that the stains were not fresh. They fell twelve hours later into the capable hands of the police surgeon, and the sanguinary smears conjured up by the evidence of the constable diminished with absurd swiftness until they became "two stains in the center of the right cuff; each about the size of a three-penny bit." This was declared by Dr. Butter to be mammalian blood. He found no more blood at all. How these small stains came there it is difficult to trace—as difficult as to trace a stain which I see now upon the sleeve of my own house-jacket as I look down. A splash from the gravy of under-done meat might well produce it. At any rate, it may most safely be said that the most adept operator who ever lived would not rip up a horse with a razor upon a dark night and have only two three-penny-bit spots of blood to show for it. The idea is beyond argument.

JANUARY 12, 1907

THE CASE OF MR. GEORGE EDALJI
SPECIAL INVESTIGATION

The following is the conclusion of Sir A. Conan Doyle's article, the first part of which appeared in yesterday's edition.

*

But now, having exhausted the white stains and the dark stains, we come to the most damning portion of the whole indictment, though a careful consideration may change one's view as to who it is who is damned by it. The police claimed that they discovered horse-hairs upon the coat. "On the sleeve," says Inspector Campbell, "I found brownish hairs, which look like horse-hairs. There are some on now." Now, let us listen to the very clear statement of the vicar upon the subject. I transcribe it in full:

"On Aug. 18, 1903, they called at the vicarage at about eight o'clock in the morning, and in compliance with their request Mrs. Edalji showed them a number of garments belonging to her son, George Edalji. As soon as they saw the old coat they began to examine it, and Inspector Campbell put his finger on one place and said that there was a hair there. Mrs. Edalji told him that it was not a hair, but a thread, and Miss Edalji, who was present then, remarked that it looked like a 'roving.' This was all that Inspector Campbell had said to them about the hair before I came down. When I saw him he told me that he had found horse-hairs upon the coat. The coat was then spread out upon the desk in the study. I asked him to point out the place where the hairs were to be seen. He pointed out a lower part of the coat, and said, 'There's a horse-hair there.' I examined the place and said, 'There is no hair here at all.' Some further conversation followed, and then suddenly he put his finger on another place on the coat nearer to where I was standing, and, drawing two straight lines with his finger, he said, 'Look here, Mr. Edalji, there's horse-hair here.' I looked at the place for a moment, and in order to have more light upon it, I took up the coat with both my hands and drew nearer to the window, and after carefully examining it I said to him, 'There is, to be sure, no hair here, it is a clear surface.' He then said that he wanted to take the coat with him, and I said, 'You can take the coat. I am satisfied there is no horse-hair upon it.'

"Now I have said it over and over again, and I say it here once more, that there was absolutely no horse-hair upon the coat. If there had been any I could not have failed to see it, and both Mrs. Edalji and Miss Edalji looked at the coat at the same time, and saw no hair of any sort upon it." Incidentally it may be mentioned in connection with this statement, in which Miss Edalji entirely concurs that we have the evidence of Miss Foxley, formerly of Newnham College, and then head mistress of the high school, that Miss Edalji was an exceedingly competent scientific observer. She adds, "Wilful mis-statement on her part is as impossible in itself as it is inconsistent with her high principles and frank, straightforward character."

Now, here is a clear conflict of evidence between two groups of interested people—the constables on the one hand, eager to build up their case; the household on the other, eager to confute this terrible accusation. Let us suppose the two statements balance each other. But is it not evident that there was only one course open for the police now to establish their point, and that if they did not avail themselves of it they put themselves out of court? Their obvious course was then and there to send for a referee—the police doctor, or any other doctor—and picking samples of the hair from the coat to have sealed them in an envelope, calling the newcomer to witness when and where they had been obtained. Such a proceeding must silence all doubt. But they did nothing of the kind. What they actually did do was to carry off the coat upon which three reputable witnesses have sworn there were no hairs. The coat then disappears from view for twelve hours. In the meantime the pony has been put out of its pain, and a portion of its hide was cut off with the hairs attached, and also secured by the police. The coat had been taken at eight in the morning. It was seen by Dr. Butter, the police surgeon, at nine in the evening. At that hour Dr. Butter picked twenty-nine undoubted obvious horse-hairs from its surface.

The prosecution have here to break their way through two strong lines of defense, each within the other. On the one hand, if Edalji had done the crime the evening before, it was his blue serge coat, and not his house-coat, that he wore, as is shown by the independent evidence of Mr. Hands. In the second line of defence is the oath of the family that there were no hairs in the morning, which is strengthened by the failure of the police to demonstrate there and then a fact which could have been so easily and completely demonstrated. But now we are faced by the undoubted fact that the hairs were there, upon the cuffs and the left breast, by evening. Why was the coat not taken straight to the surgeon? Why was a piece of the animal's hide sent for before the coat was shown to Dr. Butter?

One need not fly to extreme conclusions. It is to be remembered that the mere carrying of hide and coat together may have caused the transference of hairs, or that the officers may themselves have gathered hairs on their clothes while examining the pony, and so unconsciously transferred them to the coat. But the fact that the hairs were found just on the cuffs and breast will still recur in the mind. It would be sad indeed to commit one injustice while trying to correct another, but when the inevitable inquiry comes this incident must form a salient point of it.

There is one test which occurs to one's mind. Did the hairs all correspond with the type, colour, and texture of the hairs on the sample of hide? If they did, then they were beyond all question conveyed from that sample to the coat. The cut was down the belly, and the portion taken off was from the side of the cut. The under-hair of a horse differs greatly from the longer, darker, harsher hair of the sides. A miscreant leaning against a horse would get the side hairs. If all the hairs on the coat were short belly hairs, then there is a suggestive fact for the inquiry. Dr. Butter must have compared their appearance.

Since writing the above I have been able to get the words of Dr. Butter's evidence. They are quoted: "Numerous hairs on the jacket, which were similar in colour, length, and structure to those on the piece of skin out from the horse." In that case I say, confidently—and all reflection must confirm it— that these hairs could not possibly be from the general body of the pony, but must have been transferred, no doubt unconsciously, from that particular piece of skin. With all desire to be charitable, the incident leaves a most unpleasant impression upon the mind.

If one could for a moment conceive oneself performing this barbarity, one would not expect to find hairs upon one's coat. There is no necessary connection at all. Anxious to avoid the gush of blood, one would imagine that one would hold off the animal with the flat of one hand and attack it with the other. To lean one's coat against its side would be to bring one's trousers and boots in danger of being soaked in blood.

So much for the saliva stains, the blood stains, and the hairs. There remain the questions of the trousers and the boots. The trousers were said by the police to be damp, and stained with dark mud round the bottom. The boots were very wet. The boots were the same ones which Edalji had admittedly used during his sixty-minutes' walk upon the evening before. It was fine in the evening, but there had been heavy rain during the day, and puddles everywhere. Of course his boots were wet. The trousers were not a pair used the evening before, according to the family. No attempt was made to show blood marks on boots or trousers, though Mr. Sewell, a well-known veterinary surgeon, deposed afterwards that in making such an incision a skilled operator would wear an apron to prevent his clothes from being soaked. It is an interesting point, brought out by the evidence of some of the witnesses of the prosecution, that the mud at the place of outrage was yellow-red, a mixture of clay and sand, quite distinct from the road mud, which the police claim to have seen upon the trousers.

And now we come to the farce of the footprints. The outrage had occurred just outside a large colliery, and hundreds of miners going to their work had swarmed along every approach; in order to see the pony. The soft, wet soil was trampled up by them from six o'clock onwards; yet on four o'clock of that afternoon, eight hours after the seizure of the boots, we have Inspector Campbell endeavouring to trace a similarity in tracks. The particular boot was worn at the heel, a fairly common condition, and some tracks among the multitude were down at the heel, and why should not the one be caused by the other? No cast was taken of the tracks. They were not photographed. They were not cut out for purpose of expert comparison. So little were they valued by inspector Campbell that he did not even mention them to the magistrates on the 19th. But in retrospect they grew more valuable, and they bulked large at the trial.

Now, once again, the police are trying to make a point which in itself would help them, but which is incompatible with their other points. Their original theory was that the crime was done before 9.30. There was heavy rain on and off all night. It is perfectly clear that any well-marked footsteps must have been left after the rain stopped, or when it had nearly stopped. Even granting that the earth was soft enough, as it was, to take footprints before then, this heavy rain would blur them to a point that would make identification by a worn-down heel absurd. What becomes then of all this elaborate business of the footmarks? Every point in this case simply crumbles to pieces as you touch it.

How formidable it all sounds—wet razor, blood on razor, blood and saliva and hair on coat, wet boots, footmark corresponding to boot—and yet how absolutely futile it all is when examined. There is not one single item which will bear serious criticism. Let us pass, however, from these material clues to those more subtle ones which the bearing or remarks of the youth may have furnished. These will bear examination even less than the others. As he waited upon the platform for the 7.30 train an ex-constable, now an innkeeper, named Markhew, came up to him and asked him to stay, as Inspector Campbell wished to see him. At the same moment someone announced that a fresh outrage had been committed, upon which Markhew says that Edalji turned away and smiled. Now, it is perfectly clear that a guilty man would have been much alarmed by the news that the police wished to see him, and that he would have done anything but smile on hearing of the outrage. Edalji's account is that Markhew said, "Can't you give yourself a holiday for one day?" on which Edalji smiled. Which is the more probable version I leave to the reader. The incident was referred to by the prosecuting counsel as "the prisoner's extraordinary conduct at the station."

He went to his office in Birmingham, and there, later in the day, he was arrested by the police.

On the way to the station, after his arrest, this unfortunate youth made another deadly remark: "I am not surprised at this. I have been expecting it for some time." It is not a very natural remark for a guilty man to make, if you come to think of it; but it is an extremely probable one from a man who believes that the police have a down on him, and who is aware that he has been accused by name in malignant anonymous letters. What else would he have said? Next day and the following Monday he was before the magistrates, where the police evidence, as already set forth, was given. The magisterial proceedings lasted till Sept. 4, off and on, when a *prima facie* case was made out, and the prisoner committed to the Staffordshire Quarter Session. How far a case of this importance should have been referred to any less tribunal than the assizes I leave to legal opinion. Again the criminal made a remark which rose up in judgment against him. "I won't have bail," said he to police-constable Meredith, "and when the next horse is killed it will not be by me." In commenting upon this, Mr. Disturnal, the prosecuting counsel, said, "In refusing bail the prisoner made use of a very significant observation, and it went to suggest that the prisoner knew perfectly well what he was about when he refused bail."

The inference here is that it was pre-arranged that a friend of Edalji's would do a fresh crime, in order to clear him. Was there ever a more unfair utterance! It was, "Heads I win, tails you lose!" If no crimes occur, then it is clear we have the villain under lock and key. If crimes do occur, then it is clear that he is deep in conspiracy with others. As a matter of fact, both Edalji's decision to remain in gaol and his remark were the most proper and natural things in the world. He believed that there was a strong conspiracy against him. In the fact of the letters he had every reason to believe so. So long as he was in his cell he was safe, he thought, from this conspiracy. Perhaps another crime would be committed, and in that case, he thought, in the innocence of his heart, that it would clear him. In his wildest dreams he could never have imagined that such a crime would be fitted in as a link in the chain against him.

A crime was committed, and it occurred upon Sept. 21, between Edalji's committal and trial, whilst he lay in Stafford Gaol. The facts are these: Harry Green was the nineteen-year-old son of a farmer who lived somewhere between the vicarage and the scene of the outrage for which Edalji was convicted. He and Edalji knew each other slightly, as neighbours in the country must do, but how slight was their acquaintance may be shown by the fact that when, in the course of my inquiry, I asked Edalji what Green's writing was like, he had to admit that he had never seen it. Consider the utter want of common ground between the two men, the purblind, studious teetotal young lawyer of twenty-seven, and the young Yeomanry trooper of nineteen, one of a set of boisterous young fellows, who made a centre of mirth and also of mischief at each annual training. Edalji entered no public-house, and was at work from early morning to late at night. Where was there room for that blood-brotherhood which would make the one man risk any danger and sacrifice his own horse for the sake of the other?

Green's charger was found disembowelled. It was not a very valuable animal. In one estimate it is placed at five pounds. Whether it was insured or not there is a conflict of evidence. For days there was scare and conjecture. Then, at the end of that time, it was known that Green had signed a confession which admitted that he had himself killed his own horse. That confession undoubtedly exists, but Green, having had a week or two to think things over, and having in the meantime got a ticket to South Africa, suddenly went back on his own confession, and declared, with much circumstantiality of detail, that he had not done it, and that the confession had been bullied out of him by the police. One or other statement of Green's must be a falsehood, and I have sufficient reason myself, in the shape of evidence which has been set before me, to form a very clear opinion what the actual facts of the case were. When a final clearing of the case arrives, and there is a renewed inquiry on the basis that Edalji is innocent, and that the actual perpetrators have never been punished, there are many facts which may be laid before the authority who conducts it. Meanwhile the task which lies immediately before me is not to show who did do the crimes—though that, I think, is by no means an insuperable problem—but that Edalji did not and could not have done them. I will leave young Green there, with his two contradictory statements, and I will confine myself to his relation with the case, whichever of the statements is true.

And, first of all, here are the police who claim to hold his written confession. Then why did they not prosecute? It will not do to say that it is not a crime to kill your own horse. It is not a crime to shoot your own horse from human motives, but it is at all times a crime, as the Society for the Prevention of Cruelty to Animals would very quickly show, to disembowel a horse on a dark night, be it fifty times your own. Here is an outrage of the same sort which has convulsed the countryside for so many months, it is brought home by his own confession to the offender, and yet the police refuse to prosecute, and connive at the man's flight from the country. But why? If it was not that the prosecution of Green would bring out facts which would interfere with the successful prosecution of Edalji, then, again, I ask, why? Far be it from me to be unjust to the police, but again it is their own really extraordinary behavior which drives one to seek for hypotheses. The Home Office says that all inquiry has been made in this case, and that everything has been investigated and the matter closed. That is the official answer I received only a fortnight ago. Then can the Home Office give any good reason why Green was not prosecuted? The point is a very vital one.

Green was present at Edalji's trial, was not called, and left afterwards for South Africa. He had been subpoenaed by the police, and that, no doubt, was what prevented the defence from calling him. But had they done so, and had he spoken in public as he has spoken in private, there would have been an end of all possibility, according to my information, of the great miscarriage which ensued. It may be noted before leaving this extraordinary incident that the reason given by Green in his confession was that the horse had to be killed, having been injured in the yeomanry training, but nowhere has he ever said a word to suggest that he was acting in collusion with George Edalji.

And now at last we come to the trial. Here, as at every point of this extraordinary case, there are irregularities which will be more fitly dealt with by a lawyer. Suffice it that though the case was of such importance that it is generally thought that it should not have been at Quarter Sessions at all, it was at the lesser of the courts which make up that tribunal that it was at last tried. In Court A a skilled lawyer presided. Sir Reginald Hardy, who conducted Court B, had no legal training. I have not a word to say against his desire to be impartial and fair, but here was a young man, accused of one of a series of crimes for which the whole county was longing to find someone who might be made an example of. The jury would naturally have the same feelings as their fellow-citizens. Hence it was peculiarly necessary to have a cold legal mind to cool their ardour and keep them on firm ground of fact, far from prejudice and emotion. Yet it was in the court of the layman that the case was tried.

The ground over which the prosecution advanced is already familiar to the reader. We have the clothes which have now become "wet." They were merely "damp" in the previous inquiry, and we have the word of the vicar that this dampness was imperceptible to him, coupled with the fact that any bloodstains would then have been liquid. We have the down-at-heel boot, which was fitted into impressions which must have been made after rain, whereas the whole police theory was that the crime was committed before the rain. We have the bloodstains which sank from smears into two three-penny-bit patches, and we have the hairs which made their appearance thirteen hours after the coat had been in the hands of the police, and after it had been associated with the strip of horse's hide.

Then came the letters. There was a strong probability that whoever wrote the letters knew something of the crimes. What matter that the letters actually accused Edalji himself and vilified him in all sorts of ways? What matter that one villainous postcard in the same writing as the others was posted at Wolverhampton when he was at Aberystwith? What matter that in the original series of anonymous letters the writer had said, "Do you think we cannot imitate your kid's writing?" None of these things weighed as compared with the expression of opinion by an expert that the letters were in George Edalji's own writing. As the unfortunate prisoner listened to such an opinion he must have felt that he was in some nightmare dream. And who was the expert who expressed these views which weighed so heavily with jury? It was Mr. Thomas Gurrin. [One must not be too hard on the hapless Thomas Gurrin. His testimony in the case of Adolph Beck, a man accused of defrauding women out of their jewelry, was influenced by the fact that over ten women identified Beck as the culprit. The truth was, the real thief was a man named John Smith, who had relatively bad handwriting, as did Beck. Apparently, illegibly bad handwriting looks illegibly similar to other bad handwriting. See William Roughhead, *Classic Crimes* (London: Cassell, 1951), pp. 291–296.] And what is the record of Mr. Thomas Gurrin? His nemesis was soon to come. Within a year he had to present himself before the Beck Committee, and admit the terrible fact that through his evidence an innocent man had suffered prolonged incarceration. Does this fact alone not convince my readers that an entire reconsideration of the Edalji case is a most pressing public duty?

There is absolutely the whole evidence—the coat-boot-razor business, the letter business, the so-called incriminating expressions which I have already analyzed, and the one fact, which I admit did really deserve consideration, that a group of schoolboys with whom once a month young Edalji may have travelled were known also to the writer of the letters. That is all. I have shown what each link is worth. And on that evidence a young gentleman, distinguished already in an honourable profession, was torn from his family, suffered all the indignities of a convict, was immured for three of the best years of his life, was struck from the roll on which with such industry and self-denial he had written his name, and had every torture made ten-fold more bitter by the thought of the vicar at home, of his mother and of his sister, so peculiarly sensitive, from their position in the church, to the scoff and the derision of those around them. It is a tale which makes a man hot with indignation as he reads it.

One word as to the evidence of the family, upon which so much depends.

It has been asserted that it was given in a peculiar way, which shook the confidence of the jury. I have had some experience of the Edaljis, and I can say with confidence that what seemed peculiar to the jury arose from extreme anxiety to speak the absolute, exact truth. An experienced barrister who knew them well remarked to me that they were the most precisely truthful people he had ever met—"bad witness," he added, "as they are so conscientious that they lay undue stress upon any point of doubt."

It must be admitted that the defence was not as strong as it might have been made, which does not seem to have been due to any shortcomings of the counsel so much as to a deficiency in the supply of information. The fact is that the consciousness of innocence was in this case a danger, as it caused some slackness in guarding every point. So far as I can find, the whole story of the early persecutions of 1888 and of 1893–5 was not gone into, nor was their probable connection with that of 1903 pointed out. The blindness of Edalji, a most vital fact, was not supported by an array of evidence; indeed, I think that it was hardly mentioned at all. At all points one finds things which might have been better, but even granting that, one cannot but feel the amazement, which Sir George Lewis has voiced when the jury brought in "Guilty," and Sir Reginald Hardy sentenced the prisoner to seven years.

Now, once again, let me state the double dilemma of the police before I leave this portion of my statement. Either Edalji did the crime before ten o'clock that night or after ten o'clock that night. The latter case must be laughed out of a commonsense court by the fact that his father, the vicar, spent the night within a few feet of him, that the small vicarage was bolted and barred, no one being heard to leave it, and that the police watchers outside saw no one leave it. If that does not establish an alibi, what could? On the other hand, supposing that he did it before ten, or rather before 9.30, the time of his return home. You have to face the supposition that after returning from a long day's work in Birmingham he sallied out in a coat which he was only known to wear in the house, performed a commonplace mission at the boot-shop in the village, then, blind as he was, hurried off for three-quarters of a mile, through difficult, tortuous ways, with fences to climb and railway lines to cross (I can answer for it, having myself trod every foot of it) to commit a ghastly and meaningless crime, entirely foreign to his studious and abstinent nature; that he then hurried back another three-quarters of a mile to the vicarage, arrived so composed and tidy as to attract no attention and sat down quietly to the family supper, the whole expedition from first to last being under an hour.

The mere statement of this alternative supposition seems grotesque enough, but on the top of the gross, inherent improbability you are up against the hard facts that the pony was bleeding freely in the morning, and could not have so bled all night, that the veterinary surgeon deposed that the wound could not possibly be more than six hours old, no other veterinary surgeon being called to contradict this statement, and that the footprints on which the police relied were worthless unless left after the rain, which began at twelve. Add to this that the pony was seen standing apparently all right by the police themselves at eleven o'clock, and the case then seems to me to be overpoweringly convincing. Take whichever supposition you like, and I say that it is demonstrably false, and an insult to commonsense, to suppose that George Edalji committed the crime for which, through the action of the Staffordshire police, the error of an expert, and the gross stupidity of a jury, he has been made to suffer so cruelly.

I do not know that there is much to add, save a bare recital of the events which have occurred since then. After Edalji's conviction the outrages continued unabated, and the epidemic of anonymous letters raged as ever. The November outrage upon Mr. Stanley's horses was never traced, but there was some good local information as to the author of that crime, and a widespread conviction in the district, which may have been utterly unjust, that the police were not too anxious to push the matter, as any conviction would certainly disturb the one which they had already obtained. This incident, also, will furnish some evidence for the coming inquiry. Finally, in March, 1904, a man, named Farrington, was convicted for injuring some sheep. No attempt has ever been made to trace any connection between this man and Edalji.

In the Green case not only was there no attempt to prove complicity between Green and Edalji, but I have evidence to show that the police had a most positive statement from Green that he had nothing to do with Edalji, obtained under circumstances which make it perfectly convincing. And yet, in face of this fact, Mr. Disturnal, the mouthpiece of the police at the trial, was permitted to say, referring to this outrage: "The letters which would be read would show that the writer of them was not acting alone, but in conjunction with some other people, and he put it to the jury, what was more likely than that, if there was a gang operating in the way suggested, one of its members would commit a similar outrage in order to create evidence for the defence?" Counsel, no doubt, spoke according to his instructions; but what are we to think of those from whom such instruction issued, since they had the clearest proof that there was no connection between Green and Edalji? Such incidents shake one's confidence in British justice to the very foundations, for it is clear that the jury, already prejudiced by the nature of the crimes, were hood-winked into giving their conviction.

A few words as to the sequel. The friends of the prisoner, organized and headed by Mr. R. D. Yelverton (late Chief Justice of the Bahamas), to whose long, ceaseless, and unselfish exertions Edalji will owe so much when the hour of triumph comes, drew up a memorial to the Home Secretary, setting forth some of the facts as here recorded. This petition for reconsideration was signed by ten thousand people, including hundreds of lawyers and many K.C.'s, and was reinforced by the strongest letters testifying to Edalji's character from men who must have known him intimately, including Mr. Denning, his schoolmaster; Mr. Ludlow, the solicitor with whom he was for five years articled; the honorary Secretary and Reader of the Birmingham Law Society, and many others.

Now every man of the world will admit that the schoolmaster's testimony is of very great importance, for any traits of cruelty will show themselves most clearly at that age. This is what Mr. Denning says: "During the five years your son George was here I have never known him commit any acts of cruelty or unkindness. I have always found him a thoroughly upright and well-principled youth, in whom I could place every confidence." Grier, his school-mate, writes: "He was several years older than myself, but always treated me with great kindness. I never knew him cruel to any animal, and from what I knew of him then—for I came to know him well—I should say he was quite incapable of any act of cruelty." How foolish the loose gossip and surmise of Stafford seem in the face of page after page of testimonials such as these.

The memorial had no effect, and some inquiry should certainly be made as to how its fate was determined. It would be indeed a vicious circle if a police prosecution, when doubted, is referred back again to the police for report. I cannot imagine anything more absurd and unjust in an Oriental despotism than this. And yet any superficial independent investigation, or even a careful perusal of the memorial, must have convinced any reasonable human being. The friends of Edalji, headed by Mr. Yelverton, naturally demanded to see the dossier at the Home Office, but, as in the Beck case; the seekers after justice were denied access to the very documents which they needed in order to prove their case and confute their opponents. [The Beck Case will be referred to numerous times throughout the examination of the predicament of George Edalji. Adolph Beck, a Norwegian, was convicted of defrauding "loose women" of their jewelry by telling them that he was a nobleman who needed a mistress. If they would trust him with a piece of their jewelry, he would write out a check for them to acquire a new outfit of clothing and move in with him.

Of course, the true criminal, as it turns out a man named John Smith, decamped with the jewelry.

Beck was convicted of this crime he did not commit because of convincing eyewitness testimony from at least ten women who identified him as the deceiver. If that were not enough, the Crown produced a handwriting expert in the person of Thomas Gurrin, who features prominently in the Edalji case, who testified that John Smith's handwriting and Adolph Beck's handwriting were one and the same.

When Beck was shown to be totally innocent of the charges against him because he was an uncircumcised man, and the perpetrator of the crimes was circumcised, Mr. Gurrin allowed that he would never have testified that the handwritings of John Smith and Adolph Beck were the same if he had previously known that that couldn't have been the case! The committee of review let Gurrin off without comment.]

I have said it was as in the Beck case. I might well have gone to a more classic example, for in all its details this seems to me to form a kind of squalid Dreyfus case. [Captain Alfred Dreyfus, a French army officer who was a Jew, was court-martialed for selling military secrets to the Germans. The military tribunal that convicted Captain Dreyfus was anti-Semitic and used a handwriting expert to convict Dreyfus of treason in the year 1894. The army also used forged documents to strengthen its case. A long campaign to exonerate Dreyfus, led by French novelist Émile Zola, did not succeed in gaining his release until 1906.] The parallel is extraordinarily close. You have a Parsee, instead of a Jew, with a young and promising career blighted, in each case the degradation from a profession and the campaign for redress and restoration, in each case questions of forgery and handwriting arise, with Esterhazy in the one, and the anonymous writer in the other. Finally, I regret to say that in the one case you have a clique of French officials going from excess to excess in order to cover an initial mistake, and that in the other you have the Staffordshire police acting in the way I have described.

And that brings me to what is the most painful part of my statement, and the one which I would be most glad to shirk were it possible for me to do so. No account of the case is complete which does not deal with the attitude taken up by Captain Anson, Chief Constable of Staffordshire, against this unhappy young man. It must, I suppose, have taken its root in those far-off days from 1892 to 1895, when Edalji was little more than a boy, and when Sergeant Upton, for reasons which make a tale by themselves, sent reports against him to his superior at Stafford. It was at that early date that Captain Anson delivered those two memorable dicta: "You may tell your son at once that I will not believe any profession of ignorance," and "I will endeavour to get the offender a dose of penal servitude."

Now, I have no doubt Captain Anson was quite honest in his dislike, and unconscious of his own prejudice. It would be folly to think otherwise. But men in his position have no right to yield to such feelings. They are too powerful, others are too weak, and the consequences are too terrible. As I trace the course of events this dislike of their chief's filtered down until it came to imbue the whole force, and when they had George Edalji they did not give him the most elementary justice, as is shown by the fact that they did not prosecute Green at a time when his prosecution would have endangered the case against Edalji.

I do not know what subsequent reports prevented justice from being done at the Home Office—(there lies the wickedness of the concealed dossier)—but this I do know, that instead of leaving the fallen man alone, every possible effort was made after the conviction to blacken his character, and that of his father, so as to frighten off anyone who might be inclined to investigate his case. When Mr. Yelverton first took it up, he had a letter over Captain Anson's own signature, saying, under date Nov. 8, 1903: "It is right to tell you that you will find it a simple waste of time to attempt to prove that George Edalji could not, owing to his position and alleged good character, have been guilty of writing offensive and abominable letters. His father is as well aware as I am of his proclivities in the direction of anonymous writing, and several other people have personal knowledge on the same subject."

Now, both Edalji and his father declare on oath that the former never wrote an anonymous letter in his life, and on being applied to by Mr. Yelverton for the names of the "several other people" no answer was received. Consider that this letter was written immediately after the conviction, and that it was intended to nip in the bud the movement in the direction of mercy. It is certainly a little like kicking a man when he is down.

Since I took up the case I have myself had a considerable correspondence with Captain Anson. I find myself placed in a difficult position as regards these letters, for while the first was marked "Confidential," the others have no reserve. One naturally supposes that when a public official writes upon a public matter to a perfect stranger, the contents are for the public. No doubt one might also add, that when an English gentleman makes most damaging assertions about other people he is prepared to confront these people, and to make good his words. Yet the letters are so courteous to me personally that it makes it exceedingly difficult for me to use them for the purpose of illustrating my thesis—viz., the strong opinion which Captain Anson had formed against the Edalji family. One curious example of this is that during fifteen years that the vicarage has been a centre of debate, the chief constable has never once visited the spot or taken counsel personally with the inmates.

For three years George Edalji endured the privations of Lewes and of Portland [prisons]. At the end of that time the indefatigable Mr. Yelverton woke the case up again, and *Truth* had an excellent series of articles demonstrating the impossibility of the man's guilt. Then the case took a new turn, as irregular and illogical as those which had preceded it. At the end of his third year, out of seven, the young man, though in good health, was suddenly released without a pardon. Evidently the authorities were shaken, and compromised with their consciences in this fashion. But this cannot be final. The man is guilty, or he is not. If he is he deserves every day of his seven years. If he is not, then we must have apology, pardon, and restitution. There can obviously be no middle ground between these extremes.

And what else is needed besides this tardy justice to George Edalji? I should say that several points suggest themselves for the consideration of any small committee. One is the reorganization of the Staffordshire Constabulary from end to end; a second is an inquiry into any irregularity of procedure at Quarter Sessions; the third and most important is a stringent inquiry as to who is the responsible man at the Home Office, and what is the punishment for his delinquency, when in this case, as in that of Beck, justice has to wait for years upon the threshold, and none will raise the latch. Until each and all of these questions is settled a dark stain will remain upon the administrative annals of this country.

I have every sympathy for those who deprecate public agitations of this kind on the ground that they weaken the power of the forces which make for law and order, by shaking the confidence of the public. No doubt they do so. But every effort has been made in this case to avoid this deplorable necessity. Repeated applications for justice under both Administrations have met with the usual official commonplaces, or have been referred back to those who are obviously interested parties.

Amid the complexity of life and the limitations of intelligence any man may do an injustice, but how is it possible to go on again and again reiterating the same one? If the continuation of the outrages, the continuation of the anonymous letters, the discredit cast upon Gurrin as an expert, the confession of a culprit that he had done a similar outrage, and finally the exposition of Edalji's blindness, do not present new facts to modify a jury's conclusion, what possible new fact would do so? But the door is shut in our faces. Now we turn to the last tribunal of all, a tribunal which never errs when the facts are fairly laid before them, and we ask the public of Great Britain whether this thing is to go on.

ARTHUR CONAN DOYLE
Undershaw,
Hindhead, January, 1907.

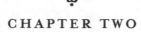

CHAPTER TWO

THE READERS REPLY:
THE PUBLIC FRAY BEGINS

The *London Daily Telegraph*'s publication of the two-part installment of Sir Arthur Conan Doyle's investigation into the conviction of solicitor George Edalji caused a firestorm of public debate. Readers from throughout the British Empire reacted by writing letters to the editor of not only the *Daily Telegraph* but to other newspapers as well. Keep in mind that in 1907, the primary method of public discourse was the newspaper. Radio was not widely available to the public, and television didn't exist. And obviously, there were no Internet chat rooms, bulletin boards, or websites where one could express one's opinions. In that sense, the daily newspaper was a more integral part of public life than it is today.

The first letter included in this chapter is a long treatise written by R. D. Yelverton, the former Chief Justice of the Bahamas. Yelverton took up the case of George Edalji with as much passion as did Sir Arthur, but his tactics were different. Yelverton led the drive to get relief for Edalji through petitions, or "memorials." As Yelverton explains, the British legal community was solidly behind the wrongly convicted solicitor.

JANUARY 14, 1907

CASE OF MR. EDALJI
PUBLIC OPINION

TO THE EDITOR OF THE *DAILY TELEGRAPH*

Sir—To say that the feelings of those who have throughout been convinced of the innocence of Mr. Edalji overflow with gratitude to Sir Arthur Conan Doyle and to your journal for the vindication of the truth but feebly expresses our appreciation of the powerful assistance which such advocacy gives to our cause. It is one of the most noble causes which it can fall to the lot of man or a journal to establish, and in which I, only a humble supporter of an innocent and cruelly-wronged sufferer, have behind me 10,000 signed memorialists, numerous friends of my own professional rank, including many King's Counsel, and upwards of 400 solicitors—some of whom knew Mr. Edalji personally. These memorials included, amongst others, a memorial from Mr. Edalji's acquaintances, clients, friends, and others in Birmingham, and more particularly from persons resident at Great Wyrley, Cheslyn Hay, Bridgetown, Walsall, and the district round. The signatures to this memorial number 3,570, and the memorial itself, with the signatures, covers 135 quarto sheets of paper. Another memorial, more general in its character, and signed by about 5,200 persons, some of them also personally acquainted with Mr. Edalji, covers 202 quarto pages. A memorial of a short character from remote districts, such as the West and North of England, is signed by one thousand persons. There is also a memorial confined wholly, except in one or two instances of solicitors who specially requested permission to sign, to solicitors resident and practicing in and around the neighborhood of Mr. Edalji's residence. With these I have before me as I write the praises of the young man, in letters from Mr. Denning (his former schoolmaster at Rugeley); Mr. Sutton Dudlow, with whom he served his articles; Mr. Grier, of the School; Cheaem, an old schoolfellow of his; Mr. Vice-Principal R. S. Heath, of Birmingham University, under whom he studied; Dr. Hosegood, medical officer of the Cannock District Council, who testifies in warm language to the young man as "strictly temperate, moral, shrewd, honest, and straightforward," and "kind towards animals"; and numerous others—persons independent and firmly determined as I am that justice shall be done.

Having been allowed to make, with your most generous permission, these preliminary observations, I will now address myself exclusively to the legal considerations, viz.: (1) The nature of the offences charged; (2) the proper procedure and the evidence which a trained lawyer would have required to establish guilt; and (3) the trial as it took place.

Mr. Edalji was indicted (1) for threatening to murder Sergeant Robinson—the threat to murder being contained in one of the ribald effusions which Sir Arthur Conan Doyle has so thoroughly exposed; (2) for maiming a pony, the property of the Great Wyrley Colliery Company.

It is unnecessary to point out to unprejudiced minds that threatening by letter to murder and the crime of cattle-maiming are amongst the most serious offences known to the law, but it is important to observe that they are both felonies created by statute, and it follows as a natural corollary that the judicial tribunal charged with such an investigation should not only be of the best procurable nature, but should be calmly and judicially guided by evidence of an independent and conclusive character. It is stated in "Russell on Crimes" that a prisoner charged with such offences should be tried at assizes. In this shameful case of Mr. Edalji he was not even tried in the first Court of Quarter Sessions. He was blasted as to character for life, as the prosecution hoped, in an Assistant Court of the Sessions, presided over by a justice of the peace without any legal training. That the trial was a "mis-trial" was admitted by the late law officers, and I challenge the Home Office to deny this. I can give names and details.

I now come to the so-called "evidence." I pass over the anonymous letter containing a threat to murder. It was too ridiculous for even this prosecution to present it, except to bolster up the other indictment, and I go at once to the charge of cattle-maiming, the nature of which has been so well exposed by Sir Arthur. I will confine myself to a commonsense, as well as legal view, as to what the evidence should have been, and then deal with it as it was.

Firstly, as to motive. Every crime, unless committed by a lunatic or for love of mischief, is actuated by a motive. Mr. Edalji is one of the sanest men I know. It could not be, neither was it, suggested that he, with a most brilliant record in honours, as a law student, went about cutting up animals for the love of mischief. Where, then, was the motive? This is the first thing a trained lawyer would have tried to discover. None was suggested—it is needless to say that there was none to suggest.

Secondly, What was the nature of the crime? To diagnose this in a charge of statutory felony such as this the prosecution should have called the veterinary surgeon in the employ of the colliery company, who examined the animal after the injury, and ordered its destruction. To him should have been produced, or suggested, the weapon which the prosecution presented as the probable instrument of the crime. He should have stated his opinion as an expert witness provided by the prosecution to guide the jury. Will it be credited that the veterinary surgeon, although in court, was not called by the Crown. No expert evidence was given or tendered by the prosecution diagnosing the crime, and it was left to the defence to put the veterinary surgeon into the box. The proposition which the vice-chairman put to the jury was this: "Pony injured; similar previous injuries to other cattle in the same neighborhood, and these referred to in anonymous letters ascribed to Edalji," therefore a crime was committed in this particular case. No evidence as to whether in harvest time the field had been searched for a scythe or broken glass or any weapons; simply the bald proposition I have stated. Did Edalji commit the crime? To support this the said vice-chairman admitted wholesale any letter produced by the prosecution, and whether stated by such prosecution to be written by Mr. Edalji or not, and then the jury were substantially told, "Gentlemen, take these letters into your consideration. Gurrin, the expert, says some of them were written by Edalji. If you believe Gurrin you will probably convict Edalji." Such a proposition has only to be stated to a legal mind to be exposed as fallacious. I have myself a strong opinion that most of these letters, if not all, were inadmissible in evidence and I will support my view by the following illustration. I receive from an anonymous writer, who possibly wishes to see me convicted, a letter in which I am fondly described as given to practicing forgery. I hand this letter to the police, requiring them to discover the author. I am myself charged subsequently to this with a forgery. According to the law of the assistant court of Staffordshire Sessions, the letter of the anonymous writer to me is evidence to go to the jury that I committed the subsequent forgery. Further, the vice-chairman was wrong in another particular. He allowed the jury to take cognisance of other cases of cattle-maiming in the neighbourhood, as supporting the guilt of Mr. Edalji in the particular crime under investigation. In this he was wrong.

In the recent case of Madame Girod the Court of Crown Cases quashed the conviction because the prosecution had, in order to support a charge of alleged theft from Messrs. Swan and Edgar, put in evidence as to a blouse and a belt alleged to have come from elsewhere and found at the defendant's lodgings. The learned judge at Clerkenwell very properly reserved the point, and Madame Girod was acquitted. But we do not need to stand upon legal technicalities; the broad fact is that Mr. Edalji is an innocent man, convicted by irregular means.

The fact that the evidence was purely circumstantial is another reason why the utmost deliberation should have been observed. The absolutely untrustworthy character of that evidence has been ruthlessly exposed by Sir Arthur Conan Doyle. Some of the letters are so gross and vile that it is absurd to ascribe them to Mr. Edalji. Police evidence through and through, without the slightest attempt at independent corroboration, was alone submitted to the jury. Persons subpoenaed by the prosecution; who had on the morning of the trial—I can give names and details—informed the prosecution that they could not support the police theory, but who were sitting in the room reserved for witnesses, were not called "because their evidence would not fit in with the case for the prosecution."

I do thank you most sincerely for allowing me to have space on your columns, and I may ask of your sense of justice and generosity to be allowed to supplement what I have here advanced by another letter. Meanwhile, I desire to conclude by saying that we demand an independent inquiry before a tribunal formed as in the recent Beck Case, and if the Royal Commissioners in that case, viz., the Master of the Rolls, Sir Spencer Walpole, and Sir John Edge would be so generous and kind as to sit in public, my friend and client, Mr. George Edalji will most willingly submit his guilt or innocence to their decision.—Yours faithfully,

> R. D. YELVERTON
> Ex-Chief Justice of the Bahama Islands
> 5, Pump-court, Temple, Jan. 12.

TO THE EDITOR OF THE *DAILY TELEGRAPH*

Sir—Having read the first installment of Sir A. Conan Doyle's investigation in the Edalji case, I must confess that I think optical experts will require some further explanations before it is clear to them. [**Conan Doyle probably came to regret ever bringing up the subject of Edalji's myopia. Throughout the ensuing months of correspondence that ran in the *Daily Telegraph*, this topic became an ever-living red herring diverting readers from better evidence and sounder arguments for Edalji's innocence.**]

To begin with, I must point out that the writer has made a slip in his suggestion that readers who are partial-sighted should place themselves in Edalji's position by wearing concave glasses of the power indicated. This would have just the contrary effect, and would make the person hypermetropic. If I wish to try and imagine how a myopic person feels I must wear convex glasses, because in the myopic eye the rays of light fall short of the retina, and to produce this effect artificially one must reduce the length of the path of the rays on the normal eye. This is, however, probably only a slip of the pen on the part of the writer.

The fact to be dealt with is the amount of the myopia. I must take exception to the statement that eight diopters is a very extraordinary amount. On reference to my record of 1,000 cases of short sight I find that nearly 200 equal or exceed that amount, and probably in an ophthalmic surgeon's casebook, dealing as he would mostly with diseased conditions, the percentage would be greater. Unless there is a morbid condition—and Mr. Kenneth Scott did not suggest this—it should easily be possible to correct the whole of Edalji's myopia by means of glasses, and at the age of eighteen it would usually be done. There are many persons wearing concave glasses of from ten to fifteen diopters power, and getting almost full visual acuity.

The ophthalmic surgeon who certifies to the defect merely gives the amount of the myopia, and does not state if it can be corrected by means of glasses as a whole or in part, or if the eyes are in such a diseased condition that it cannot be corrected at all, and this is the crux of the whole optical question.

Merely to be myopic to the extent of eight diopters proves nothing, because, under most circumstances, it can be corrected, and, further, it is well known that the pupil of the myopic eye is generally larger than the normal, consequently with the defect remedied by means of sonal lenses, which fit close to the eyes, it is possible that, owing to the admission of more light, the person might actually see better in semi-darkness than the individual with good eyes.

Please allow me to state that I have no personal bias in the case, and am dealing with it purely as a scientific problem, which can probably be explained by Sir A. Conan Doyle.—I remain yours faithfully,

> JAMES AITCHISON
> 12, Cheapside,
> E.C., Jan. 11.

The *Daily Telegraph* promotes its series and its author.

COMMISSION OF THREE
SIR A. CONAN DOYLE'S SUGGESTION

Many who have read Sir A. Conan Doyle's able analysis of the Edalji case will wonder (says the *Evening Standard* and *St. James's Gazette*) how it is that the creator of "Sherlock Holmes" has become the champion of the young Birmingham solicitor. Asked by one of our representatives, who visited him at his house at Hindhead, to explain the matter, Sir Arthur readily complied:

"A little over three weeks ago," he said, "Edalji sent me cuttings of some articles which he wrote on his own case in a Midland paper. For several days the cuttings lay on my writing table just as they had been taken out of the envelope, and they might have remained there like others, only glanced at, had I not found myself one evening with nothing very much to do.

"So I took the cuttings up, and began to read them—very languidly at first. Then some statement he made struck me, and after that there were several others which held my attention. I became really interested, and saw that here was a man who was telling the truth in a case which needed further investigation.

"Well, I met him by appointment later, and then I decided to take up his case. I am firmly convinced that if ever a man was innocent Edalji is. I have been to Great Wyrley, and gone carefully over the scene of the outrage, as well as read a number of letters and papers. Since I first took the matter in hand I have been working, I suppose, twelve hours a day at it."

"And have you followed those methods which you made 'Sherlock Homes' use?"

Sir Arthur laughed. "Ah!" he said. "There is a good deal of difference between fact and fiction; but I have endeavoured to get at facts first before coming to any conclusion."

"Then you started without any predisposition in Edalji's favour?"

"Yes. I kept my mind perfectly open. In fact, on several occasions I came across side-issues which might have led to proving Edalji's guilt, and I left my main investigation to follow them up, in each instance, however, finding innocence clearly proved.

"It is rather a difficult legal question to know how to get the case reopened. There is no court of appeal for a re-trial; but I am in favour of a commission of three being appointed, not only to sift thoroughly all the evidence, but also to hold an inquiry into the police conduct of the case."

In his concluding remarks, Sir Arthur again emphasized his confidence in Edalji's innocence, and remarked that now he had gone into the case and taken it up he would fight on his behalf to the end.

The *Daily Telegraph* continued to promote itself by quoting extensively from other papers that could not ignore the national controversy.

PRESS COMMENTS

Sir A. Conan Doyle's articles on the Edalji case, published in the *Daily Telegraph* last week, have been extensively quoted both by the London and provincial Press. Among the prominent references to his investigation are the following:

PALL MALL GAZETTE

Sir Arthur Conan Doyle's examination of the Edalji case, as published in the *Daily Telegraph* will leave an uneasy impression in many quarters as to the conclusion reached by a Staffordshire jury, and the sentence of seven years' penal servitude pronounced by an untrained county magistrate. The chief points pressed by the investigator are that Edalji's defects of eyesight make it impossible for him to have scoured the country at night in order to mutilate cattle; that there is evidence of persistent prejudice towards him on the part of the police, from the chief constable downwards; that another man who confessed to an act of mutilation was not prosecuted, but permitted in a most mysterious way to leave the country; that evidence as to handwriting was accepted from the "expert" who assisted in the conviction of Adolf Beck; and, finally, that Edalji, who had a perfectly blameless record, was unconnected with the crimes in question by a particle of direct evidence. The facts to which Sir Arthur Conan Doyle draws attention with regard to the police attitude are of such a serious character that it seems impossible for the matter to be left where it stands.

LLOYD'S NEWS

With the Beck case still fresh in the public memory, it is not surprising that such interest has been aroused by "Sherlock Holmes's" investigation of the Edalji case. Sir A. Conan Doyle has unquestionably shown in his own methods some of the ingenuity and resource which distinguish his ever-famous detective. It is true, when he was asked on Saturday whether he had taken Sherlock Holmes for his model, he remarked that there is a good deal of difference between fact and fiction—an implied criticism by his creator on Sherlock Holmes which that great man will no doubt survive. In any case, Sherlock Holmes could not have taken more pains to get at the truth. Was Edalji guilty of horse-maiming at Great Wyrley, on account of which he was sentenced to seven years' penal servitude in 1903, or was he not? Sir Conan Doyle is confident he was not. If he was, then it must be agreed he deserved every day of his seven years. If he was not, there must be something more than release after three years on ticket-of-leave. There must be "apology, pardon, and restitution."

EVENING NEWS

It was certainly a happy idea on the part of the *Daily Telegraph* to secure the services of Sir Arthur Conan Doyle, the creator of Sherlock Holmes, for an investigation into the case of George Edalji, whose conviction for cattle-maiming outrages at Great Wyrley, in Staffordshire, and whose subsequent release from penal servitude are still fresh in the public mind. Ever since the conviction of Edalji for the hideous outrages which shocked and horrified the whole country, untiring efforts have been made to show that he could not have been the guilty person and the more the case was investigated the clearer did it become that the unfortunate man never had anything approaching fair play at his trial. But it has been left for Sir Arthur, ably using the system of reasoning which has brought him so much literary fame, to demonstrate with perfect lucidity that the conviction was entirely unjustified, and not only to prove that Edalji might have been innocent, but that he was so in very fact.

The most unpleasant part of the case, and one with which Sir Arthur deals in an admirably judicial spirit, is that concerned with the action of Captain Anson in the matter. That this police officer had conceived a strong prejudice against Edalji years before the Great Wyrley outrages occurred appears to be only too clear, and although Sir Arthur has "no doubts that Captain Anson was quite honest in his dislike," he leaves us in no doubt as to the effect of that dislike upon the official conduct of the case against the unfortunate prisoner. With regard to the testimony of Mr. Gurrin, it can only be said that, actuated as he doubtless was by the best of motives, that gentleman has only succeeded in proving that his testimony of handwriting experts is, in at least nine cases out of ten, absolutely unreliable, a fact which the Beck case and others before it had already established.

It is, of course, impossible to enter here into the means by which Edalji's conviction was obtained, but these facts are clear, and may be stated in a few words.

1. Edalji was convicted.

2. Edalji's friends claimed to have proved his innocence.

3. Edalji was released for no reason assigned after less than half his sentence had run.

Why was he released? Was it because the Home Secretary thought that Edalji's guilt had not been proved? Surely that could be the only reason for extending "mercy" to a man convicted of so hideous an offence, but if the man had not been guilty in the eyes of the heads of our legal system he must be treated as innocent, he must receive a pardon and compensation for the grievous wrong which has been inflicted upon him. There is no half-way house, and the present attitude of the authorities constitutes a grave offence against all English ideas of right and justice.

THE OBSERVER

To risk a unique reputation is always a bold thing, and when such reputation is an honest one our attention must needs be arrested. Yet this is what Sir Conan Doyle has done—he, our champion fictional detective, he in whose hands the unravelling of criminal mystery has never been known to fail; he, more than any man in England, who, were he not positive of a man's innocence, has most to lose by seeking to establish it. The plunge has been taken, and the creator of Sherlock Holmes now stakes his reputation on the innocence of the man Edalji, condemned to seven years' penal servitude by a county magistrate. The exculpating points advanced by the investigator are in themselves of great weight and significance. Chief among them is the question of Edalji's eyesight, which was so defective that Sir Conan considers it would have been physically impossible for him to have scoured a very difficult country by night, as alleged; and, further, that there is convincing evidence of systematic persecution towards Edalji on the part of the police, from the chief constable downwards.

Unquestionably Sir Conan Doyle must feel inwardly satisfied with the justice of his case, otherwise he would never have spoken so frankly. Obviously the matter cannot be left where it is. The public will have to insist on a careful and immediate inquiry. If Sir Conan Doyle proves his contentions he will have done a much injured man a great service and the public a public one. It is now the duty of the law to pronounce true judgment.

STAFFORDSHIRE SENTINEL

The opinion of most of those who were in court at the trial was that, though there was a strong case of suspicion, the evidence did not go far enough to warrant a conviction. In Scotland a verdict of "not proven" would probably have been returned, and if there had been a Court of Criminal Appeal available in England the conviction might very likely have been quashed. Sir A. Conan Doyle's narrative renders clearer than ever the contention that there ought not to have been a conviction upon the evidence. In England a man must, of course, be regarded as innocent until he has been proved guilty, and whether George Edalji was "proved" to be guilty is certainly open to very serious question.

Mr. Edalji defends himself, Conan Doyle replies to Aitchison's letter, and other writers contribute to the controversy.

JANUARY 15, 1907

THE EDALJI CASE
LETTERS FROM MR. EDALJI AND SIR A. CONAN DOYLE

THE QUESTION OF EYESIGHT

TO THE EDITOR OF THE *DAILY TELEGRAPH*

Sir—Allow me to heartily thank you for the great space you have devoted to Sir Arthur Conan Doyle's able and lucid articles on my behalf.

Regarding Mr. Aitchison's letter in to-day's issue, while I am unable to discuss the scientific questions he raises, I should like to draw attention to the following facts:

I have several times been to optical experts and ophthalmic surgeons, with a view to getting glasses to suit me, but until Dr. Kenneth Scott made a very long and careful scrutiny of my eyesight I have never got glasses of any use to me. Last November I got two well-known ophthalmic surgeons to examine my eyes. Both prescribed glasses of practically the same description. For several weeks I thoroughly tried those recommended by one of these gentlemen (a man, let me add, of the highest standing in his profession), but found them absolutely useless. After a prolonged investigation, Dr. Scott discovered defects which I presume others had failed to detect, told me I must not use the glasses I had, and prescribed very different ones, and with them I can see better than ever I did in my life. But even these do not give me normal sight, as I find other people can see things without glasses at a far greater distance than I can with them. Another well-known ophthalmic surgeon declares my sight to be considerably less than one-tenth of the normal.

Now, for the question about seeing in semi-darkness. On a main road, provided I know it thoroughly, I can find my way as well as most people after dusk without glasses at all. But the point in my case has nothing to do with semi-darkness or main roads, or even roads of any description. After the theory of the police that I committed the outrage between nine and 9.40 had been proved to be untenable and utterly ridiculous on the face of it, the prosecuting counsel in his closing speech (to which there was no opportunity for my advocate to reply) promptly threw it aside, and declared that if I did not commit the atrocity when I was seen out (on the main road only) I must have done it when I was not seen out at all; and that owing to the unusual darkness, which the police had suggested equalled, if it did not exceed, that which troubled Egypt, the three constables actually guarding the field (two of whom, Bradley and Weaver, the prosecution found it convenient not to call) could not have noticed me! There were also twenty other constables patrolling the immediate neighbourhood of the occurrence, and so we get the preposterous hypothesis that in complete darkness I sallied forth on this diabolical errand, found my way along a colliery tramway, with obstacles at almost every step, across the London and North-Western main line, over long rows of metals and sidings intersected with points, wires, and signalling contrivances of a varied description, then along the line over projecting "sleepers" to a flight of steps, and down the steps and under an archway into the field. All this way I should have to proceed so noiselessly as not to attract the attention of the army of watchers around me, and in the field make myself invisible to the three detectives there, find the animal, inflict the terrible injuries without the pony making any movement, or sound likely to attract attention and then return by an absolutely impossible route at night, over the fields, hedges, and ditches, where the alleged footmarks were found. Never in my life had I been in this field till last October, when I went purposely to see it. It has been asked why I called no expert evidence about my sight at the trial. The explanation is simple enough; so satisfied were my advisers that there was not a particle of anything worthy of the name of evidence against me, and that no jury would ever dream of convicting me that I was told I was incurring useless expenses in calling any witnesses at all. However, I myself insisted on calling those witness who so completely upset the theory of the crime being committed before 9.40, and I reluctantly refrained from calling any expert as to my eyesight or handwriting.

To show that I gave full information to my advisers about the state of my eyes, I extract the following from counsel's brief, which I have before me:

> He is by no means an athlete, and, in addition, is very short-sighted. This would make it difficult for him to get out at night, find his way across country, and scale hedges and ditches, and also find the animals, while a strong man, used to horses and cattle, in the full possession of his eyesight would doubtless experience much difficulty and danger in catching and wounding them without their retaliating.
> —Yours truly,

> G. E. T. EDALJI
> Jan. 14.

TO THE EDITOR OF THE *DAILY TELEGRAPH*

Sir—I regard the optical part of my argument as so important that, with your permission, I will at once answer the remarks of Mr. Aitchison.

I fear that I expressed myself clumsily in the paragraph in which I showed how the normal eye might be reduced to the condition in which Mr. Edalji's eyes always are. Every minus sign in the prescription would, of course, become a plus. My own sight is normal, and I can answer for the feeling of helplessness which such a glass produces. I tried it upon a Press man, and defied him to reach the lawn-tennis ground in front of the house. He failed. Mr. Aitchison underrates the degree of myopia, though it is quoted in full in my paper. On one axis it becomes -10.50, which surely is a very high degree, and the more serious when combined with astigmatism.

The effects of correction are beside the question, as Mr. Edalji did not wear glasses. I have a police admission to that effect.

To my mind it was as physically impossible for Mr. Edalji to have committed the crime as it would have been if his legs, instead of his eyes, were crippled. I have asked the editors of three of the leading medical papers to put the question of possibility before those of their readers who practice eye work. When the replies have come in we shall see what the opinion of the oculists of Great Britain is upon the subject.—Yours faithfully,

ARTHUR CONAN DOYLE
Undershaw,
Hindhead, Surrey, Jan. 14.

Sir—I have read with the greatest interest the articles by Sir Conan Doyle on the Edalji case, and am absolutely convinced that a serious miscarriage of justice has occurred. But as Sir Conan Doyle, in having this matter brought before Parliament, as he undoubtedly will, should be able to prove every item in his brief, I venture to point out to you an error he has made (and rather a serious one on account of the importance which he attaches to it) regarding the question of Mr. Edalji's eyesight. I personally happen to have the misfortune to suffer from myopic astigmatism in a degree which is actually greater by about one dioptric more than Mr. Edalji's, and yet with correcting glasses my vision is brought up to almost exactly normal. If mine, why not Mr. Edalji's? And then the important point with which Sir Conan opens this able defense falls to the ground; he lays great stress on Mr. Edalji not being able to see things at a distance of more than a few inches, and being unable, on account of his eyesight, to find his way about difficult and unfamiliar ground, too. Yet there is nothing easier for the Staffordshire police—and remember, they are really on their trial now—than to prove that with proper spectacles his vision was that of a normal individual.

It is because I am so anxious that Sir Conan Doyle shall not have one weak spot in his splendid championship that I venture to bring this point to your notice—Yours, too,

I. A. BARRY, F.R.C.S.
Church-road, Hove, Jan. 12.

TO THE EDITOR OF THE *DAILY TELEGRAPH*

Sir—There are some points connected with the anonymous letters which I think Sir Conan Doyle has not sufficiently signalised in his very able articles on the Edalji case. These letters, I think, ought not to have been admitted in evidence. Edalji was not accused (except in speeches, into which they were improperly introduced) of being one of a gang of horse-maimers, or of being concerned, whether as principal or accessory, in any offense of the kind with one exception—the crime committed on Aug. 17, 1903—and the prosecutors ought not to have been permitted to give any evidence that did not bear on the commission of that crime. However, an inquiry intended to clear up the entire case should no doubt include the anonymous letters, but it should also include the entire series of crimes which were alleged to have been the work of the same criminal, or, at least, of the same gang. The unfairness of giving the letters in evidence, while giving no evidence of the crimes referred to in them, must be obvious to everyone. These crimes were treated as matters of public notoriety, and it was alleged that the letters showed such an intimate acquaintance with them that the writer must have been either the perpetrator or a member of a gang of perpetrators. But the public notoriety of crimes is a very different thing from accurate knowledge by the public of the details of each crime which would be necessary in order to show that the writer of the letters was intimately acquainted with these details; and this theory that the letters proved the intimate acquaintance of the writer with the crimes seems to have passed unquestioned at the trial; whereas, had evidence as to the crimes been given, the variances would have at once become apparent.

Sir Conan Doyle has pointed out one of these variances, but not, I think, sufficiently signalised it. The writer of one of these letters stated that Edalji had killed a horse at full moon on the night of April 11. Sir Conan has pointed out that no horse was killed on that night, the actual outrage having occurred on the night of the 2nd. But he does not seem to have observed that the full moon really took place on the night of the 11th, and that on the night of the 2nd the moon was not even half full. Nor, in fact, had there been any outrage at full moon up to the time that the letters were written, the nearest approach being that on the night of May 14, when the moon had been full on the 11th. The writer seems to have heard from somebody that there had been an outrage at full moon, and knowing about Edalji's defective sight, he fixed on the full moon for the outrage with which he was alleged to be personally concerned, and in doing so hit on a full moon, when no outrage occurred. The outrages, it will be noted, commenced in February. There were no anonymous letters till July. Putting out of sight for a moment Mr. Gurrin's evidence as to the handwriting, I think there could be no doubt that the object of the writer was to implicate Edalji in a series of outrages which had hitherto baffled the police. But why did not the writer try to do this at an earlier period? Or why, if Edalji himself were the writer, did he not commence earlier?

The reason seems to me to be that the writer was not in the Great Wyrley district until about July 1, and was misinformed with regard to the details of some of the preceding outrages, as would have appeared if evidence as to these details had been given. I think most of your readers will fail to see any motive for Edalji writing an anonymous letter stating that he had killed a horse at full moon on April 11, when the police, who were intended to see the letter, knew very well that no horse had been killed at that date, though, for some unexplained reason, nothing was said about this gross blunder at the trial, when the letters were relied on as proving that the writer was intimately acquainted with the preceding crimes. For my own part, I do not think he possessed any special knowledge whatever. He was an enemy of Edalji's, and wrote for the purpose of implicating Edalji; but it occurred to him that Edalji might have a satisfactory alibi as regards some of the crimes, and that perhaps others might occur when he was in prison. Hence the theory of a gang naturally occurred to him, and his plan succeeded. Edalji was tried and convicted of the very first crime that occurred after the letters were written, and the letters formed a large part of the evidence against him, though in my opinion they ought to have been rejected.

Do the police still stick to this gang theory? If so, why have they never made any attempt to show that Green and Farrington were members of the gang? And why did they let Green escape? If he were of the gang, the injury done to his horse should not have been treated as an isolated incident. (And as Green was a youth of nineteen, the chances are that the horse which was killed, though he was in the habit of riding it, belonged to his father, not himself, so that the suggested defence—viz., that a man might lawfully kill his own horse—would have been inadmissible. On this point, I may also mention that the sheep killed on the night of May 14 belonged to the elder Green.) Or will the police contend that there was really a gang, though neither Green nor Farrington were members of it, and though they have hitherto failed to detect and bring to justice any member of it except Edalji?

But for this gang theory, started by these letters, the continuance of the outrages after Edalji's imprisonment must have satisfied the Home Secretary that he was the wrong man. On what evidence, then, does this theory rest? And how is it that the police have failed to trace this gang?—Truly yours,

An Irish Barrister

⚜

CHAPTER THREE

MR. A. H. HENDERSON-LIVESEY
STIRS THE WATERS: THE PUBLIC
FRAY ESCALATES

In the days following the publication of Conan Doyle's investigation into the Great Wyrley animal-maiming case, public opinion seemed to be leaning toward Edalji. However, the debate became much more heated when the *Daily Telegraph* published a letter by Mr. A. H. Henderson-Livesey. History has failed to record who A. H. Henderson-Livesey was or what credentials he had, but his letter was the first to bring Sir Arthur's conclusions into serious question. He challenges Conan Doyle on the question of Edalji's eyesight, a challenge which was well-founded, given that Conan Doyle tended to overstate his own credentials as an eye doctor.

But Henderson-Livesey also defended the local police and their methods so effectively that Conan Doyle's judgment and integrity were called into question. At the end of his letter, Henderson-Livesey chides Conan Doyle and suggests that he "apply to the case more accurately the methods of 'deductive analysis' of his great creation . . ."

Needless to say, Sir Arthur wasn't going to sit still for that. He fired back several letters defending his statements and sought the support of the medical community in his conclusions about Edalji's eyesight. This time, however, the controversy grew even more intense. Other daily newspapers

87

began calling for an official inquiry into the case, and for the first time since the publication of Conan Doyle's investigation, Edalji himself fully entered the fray. A. H. Henderson-Livesey fired back, defending the statements he'd made in his letter which were, themselves, now under attack.

Ultimately, Edalji's public defense would become a family matter: both the Reverend Edalji and his wife, Charlotte, would join the letter-writing campaign, each protesting in the strongest language possible that their son was innocent.

TO THE EDITOR OF THE *DAILY TELEGRAPH*

Sir—Sir Arthur Conan Doyle's remarkable articles on the case of George Edalji will, no doubt, occasion widespread national interest, but it is to be hoped that in the controversy which must ensue in the Press and elsewhere two facts will not be overlooked. The first is, that those officials who were engaged in the case, and who are still in the public service, are debarred from replying to Sir Arthur in the public Press; the second is, that written as the articles are, three years after the trial, when the details have been forgotten by the great majority of people, nothing is easier than, by a judicious selection and display of certain facts, to make the evidence upon which the conviction was based appear weak and unconvincing. Any man equipped with only a modicum of forensic ability could deal in a like manner with any conviction obtained upon circumstantial evidence a few years back.

One would like to deal seriatim with Sir Arthur's contentions, were it not that such a course would necessitate a really outrageous demand upon your very valuable space. The utmost, therefore, that can be done in a letter of this kind is to call attention to one or two points in the articles which, to say the least of it, are extremely unconvincing.

First, as to Edalji's blindness, which the author rightly regards as a point of overwhelming importance, the medical evidence which is put forward is the result of an examination made since the prisoner's release. It may be taken as an accurate account of the state of the man's eyes now, but what proof is advanced that they were in that condition when the crimes were committed? A man with slightly defective eyesight may well become blind in the space of three years, especially when those years are passed in confinement.

The author skips over this vital point by a perfunctory reference to "a permanent structural condition," but what is it that the public are asked to believe? That here was a man "as blind as a bat" accused of a crime which could not possibly have been committed by a man so afflicted. It was open to prisoner's counsel to challenge the prosecution to have the man examined by the highest authorities in the land, and could such evidence have been produced the case must have collapsed.

Why was this evidence not called? Because, whatever may be the condition of the man's eyes now, he certainly was not blind, or nearly blind, three years ago.

If this is not so, it must be said that the articles bring condemnation upon anyone: they heap it in three-fold measure upon the prisoner's relatives, his friends, his legal advisers, and all who were connected with his defence. It is unthinkable that all these people could have this vital element in their case.

The second point to which I desire to draw attention is this: in the first article the author has referred to a long-standing persecution of the Edalji family by means of anonymous threats, and plainly suggests that the outrages were committed by the sender of these threats, for the express purpose of fastening their authorship upon George Edalji, and thus bringing about his ruin. How, then, does he account for the continuance of the outrages after the man's conviction? Is it conceivable that all this devilish ingenuity would be shown to bring about a certain result, and then a line of conduct taken which, in all probability, would have the ultimate effect of nullifying the result? It was suggested by the prosecution—quite reasonably—that the outrage that was committed during the trial was committed by the prisoner's friends, to throw the police off the scent, but, says Sir Arthur, this is absurd, because an outrage was committed after the man had been committed to prison. The reasoning here is somewhat involved. Would the interest taken in the man by his friends cease with his conviction? If an outrage during the trial to confuse the police, why not one after conviction to further heighten the effect?

Now, Sir, as to the hair on the coat. If the police went to the vicarage with the express object of making evidence to incriminate Edalji, why should they show the coat to the vicar at all? Why should they not have taken the coat without comment, and put the hair on at the station? The author sets the testimony of the family to the effect that they did not see hair on the coat against that of the police to the effect that they did. Can this be justified? Can it be alleged that the desire of the police to obtain a conviction was greater, or as great, as the desire of the man's own father, mother, and sister to save him from penal servitude? Is it reasonable to expect that the vicar's family would admit that they saw hairs on the coat, even if scores were there? Such a belief would be held in defiance of all one's knowledge of human nature.

The fact that the police showed the vicar the coat is a distinct point in their favor.

Then as to the kind of hair on the coat, Sir Arthur's argument here can only be described as far-fetched. How can it be confidently suggested that under such circumstances as those which pertained at the commission of the outrage the hairs which adhered to the perpetrator's coat would necessarily be brittly hairs? Is it not as reasonable to suppose that the man before committing the foul deed would caress the animal and possibly stroke its hide?

The author asks why the police cut off the animal's hide. Many of us would like to know this, and quite conceivably the police have an excellent answer. In any case it is difficult to see how the fact strengthens the case against them. The creator of Sherlock Holmes does not need to be informed that it is not necessary to cut off an animal's hide to obtain a few hairs.

As I do not desire this letter to make the acquaintance of your blue pencil, I will bring it to a close. The case certainly presents many unsatisfactory features which may be inquired into with advantage, but before Sir Arthur Conan Doyle establishes his contention as to George Edalji's innocence he will have to apply to the case more accurately the methods of "deductive analysis" of his great creation and exhibit a little less of that gentleman's animosity to the "official police."

A. H. HENDERSON-LIVESEY
5, The Avenue, Bedford Park, W.

TO THE EDITOR OF THE *DAILY TELEGRAPH*

Sir—There are some points in Mr. Henderson-Livesey's letter in your issue of today which call for a prompt answer from me. In my letter which appears this morning I have shown that it was not due to any laxity on my part that no expert was called regarding my eyesight. I repeat that I was advised the evidence against me was so palpably ridiculous that it was needless for me to call even a single witness to refute it. Immediately after my conviction, both my friends and myself applied to the Home Office to make a scientific examination of my eyes, but it was not till after a year's delay that it was done. The Home Office persists in refusing to furnish me, or my advisers, with any information about the report sent in by the gentleman who made this examination. The inference is obvious. I now publicly challenge the Home Office to produce this report.

Next, as to the insinuation that prison life made my eyes worse. For the credit of our prison system let me remark that my three years confinement in no way affected my sight, and, further, that I had not the slightest illness of any sort while in prison. The medical officers at Lewes and Portland, where I served practically the whole of my time, were well acquainted with the state of my eyesight. At Lewes I was only employed in part-making horses' nose-bags, which merely consists in a kind of plaiting on a board; and on account of my sight the words "Half task at cell labour" were written by the doctor on my door-card. At Portland there was no "task," but the doctor said that on account of my sight he could not—save at my own risk—put me on anything except picking coir (on a board with a comb), and this was my only employment while there. On the day after my arrival at Portland I was informed that, on account of my astigmatism and myopia, I should not be allowed to go up and down stairs, and was accordingly specifically "located on No. 1 Ward" by the doctor.

Your correspondent says: "Why should they [the police] not have taken the coat without comment, and put the hair on at the station?" My answer to this is that when they took the coat they did honestly think that two or three brownish threads which were on it were horse hairs, and it was these which they indicated to my friends. Surely, seeing that they mistook cocoa stains for blood, milk for saliva, a botany spud for a dagger, and a railway key for a pistol, and made a number of other equally absurd mistakes, there is nothing surprising in their also making one about the hair.

Lastly, it is surely unnecessary for me to point out that neither I nor my friends have ever ceased to petition the Home Office for a reconsideration of my cause; that during the time of my imprisonment the Hon. R. D. Yelverton and others have indefatigably worked on my behalf, and that the editor of "Truth," besides forwarding to the Home Office an exhaustive memorial—dealing with every point on the case—also published in that journal a long series of admirably clear articles analyzing the whole of the evidence.

Everything that could be done was done to bring the whole of the evidence before the public without a delay of three years, or even three weeks.—Yours truly,

      G. E. T. EDALJI
      Jan. 15.

TO THE EDITOR OF THE *DAILY TELEGRAPH*
Sir—With your permission, I will deal with points as they are presented. Let me, therefore, say a few words as to Mr. Henderson-Livesey's letter.

1. The astigmatic myopia depends upon a congenital shape of the eye, and could not have been brought on by prison life. Mr. Edalji's sight is no worse now than it has ever been. That is, as Mr. Livesey says, a point of overwhelming importance, and there can be no doubt about it at all. I quite agree that its exclusion at the trial is a very serious reflection upon the way in which the case seems to have been presented.

2. The second of Mr. Livesey's objections, as to the continuance of the outrages after Edalji's conviction, will need a complete knowledge of the case before we can explain it. I have by no means committed myself unreservedly to the theory that the letters and the outrages are by the same hand.

It is quite possible that the writer of the letters took advantage of the existence of the outrages in order to vent his spite. That would explain the continuance of the outrages after the object of the letters had been attained. It is of interest to know that when the outrages continued after young Edalji's confinement the police were bombarded with anonymous letters suggesting that his father had done them. It was all part of the conspiracy against the family.

As to the hair on the coat, Mr. Livesey seems to miss my point, which is that when the police found that three witnesses then and there denied the existence of hairs—an unthinkable thing, if the hairs were actually staring them in the face—they should have brought in a doctor or other reputable witness to sustain their contention. With some moderation, I do not place the testimony of the vicar, his wife, and his highly educated daughter above that of two village constables, but I do claim that in such a conflict of opinions there should have been a referee.

I did not ask why the police cut off a piece of the animal's hide. It is obvious that they did so in order to give the doctor the means of comparison. They could not carry the pony down to the surgery. As to my argument about the type of hair, Mr. Livesey seems to have quite missed the point. I said nothing of "brittly" hairs, whatever that may mean. My contention was that a man coming in contact with a pony would carry away with him an assorted lot of hairs (if any), and not a lot which corresponded with one small piece of skin.

I should be glad for one instant before closing to ask your readers to raise their thoughts from small details for a moment, and to realize the general hypothesis upon which the police case rests. Merely to state it is to make it grotesquely impossible. It is that a purblind young lawyer, a total abstainer, and earnest student, devoted his days to professional work in Birmingham and his nights to crawling about the fields ripping animals open with no conceivable object in view, and being in all other respects a perfectly sane man. You have further to believe that after these exploits he sat down and wrote anonymous letters to the police, accusing himself of having done the deed. That is the charge on which Edalji has been convicted.—Yours faithfully,

ARTHUR CONAN DOYLE
Jan. 15.

TO THE EDITOR OF THE *DAILY TELEGRAPH*

Sir—Perhaps one of your many readers may be able and willing to give information upon this point. Is it a fact that on the occasion of one of Mr. Edalji's professional examinations it was with the utmost difficulty that he was able to ascertain the numbered desk at which he had to sit? I understand that, owing to the badness of his eyesight, he was, to quote my informant, "guided to his place" by one of the attendant officials. With regard to the dates April 11 and April 2, it might be interesting to know if either the "th" or "nd" were present, or was 11 merely an illiterate way of expressing 2. In this most painful and unfortunate case facts which can be fully attested are what the public require. These facts, if duly authenticated, will, when marshalled, constitute the case for the consideration of the Home Office. As it is admitted almost universally that things occurred with regard to the prosecution, trial, and sentence which have raised doubts in the minds of men as to their propriety, facts and facts only are concerned with the agitation now in progress. That Sir A. Conan Doyle wrote "Sherlock Holmes" has nothing whatever to do with the case in hand. Either the sentence was just or it was unjust. If the former, the stigma will remain; if the latter, redress should, and I believe will, follow now. But let us keep to the point and avoid discussion of "wider issues," etc.—Yours faithfully,

C. R. B. B.
Wandsworth, S. W., Jan. 15.

TO THE EDITOR OF THE *DAILY TELEGRAPH*

Sir—Surely the conscience of England has already been shocked by various instances in recent years of miscarriage of justice, not alone in our country, but in many others, that it behoves all Englishmen to insist, and most strongly, that all care shall be taken that similar cases do not happen again if in any way such may be possible. *Humanum est errareis* [**To err is human—Plutarch.**] a very old proverb, as true today, as true it was, when first written.

With your permission, Sir, I propose to put the following points for consideration as regards the unfortunate Mr. Edalji: (1) His conviction was brought about largely by prejudice imported into his case, and admitted before the jury by a layman presiding in a criminal court; (2) His conviction was aided by allowing an expert witness to state as facts things which, from the nature of the case, are but matters of opinion; (3) His conviction was assisted by the neglect of ordinary precautions against accident or design.

1. Now as to my first point—prejudice. This is clearly demonstrated by the action of the Chief Constable. He held the view that the man was guilty, and capable of any criminal act, long before Mr. Edalji was of any age before, apparently, he could legally be "culpable" in the technical sense. The lawyer holds, in this country, that every man is innocent until he is proved guilty. This Captain Anson did not hold. Moreover, the highest judges in the land have laid down as a rule of law that it is the duty of the police to bring forward evidence that makes for an acquittal just as much as evidence that makes for conviction. This certainly was not done at the trial now under consideration.

2. My second point is that the expert witness stated as facts matters which are questions of opinion. Mr. Gurrin said certain letters were in Edalji's handwriting. Whether they were or not was the province of the jury to decide. While stating this brings in the question whether experts ought not to be treated as a separate class of witnesses. They invariably give evidence on the side that pays their fees. This is but in accord with human nature. Nevertheless, I contend that all expert evidence should be treated with "honourable suspicion," and tainted by a desire to make the most of any points telling in favour of the side which calls such evidence. In many cases I have heard the expert state to a jury his views as if he were stating clear and well-ascertained facts.

3. His conviction was helped by the neglect of ordinary precautions against accident or design. This I so state because, unfortunately, neither the police nor Mr. Edalji, sen., provided that the coat given up, and on

which horse hairs are alleged to have been found, was placed in a sealed packet before being handed to the analyst. Why even in the case of suspected milk a sample is taken, and one half placed in a clean jar and sealed, and the other half similarly treated. Then one jar is retained by the milk seller and the other by the inspector, and so handed to the public analyst. And it is procedure in a trifling matter, but in one of the gravest importance no such care is observed. The milk seller can protect himself by the results of the analysis of his sample, though, the coat, I admit, could not have been divided to insure equal results, but there is an analogy, I maintain, and if the obvious precaution had been taken to carefully seal the coat in some impervious material it must have reached the analyst in the same state as when it left the vicarage. These matters do not appear to have had any weight with the gentleman who presided at Edalji's trial. It is only through the Press that tardy justice can be compelled to remove the bandage from her eyes.—I am, Sir, your, etc.,

R. R. S. WAUKER
Foxford, Suffolk, Jan. 14.

TO THE EDITOR OF THE *DAILY TELEGRAPH*
Sir—There is just one point in Sir Conan Doyle's able defence of Mr. Edalji which has occurred to me, in common, no doubt, with others of your readers of the articles in last week's issues. This is concerning Mr. Edalji's defective eyesight.

Sir Conan Doyle in his exposition does not allude at all to Edalji having used spectacles or glasses, and, as Mr. Aitchison in his letter in this morning's *Daily Telegraph* points out that not only could Edalji's myopia be entirely corrected and full visual acuity be obtained from the use of glasses, but that by this means he might even see better in semi-darkness than does the average person with good eyes.

Though from one point of view this question would appear to be against the interests of Mr. Edalji's innocence, further inquiry into the point might prove the defective eyesight to be a strong point in his favour, clearing away at the same time the apparent weakness in Sir Conan Doyle's argument.

As my remarks would infer, I am amongst the vast number of those who are absolutely confident of Edalji's innocence.—I am, dear Sir, yours faithfully,

> A. E. LEGGE
> Sunny Bank, South Norwood, S.E., Jan. 14.

TO THE EDITOR OF THE *DAILY TELEGRAPH*

Sir—The idea of Mr. Edalji being in collusion with the group of schoolboys who had been proved guilty of writing some of the anonymous letters, is too ridiculous. I often saw the Wyrley train come into Walsall Station, but never once did I see Mr. Edalji alight from the same carriage as the schoolboys; they were, truth to tell, a rather disreputable looking lot, and such as no young solicitor could very well be familiar with; I never saw Mr. Edalji even speak to them or pay the slightest attention to them in any way.

I often travelled between Walsall and Birmingham in the carriage with Mr. Edalji at the time of the outrages, and he always appeared to me to be particularly studious and quiet—in fact, a regular bookworm—and the very last man, from every point of view, that any reasonable person could associate with the cattle outrages. In the search, which is bound to come, for the real culprit, the fact that village gangs used to be found in the district, at the time of, and previous to the outrages, should not be lost sight of, for instance, in the village of Pelsall, three miles away from Wyrley, a gang existed, known locally as the "Black Watch," who would for a period of say, three weeks confine their attention to pushing down forecourt walls. Next they would turn their attention to young trees which the parish council had planted on the common, and would, night after night, cut down a certain number. These gangs consisted of young miners and others, capable of anything, and against whom, it is almost unnecessary to say, the police were useless. The suggestion that Mr. Edalji was a member of such a gang seems monstrously absurd.

Not a single thinking person in the Midlands can now believe in Mr. Edalji's guilt, and the remembrance here of Sir Arthur Conan Doyle's present noble effort will always be treasured.—I am Sir, your obedient servant,

J. E. WILKES, Assoc. M.Inst.C.E.
Pelsall, Staffordshire, Jan. 14.

TO THE EDITOR OF THE *DAILY TELEGRAPH*
Sir—I can fully endorse the opinions of Mr. Aitchison in today's issue regarding eyesight. I am personally acquainted with a gentleman not many years older than Edalji, who has the greatest difficulty in seeing his way about by day, but, as he is a traveller and a great walker, does most of his business by night. I have known him to frequently walk back over fifteen miles or so two or three times a week in absolute darkness without a light and often in strange country lanes and roads. I may say he does not wear glasses, and often carries heavy loads. I think the sight theory falls to the ground.—Yours faithfully,

AMOR
Bruton, Jan. 14.

TO THE EDITOR OF THE *DAILY TELEGRAPH*
Sir—I have read with great interest the case of Mr. George Edalji exposed in the *Daily Telegraph* of the 11th and 12th inst., and have from the beginning of the trial thought him innocent, but notwithstanding there has been so much proved in his favour, there remain also some very striking points against him. Surely, there must have been other causes than that stated by Sir A. Conan Doyle for the many objectionable anonymous letters received at the vicarage from time to time, taking it they were not written by the accused. Again, George Edalji having distinguished himself as a clever law student, could he not supply his counsel with useful information regarding his defence, and was he not able to defend himself from the unfair charges brought against him? Did not a man of his ability, being innocent, know the result of the dangerous

remark made at his arrest: "I am not surprised at this. I have been expecting this for some time." Do not these words seem familiar as being similar to the expressions of many criminals at the time of their arrest?

Now take the case of the horse-hairs upon the coat—the dispute between the inspector and the Edaljis. Why was not a witness called in from outside to prove their assertion that the coat was free from horse-hairs? And then there is the evidence of the Edalji family. One would expect a good and sound witness for the defence in a clergyman, who is accustomed to speak in public, and is looked upon to know what he is talking about.

There is no doubt that the case is a difficult problem, for it seems very strange that a clergyman and his family, above all people, should be treated by surrounding neighbours as the family of the Rev. S. Edalji, of Great Wyrley.—Yours faithfully,

W. GARNET ARMSTRONG
Jan. 14.

PRESS COMMENTS

The daily papers began to agitate for an official inquiry by the Home Office secretary, Mr. Herbert Gladstone, son of the late four-time prime minister of England Mr. William Gladstone.

THE DAILY CHRONICLE

There is not only the possibility (or, as it seems to us, the probability) that an innocent man has been wrongfully convicted. There is also the possibility that the real culprit, or culprits, may be still at large. Sir Conan Doyle, besides being convinced that Mr. Edalji is innocent, has, it is clear, formed an opinion as to the quarter in which the real culprit is to be found.

[Conan Doyle was indeed investigating the Great Wyrley outrages himself and later presented his findings to the Home Office. He came to believe that two brothers living in the vicinity had conceived a great hatred for the talented but odd-looking Edalji and had been both the source of the outrages and of the anonymous letters.

Royden and Wallis Sharp were named in findings Conan Doyle presented to the Home Office. The circumstantial case against the two is so strong that even the most desultory investigation into their lives either would have convicted them or exonerated them, but by this time the Home Secretary seemed more concerned with protecting officials involved in the Edalji case than in finding the real culprits.

For more information on the Sharps, it is most useful to read Pierre Nordan's biography of Sir Arthur Conan Doyle titled *Conan Doyle: A Biography*, published in 1966 by Holt, Rinehart and Winston of New York. Conan Doyle's actual letter to the Home Office remains under copyright.]

That is as it may be. The things of paramount importance are that the wrong, if such it be, that has been done to an innocent man should be righted; and that if such wrong has been due to faults on the part of the local police, the responsibility should be brought home to the proper quarter. We hope that Mr. Gladstone will see his way to appoint the commission of inquiry for which Sir Conan Doyle has pleaded so powerfully.

LIVERPOOL DAILY POST

It is expected that the Home Secretary, as the result of Sir Conan Doyle's investigation of the Edalji case, will order a special inquiry to be made. The matter can hardly rest where it is in view not merely of the opinion formed by Sir Conan Doyle, but of the actions of the Home Office itself in releasing Edalji long before the expiry of his sentence. What form the inquiry will take is another matter. An investigation by Home Office officials would scarcely satisfy the public, and probably, therefore, the best thing to do would be to appoint a small commission, consisting of two lawyers and a layman, to review the whole evidence in the case and report to the Home Secretary.

Sir Arthur Conan Doyle failed to make his case on the medical front.

MEDICAL VIEWS:
SCIENTIFIC INVESTIGATION

MEDICAL PRESS AND CIRCULAR

The notorious case of Mr. Edalji has been brought once again pointedly before the attention of the public. This time the challenge has been made in the *Daily Telegraph* by Sir A. Conan Doyle. In two long articles published on the 11th and 12th of the current month, he deals exhaustively with the whole case in his usual clever, concise, and powerful manner. One of his strongest grounds may be attributed to his early medical experiences, when, it is a matter of common knowledge, he was specially interested in the study of diseases of the eye. With that part of his argument we shall deal later. As regards the main portion of this most interesting document we are in complete accord.

Our readers for 1903 need not be reminded that in that year we drew up a petition to the then Home Secretary, Mr. Akers-Douglas. The nature of our views may be gathered from a special editorial notice in our issue of Nov. 11, 1903, under the title of "The Wyrley Cattle Maiming Outrage." "We feel it a public duty," the notice ran, "to call urgent attention to the cattle maiming case at Wyrley. A young Birmingham solicitor lies in prison condemned to penal servitude as the perpetrator of a number of senseless and absolutely brutal and wanton outrages on cattle. The evidence on which he has been convicted was purely circumstantial, and, as such, open to the fallacies that must necessarily accompany that class of evidence. During his imprisonment, and while awaiting trial, a further cattle maiming outrage was committed at Wyrley, the village where the accused lived. Since his conviction still other cattle have been maimed and killed. On this ground alone, therefore, we submit that his sentence demands revision. But if an educated solicitor killed cattle in the senseless and purposeless manner under which the Wyrley outrages were committed, we submit, unhesitatingly, that he was, on conviction, fitted for a lunatic asylum rather than a prison. There has been a grave miscarriage of justice, and we appeal to the Home Office for immediate action by way of revision of the sentence in this case.

If necessary, we are prepared to nominate the necessary scientific body of investigation as to the state of mind of a cattle maimer of the kind involved in the assumption of the recent sentence." This petition was signed by many medical men, including such eminent authorities on mental disease as Dr. Savage, Professor Clouston, Dr. Bevan Lewis, Dr. Younger, and by such prominent men as Dr. F. J. Waldo, Dr. Ward Cousins, Dr. F. J. Smith, Dr. Danford Thomas, Dr. H. Jellett, and Mr. E. H. Tweedy. The petition was formally acknowledged by the Home Secretary, but no official reference has been since made as to any official investigation of the state of mind of Edalji. From time to time we have referred to the case of this unhappy man. In February, 1905, we noticed the review of the affair published by *Truth*, and joined in the emphatic demand that it should be re-investigated. We then said: "It is difficult to escape the conclusion that either Mr. Edalji is an innocent man, as the continuance of the outrages after his imprisonment suggests, or that he is a poor madman who should be cared for in an asylum." Since then a new Home Secretary, Mr. Herbert Gladstone, has appeared upon the scene, and a few months ago Mr. Edalji was released. That event means presumably that his innocence was at length officially recognized.

Now comes the demand from many parts of the country that he should be given a free pardon—that formal warrant of innocence which is ironically granted by the Crown in the case of subjects convicted of offences they have not committed. It is to be hoped that this timely act of grace will be performed in order to minimize as far as possible the far-reaching moral disturbances arising from so palpable a miscarriage of justice. One point insisted upon by Sir Conan Doyle is that, owing to the physical defect of vision created by severe astigmatism, Mr. Edalji was physically unable to roam about at night, and cover the distance requisite to encompass the evil deeds of which he was found guilty. The argument is so highly technical that it is hardly possible to deal with it off-hand on general grounds. We have accordingly referred it to Mr. Sydney Stephenson, the editor of the *Ophthalmoscope*, whose remarks will be found following the present article. We may perhaps venture to make a slight criticism upon Sir Conan Doyle's challenge to any police-constable to cover the same ground at night within the requisite period of time if provided with spectacles made so as to astigmatise his vision to a degree corresponding to that of Mr. Edalji's. It seems to us fairly evident that the conditions of experiment would not be identical enough to warrant sound conclusions therefrom. In the one case we have a man who has had astigmatism from birth, and who has learned to interpret more or less correctly the distracted world in which he lives; while in the other the constable is plunged suddenly into a topsy-turvy environment. But, apart from that particular theory, Sir Conan Doyle has presented the world with a convincing case of the innocence of Mr. Edalji. We welcome his contribution, not only as coming from a medical man, but also as a vindication of the strong attitude taken up from the first by the "Medical Press and Circular." It has always seemed to us that the public must look to the medical profession for much of the future advance in criminal law reform, of which so much has been heard of late years. We hope in the course of a few days or weeks to be able to announce a free pardon from the King for one whom we cannot but regard as the hapless victim of a prolonged storm of adversity.

*

[The following note has been kindly sent by Mr. Sydney Stephenson. It is in answer to an editorial request for an opinion on Sir A. Conan Doyle's theory that Edalji's astigmatism was of such an extreme kind as to have precluded the possibility of his committing the Wyrley cattle maiming outrages in the darkness of night-time. We have, further, the express assurance of Sir A. Conan Doyle that Mr. Edalji did not wear glasses, but that information did not reach us in time to communicate with Mr. Stephenson before going to press.—Ed. "Mr. P. and C."]

TO THE EDITOR OF THE *MEDICAL PRESS AND CIRCULAR*
Dear Sir—Might I ask you in the cause of justice to permit me to put the following question to those of your readers who are engaged in eye practice:

"Do you consider it physically possible for Mr. George Edalji, whose degree of myopic astigmatism as determined by retinoscopy under homatropine is—

Left eye   −8.25 Diop. spher.
            −1.75 Diop. cylindaxis 90 deg.
Right eye −8.75 Diop. spher.

to have set forth upon a pitch-dark night, with neither moon nor stars, to have crossed country for half a mile, climbing fences, finding gaps in hedges, and passing over a broad railway line, to have found and mutilated a pony which was loose in a large field, to have returned half a mile, and to have accomplished it all under thirty-five minutes—the limit of the possible time at his disposal?"

A consensus of scientific opinion upon this point would greatly aid me in getting justice for this young professional man condemned for an offence which, in my opinion, he could not possibly have committed.—I am, Sir, yours faithfully,

> ARTHUR CONAN DOYLE
> Undershaw, Hindhead, Surrey, Jan. 13.

TO THE EDITOR OF THE *MEDICAL PRESS AND CIRCULAR*

Dear Sir—Sir Arthur Conan Doyle's question, conveyed in his letter of Jan. 13 last, raises wide issues. He inquires whether it is possible for anybody with, roughly, about nine diopters of myopia, together with 1.75 diopters of astigmatism in the right eye, to do what the police allege the convict George Edalji accomplished—namely, to have set forth on a pitch-dark night, to have crossed the country for half a mile, climbing fences, finding gaps in hedges, and passing over a railway line, to have found and mutilated a pony which was loose in a large field, to have returned half a mile, and to have accomplished it all under thirty-five minutes, the limit of the possible time at his disposal.

Assuming that Edalji was familiar with the countryside, and active in his movements, it seems to me that the short-sight from which he suffered would handicap him but little in his errand. Indeed, if the error of refraction were compensated by means of proper glasses, Edalji would probably be much in the position of a man with natural sight. It is known that some short-sighted persons are liable to a degree of so-called night blindness, and it is possible that Edalji suffered in this way. I do not gather from Sir Conan Doyle's letter whether this was or was not the case.—Yours faithfully,

SYDNEY STEPHENSON
Editor, *Ophthalmoscope*
Jan. 14, 1907.

JANUARY 17, 1907

THE EDALJI CASE
QUESTION OF EYESIGHT
REV. MR. EDALJI'S LETTER

TO THE EDITOR OF THE *DAILY TELEGRAPH*

Sir—It would seem from Mr. Henderson-Livesey's letter in this morning's *Telegraph* that he thinks that the police first offered voluntarily to show me the coat in question, and that, therefore, it was a point in their favour. Allow me to say that when I saw them on the morning of Aug. 18, 1903, I found that they had already packed up the coat with a vest, and were about to take it away, but I insisted upon it being seen by me before they took it away, and then they opened the parcel and allowed me to examine it.

Let me also add that my son more than once asked Inspector Campbell at the Cannock Police-station to show him the coat, but was not allowed to see it. Let it be noted here that the garment in question was in possession of the police for twelve hours after it was taken from my house, and that it was during those hours that my son asked them to show it to him, and they could have done so if they had any wish to be fair and straightforward.

As regards my son's eyesight, it must have been as defective three years ago as it is now, for it was only about a week after his conviction that he wrote to us asking that we should request the Home Secretary to have his eyes examined, as he felt sure that his sight was too weak and defective to have made it possible for him to go to the field in question on such an exceedingly dark night as the night of Aug. 17, 1903, was. We applied, in December, 1903, to the Home Office for this examination, but they did nothing for a whole year after the application was made. In January, 1905, however, an expert was ordered to examine the eyes, and we were informed in the following month that his report was received. As no particulars of the report were given in the letter, I wrote to ask for a copy of it, but was informed that it was a confidential document, and I could not have a copy.

I must also state here, as an absolutely undeniable fact, that although my son's eyes were weak and defective before his arrest and imprisonment, he never used any glasses, and it is only recently, after his release, that he has, on the recommendation of his medical advisers, begun to use them.—I am, Sir, your obedient servant,

S. EDALJI, Vicar of Great Wyrley
Jan. 15.

TO THE EDITOR OF THE *DAILY TELEGRAPH*
Sir—In reply to "C. R. B. B.," it is a fact that more than once I have found a difficulty in finding my numbered desk at examinations.

I must refer Mr. Armstrong to my letters in yesterday's and today's *Daily Telegraph*. I gave full information necessary for my defence, and though I was advised that it was a needless expense to call any witnesses at all to rebut the ridiculous evidence of the police, I did insist on calling eleven witnesses, but refrained from calling several others. As to the alleged remark about "expecting this for some time," seeing that Sir R. Hardy (who failed to notice any other points in my defence except absence of motive) plainly told the jury that even if I did make this remark it was, under the circumstances, more consistent with innocence than guilt, I do not think I need discuss the matter further, but I am prepared to do so if required.

As regards Amor's remarks it would be better if he stated the precise degree of myopic astigmatism with which his friend is troubled. I expect his case is very different from mine. In my petitions to the Home Office I have always pointed out that I cannot see in the dark.—Yours truly,

> G. E. T. EDALJI
> Jan. 16.

TO THE EDITOR OF THE *DAILY TELEGRAPH*

Sir—I read with much interest Sir A. Conan Doyle's remarks on the Edalji case, though I am sorry I do not agree with some of his conclusions. In clearing one person he has thrown the guilt on another. It is worthy of notice that the Rev. Mr. Edalji was fourteen years in the village before the anonymous letters commenced, by which time George had attained the age of twelve. The passages in the letters eulogizing Police-sergeant Upton are doubtful compliments, as they allege that Upton neglected his duty for the sake of the writer. Now, this is stated in a way which would produce the impression that it was written by a woman. All the letters apparently point to Elizabeth Foster, or, as suggested, her male allies, as the authors. But if she really wrote the letters in 1888, why should she require the assistance of male allies in 1893—five years after the offence for which she had merely been bound over? What motive had she for such malignant fury? It is suggested that the object of the letters was to attach opprobrium to the family and ultimately disgrace George Edalji. But why she should have switched her malice from the vicar in 1888 to George, his son, in 1893 and 1903, is difficult to say.

The aim of this conspiracy is to disgrace George Edalji—why should such palpable indications of the connection with Elizabeth Foster be displayed in most letters, and why should the conspirators endanger their chance of success by proclaiming that they can and will imitate George Edalji's writing? Surely this does not fit in with the cleverness of the conspirators or conspirator. Why was no effort made to fix the guilt on Elizabeth Foster, or at least prove she was not an accomplice? The most natural course to take. Is it likely a person who had written such letters would have been such a fool as to imperil his liberty by playing foolish practical jokes in the vicarage grounds? Sir A. Conan Doyle calls attention to a significant passage in one letter: "Before the end of the year your kid will either be in the grave-yard or disgraced for life"; yet it was not until ten years afterwards he was imprisoned, and fifteen years after Elizabeth Foster was bound over to keep the peace. It is rather obvious that the illiterate Farrington could not have been the writer of the letters. The writer knows of George Edalji's connection with a group of schoolboys. The author of the Greatorex letters imputes an outrage to Edalji on a date a week in error. Surely if the writer was concerned in the crimes and wished to attach the guilt to Edalji he would have been more careful in his dates.

If Edalji wished to clear himself I don't think he could better have done so than by writing these letters, for it apparently seems so impossible that a man should incriminate himself that people would think someone else wrote them. The effect of the postcard of Aug. 4, 1904, had the effect of fixing a suspicion on Elizabeth Foster by the phrase, "Rather go back to your old game of writing anonymous letters and writing on walls." This is not the phraseology of a domestic servant, nor would she be so foolish as to bring suspicion on herself. The writers of these series of letters must have been clever and possessed of great imaginative power. The imitation of the school-boy's letter is rather clever, though the testimony it contained was nullified by his absence in the Isle of Man—rather an oversight for such a clever conspirator.—I am, Sir, yours faithfully,

W. P. COOK

TO THE EDITOR OF THE *DAILY TELEGRAPH*
Sir—Commenting on my letter on Edalji's eyesight, Sir A. Conan Doyle stated that he was appealing to the leading ophthalmic surgeons through the medical Press. He has now received his answer from no less an authority than

Mr. Sidney Stephenson, the editor of the "Ophthalmoscope," and this is a confirmation in almost my own words of the view I stated on Monday. It is a pity that, having such a good case in other respects, Sir Arthur should persist in his argument that Edalji could not have committed the crimes because of his defective eyesight; and his further statement today, that "Mr. Edalji's sight is no worse now than it has ever been," is a most extraordinary one. If this is so, he is probably the only person in existence who, commencing with over eight diopters of myopia as a child, has reached adult age without its increasing.

Of course, we all know that freaks in every one of the human organs or senses have existed, but I am within reasonable limits in saying that a newly born child with myopia or short sight is practically unknown. Nearly every child born is, on the contrary hypermetrope—i.e., the eye is too short from front to back—and myopia is arrived at by the eye evergrowing, which may be described as a product of civilization due to the restricted surroundings and strenuous conditions of modern life. Examination of the eyes of savage tribes has shown that short sight is an unknown condition with them. This being so, Edalji must reasonably be supposed to have been much less short-sighted as a child, and probably at twelve years of age the defect did not amount to more than five diopters, as against between eight and ten now.

I note the continued reference to the astigmatism and must state why I ignored this when first writing. Sir Arthur makes this more difficult, because in his original statement he gave the right eye as possessing the double defect, but in his letter to the medical Press, which I have here taken to be the correct one, he reverses the terms. We have no information that the right eye is more degenerate than the left, and if it is as free from disease of the tunics as its fellow, then, being free from astigmatism also, it becomes the working eye, because it is a matter of universal experience that in cases of myopia, when one eye is astigmatic and the other not, and when the myopia is about the same in each, practically the whole of the work is done by the non-astigmatic eye, and the condition of the left eye can, so far as considering its work is concerned, be neglected. Therefore figures based upon the astigmatic eye are beside the mark. Edalji's ocular defect has to be judged solely upon the condition of his right eye from a purely optical point of view.

This unhappy man was convicted on circumstantial evidence and unless the actual culprit can be discovered, it is upon circumstantial evidence that we must rely for his pardon. It is consequently clear that we must have sound arguments, which will stand analyzing and must not merely theorize.

I only claim, outside optical matters, to possess the average knowledge and powers of deduction of my fellow-men. I have carefully read the evidence placed before us by Sir A. Conan Doyle, and think that, apart from the eyesight question, he has made out a most convincing case, and shown the necessity for a Home Office reinvestigation. The theory that Edalji could not have committed the crime because of his defective visual acuity is, however, untenable, and must be dropped; but there still remains the question of disease, with impaired visual acuity. In my letter I asked if there were any morbid conditions which prevented the full benefit being obtained from glasses; this question is still unanswered by any independent authority, but its importance is shown by the fact that Mr. Sidney Stephenson practically asks the same question when he says:

It is known that some short-sighted persons are liable to a degree of so-called night blindness, and it is possible that Edalji suffered in this way.

This again, is only supposition, as we have no evidence before us.

It appears to me that this question should be settled in a practical manner, which will remove all doubts and give sound evidence to work upon, and to this end I offer my services, in conjunction with an independent ophthalmic surgeon, to make an examination of Edalji's eyes under such conditions as will ensure a reliable report, which we will furnish for publication.

If Mr. George Edalji is willing to agree to this I will make an appointment for the purpose, feeling sure that his case will be considerably strengthened thereby.—I remain, yours faithfully,

JAMES AITCHISON
Cheapside, Jan. 16.

The plot thickened considerably as personal observers of the situation in Staffordshire weighed in.

THE TRAGEDY OF PREJUDICE
IMPRESSIONS OF MR. EDALJI

A member of the staff of the *Birmingham Express and Star* wrote:
As one who attended the trial of George Edalji on behalf of this paper, and also had an opportunity of investigating several of the outrages on the spot, I cannot refrain from alluding to the case sensationally resurrected by Sir Arthur Conan Doyle. . . . I was one of those who at the end of the trial were not satisfied that the evidence was strong enough to convict, and to whom the verdict of the jury came as a surprise. I wrote at the time that the Scottish verdict of 'Not proven' would have met the case; and I am still of opinion that the police failed to bear out their theory by evidence.

Local prejudice undoubtedly played a prominent part in the conviction. When Edalji was first brought up before the magistrates at Cannock the cab in which he was conveyed to the court-room was attacked by the crowd and the door torn from its hinges. It is also certain that much of this prejudice was due to his nationality—for the average rustic can see no good in a foreigner, and to him an Asiatic comes in the guise of an emissary of the devil. The fact that George Edalji was reserved and studious would heighten rather than dispel the antagonism of the countryside.

On the other hand, it must be admitted that the popular conclusion was an obvious one. The series of outrages which stirred the district were of no ordinary nature. Cattle stealing would have been understood, but cattle maiming was an unprofitable cruelty. The crimes showed a wanton lust of blood such as is rarely associated with Englishmen, and it is scarcely to be wondered at that in their prejudice the people of Great Wyrley and the surrounding district should have fixed a strange crime on what they considered to be a strange personality. Many and wonderful were the theories I heard pro-pounded in the local ale-houses as to why Edalji had gone forth in the night to slay cattle, and a widely-accepted idea was that he made nocturnal sacrifices to strange gods. Of course, to an educated man this and similar stories are ludicrous, but they go to prove the nature of the local feeling against Edalji.

One thing that impressed me strongly in the prisoner's favour was his bearing throughout the trial. I have seen many men called upon to answer for their deeds in a court of justice, but I know of none who assumed the role of an innocent man so readily as George Edalji. Whether it was in the stuffy lit-tle court-room at Cannock, with its petty officialism and weary routine, or in the more dramatic atmosphere of the sessions court, the prisoner bore him-self with the air of a man conscious of his innocence, and neither by word nor deed did he betray the workings of a guilty conscience. He was consistent in his statements, ready with his answers, and calm and collected in this demeanor. At the end of the trial I saw his mother faint and his father behave like one distracted; but the prisoner himself controlled his emotions, and received his sentence unmoved. "Guilty or not guilty," I remember saying, "here is a strong man, a man of great possibilities."

In my opinion, one man was mainly responsible for the conviction of Edalji, and that was Mr. Gurrin, the handwriting expert. The whole trial seemed to hang on those anonymous letters, and when Mr. Gurrin and his magnifying glass entered the box he carried the jury with him. Sir Reginald Hardy, in his summing-up, laid great stress on these letters, and the jury on their retrial took them away for careful consideration in the light of the expert's evidence. The issue was plain as a pikestaff. If Edalji wrote those let-ters, or some of them, he must be connected with the crimes. Mr. Gurrin's evidence went to show that he had written one or more of these letters, and the jury acted accordingly. But Mr. Gurrin had admitted that his skill was at fault in one notorious case, and it may be he was deceived in this case also. But be that as it may, Mr. Gurrin was the trump card of the prosecution, and they played it successfully. Mr. Vachell, the able defending counsel, could not confute expert evidence with expert evidence, and Mr. Disturnal, the prose-cuting counsel, was not slow in using his advantage.

Sir Arthur Conan Doyle, towards the end of his article, makes a telling attack on the Staffordshire police, and on this point I should like to refer to my own experience. For the police force generally I have a great respect, but I must make an exception in the case of the officers and men who took charge of the Great Wyrley district during the cattle-maiming scare. Day after day, I was brought in contact with the police in this area, and day after day my respect for their intelligence sensibly sank. The mind of these rustic policemen worked slowly, and the fruit of their thinking was exceedingly small. In the routine of a rural beat I dare say they would be capable of all that was expected of them, but face to face with a mysterious crime, in which cunning was to be met by cunning, and wit matched against wit, they failed miserably. I have watched these men at their work, and I have been moved to laughter, for to see them playing at being detectives was to imagine an elephant imitating a tiger in the tracking of a deer. If George Edalji is innocent of the Wyrley outrages, I for one am not surprised the real criminal has not been caught, for he is a man of daring and resource, and a man who has peculiar knowledge of the limitations of the police whose lot for the time being was cast in and about Great Wyrley.

If further investigation proves the innocence of Edalji, then, in common fairness the case of Farrington, the collier, must be reconsidered. Edalji was convicted on a mass of circumstantial evidence, but Farrington was condemned simply on the evidence of a trousers button. The whole case against him stood or fell by that button, and when I say that the button found near the carcass of the maimed sheep was one in common use, it will be seen that that was scarcely strong enough evidence to deprive a man for three years of liberty.

I was present at the trial of Farrington, and I was even less convinced that the evidence merited conviction than I was in the case of Edalji. In neither case, in my judgment, was the English idea that a man is presumed to be innocent before he is found guilty carried out to the letter. Certainly we have not heard the last of the Edalji case, and I for one would not be surprised if we were on the eve of revelations—revelations even more sensational than the alarming and mysterious outrages which shocked a country and terrorized a district.

TO THE EDITOR OF THE *DAILY TELEGRAPH*

Sir—Strong as Sir A. Conan Doyle's arguments appear at first sight, a critical examination shows many weak points. Mr. Henderson-Livesey has called attention to some of those today, and I should like to point out two more.

1. Sir Arthur says that Mr. Edalji could not have got out of the house on the night of the 17th for two reasons; first, because he was sleeping in the same room with his father, a light sleeper, with the door locked, and secondly, because the police were watching the house. The first reason depends upon the lightness of Mr. Edalji senior's sleep, which cannot be ascertained, and, in any case, it is surely too much to say that escape would be impossible under such circumstances. As to the second reason, Sir Arthur describes the closeness of the police watch, and then says: "This was before the night of the outrage, but it is inconceivable that if there was so close a watch then, there was none on the 17th." This appears to mean that he does not know for certain whether the house was watched on that night or not. But this is the all-important fact, and unless it can be definitely ascertained, the argument falls to pieces.

2. As to the postcard of Aug. 4 it is said that Edalji could not have posted it, because he was on an excursion to Aberystwith from early morning to late evening, and the theory that it might have been posted on the night of the 3rd at a country box is brushed aside by saying that it is absurd to suppose "that what was posted on the 3rd took two days to go twenty miles." But is it so absurd? There are plenty of country boxes where there is only one collection in the day. I do not know whether there is such a box near Wyrley, but if there is, a card posted on the night of the 3rd would be collected on the evening of the 4th, post-marked at that time, and delivered in Birmingham on the morning of the 5th, as actually happened. The prosecution seem to have believed that such a box existed. Unless Sir Arthur can state that they were wrong, a fact which could easily be ascertained, this argument also is valueless.

It is quite possible that Sir Arthur has got the information necessary to clear up these two points and those referred to by Mr. Livesey, and that considerations of space have prevented him from publishing it. If so, I trust that he will do so in a supplementary article, for the point about the police watch would be practically conclusive if it were established.

INNER TEMPLE
Jan. 15.

JANUARY 18, 1907

THE EDALJI CASE
LETTER FROM THE MOTHER

TO THE EDITOR OF THE *DAILY TELEGRAPH*

Sir—I am deeply grateful to Sir Arthur Conan Doyle for so nobly taking up the cause of my son, and to you for so kindly placing your columns at his disposal, and giving room for so many letters on this sad case.

I shall be glad if you will give me space for a few remarks on one part of Mr. Henderson-Livesey's letter in your paper of the 15th.

I always spoke to the solicitor employed for the defence of the extreme short sight of my son, which has been from a child. I considered that sufficient proof at once, if there had been no other, that he could not have gone to the field, with a so-called "road" impossible even to people with good sight, at night. I felt this so much that I was distressed that no opportunity was given me when giving evidence to speak on his defective sight. The time allowed me was very short; it was late in the evening, and I suppose people were tired of the case, but because I was his mother, and therefore an interested person in proving his innocence, it is hard that what I did say should be thought not to be true.

I am sure that there were no hairs on the coat when the police took it away from this house.

My son's sight was always so defective that he bent very close to the paper in writing, and held a book or paper very close to his eyes, and when out walking he did not recognise people easily. When I met him anywhere I always felt I must look for him, not he for me. I believe people sometimes thought he would not speak to them, but the fact was owing to his bad sight he did not recognise them.—Yours truly,

> CHARLOTTE E. S. EDALJI
> Great Wyrley Vicarage, Jan. 16, 1907.

TO THE EDITOR OF THE *DAILY TELEGRAPH*

Sir—Mr. Cook makes a rather misleading reference to my "connection" with a group of schoolboys. What was proved was that though I was daily using the same train as the boys yet I had not travelled with them more than twelve times in the course of a year. As there were only ten third-class compartments on these local trains, there was nothing surprising in my being about once a month in the lads' company. It was also proved I had not travelled with them for seven weeks prior to the crime; that I was not in the habit of conversing with them; but that one morning, when an outrage had been discovered, and somebody in the train asked to whom the horses belonged, I remarked that I believed they were Blewitt's. This was a matter of general knowledge at Wyrley Station, and I had been told it by several people, yet the prosecuting counsel said, "I ask the jury to consider if this significant remark is not damning evidence of his guilty knowledge."

There was contradictory evidence as to whether my home was actually watched on the night of the outrage, and it was difficult to get at the truth, as the police made no notes as to when or where they watched, and only verbal instructions were given by the inspector to his men. But it was clearly proved that twenty men were watching the "immediate neighbourhood of the occurrence," and that three constables were actually employed to guard the field, only one of whom the prosecution dared to call.

With regard to the postcard of Aug. 4, let me remark that a postmark is *prima-facie* evidence that the card was posted on the day and at the place thereby indicated. It was not my duty to prove it was actually posted at Wolverhampton on Aug. 4, but it rested with the prosecution to show that it was not. Instead of doing this, they only proved that letters posted at a place called Shareshill do bear the Wolverhampton postmark, which, of course, proved nothing with regard to this particular card in question.—Yours truly,

G. E. T. EDALJI
Jan. 17.

TO THE EDITOR OF THE *DAILY TELEGRAPH*

Sir—I observe that Mr. Aitchison has now come to the conclusion that it is feasible that Mr. George Edalji, by the use of one eye only—that eye having 8 diopters of myopia, accomplished a nocturnal journey of half a mile each way, which I can guarantee (having myself made it) to be a rough and difficult one by daylight.

Mr. Hands, the bootmaker, deposed to seeing Mr. George Edalji at 8.35 in the village. He was again seen at 9.25 near the vicarage gate by an independent witness. There are fifty minutes unaccounted for; but it is about a mile from the village shop to the spot where the winding track leaves the road for the field. It follows that Edalji could not have had more than thirty-five minutes for his double journey of half a mile each way, to say nothing of finding and mutilating the pony. All this by the aid, according to Mr. Aitchison, of one highly myopic eye. The thing is to my mind perfectly impossible. I have already challenged anyone to cover the ground in the time with glasses which would represent Edalji's sight, but I now add to this a challenge to Mr. Aitchison to do it with his normal sight upon any night when the moon is not full. Let him go to Wyrley, as I did, and try it for himself. When he returns, he will be less dogmatic as to what is possible and what is not.

I am obliged to Mr. Aitchison for pointing out that the baby's eye is not quite the same as the adult's. When I spoke of there being no change in Mr.

Edalji's eyes, I meant his adult eyes. There are some things one takes for granted, unless one is talking to a very youthful audience.

Mr. Aitchison offers himself as a referee upon the eye question. I am sure Mr. Edalji and his friends would agree to any test suggested by the Home Office, but they feel that the more eminent the authority the greater would be the public confidence.

One correspondent raises the point that there may somewhere be a post-box by which a letter can be delayed in such a fashion as to take forty-eight hours to go twenty miles. If there is so strange a thing, it is for the prosecution to prove that it was used. No attempt was ever made to do so. At present their improved assertion is that a young lawyer wrote a post-card to his own offices accusing himself of scandalous offences, but that he took immense pains, by the use of some unusual country post, to prove that he could not himself have written it. Is it a credible incident?

In the other point raised by the same correspondent the onus of proof again lies with the police. The vicar swears he was with his son all night. The household had heard no one leave. There is good reason to think the house was watched outside. There is certainty that twenty watchers were in the vicinity. Under these circumstances, the alibi holds unless the police can give some evidence that anyone saw the accused outside the house. None such has ever been given.

Mr. Cook opens the question of who did do these deeds. I think that the time for that discussion has not yet arrived; but I claim that it has already been shown to every man who is capable of reasoning that Mr. George Edalji did not do them, and could not possibly have done them.—Yours truly,

ARTHUR CONAN DOYLE

TO THE EDITOR OF THE *DAILY TELEGRAPH*

Sir—Most of your correspondents appear to be carried away upon the wave of indignation which Sir Arthur hoped for, and has so successfully raised.

It appears to me that if those who have written letters to your paper would wish to further the ends of justice they should confine themselves to a critical analysis of Sir A. Conan Doyle's case, rather than express their own feelings, and with this end in view I argue the following on the hypothesis (rightly or wrongly) that Edalji is guilty.

Referring to the last paragraph in the sixth column of last Friday's *Daily Telegraph* are the words, "This referring to the watch kept on the vicarage was before the night of the outrage, but it is inconceivable that if there was so close a watch then there was none on the 17th." I admit it is very likely that most people may agree with Sir Arthur's views as above quoted, but it is absolutely certain that the Staffordshire police will disagree with him in order to support the conviction they obtained. Again, I would call your attention to Mr. Edalji's letter, he says: "I myself insisted on calling those witnesses who so completely upset the theory of the crime being committed before 9.40"; now we come to the point at which the question arises, where was Edalji between 9.40 p.m. and 6.20 a.m., at which latter hour the pony was found with a cut in its side. The happenings between this period of time require strong corroboration, and must be supported by better evidence than Sir A. Conan Doyle adduces.

By way of comment, I might point out that nearly all coats are lined to a certain extent with horse-hair cloth—would this account for the finding of the horsehairs (if any) before the same was taken possession of by the police? Cases have been known when the horse-hair has worked from the inside to the outside of coats, and especially in old garments.—Yours faithfully,

W. T. SHAPLEY
Bristol, Jan. 15.

TO THE EDITOR OF THE *DAILY TELEGRAPH*

Sir—Sir Arthur Conan Doyle's plea for justice so cruelly and shamefully outraged, in the first instance, by prejudice and stupidity, and, in the second place, by brutal indifference on the part of those whose duty it is to do all in their power to secure it, must send the blood tingling into the face of every honest man in the kingdom. It would be an insult to us as a nation to suppose that his words, "an entire reconsideration of the Edalji case is a most pressing public duty" will not find response wherever a true English heart beats. It is pitiable, it is appalling, to reflect what such a case as he has unfolded involves—the tremendous responsibilities entrusted to men utterly unworthy and ludicrously incompetent to discharge them, the shame, the misery, the agony which it is in their power to inflict, the facility with which a web can be woven round any man, however innocent, the hopelessness of extrication when once involved in its meshes.

Not less terrible is the helplessness of those who have the wit to discern truth and who are eager to assist justice. However infamous may be the means employed to obtain a victim when the police, to disguise, or, rather, retrieve their own imbecility and failure, are bent on obtaining a victim, the means employed for baffling any attempt as re-investigation are more infamous still. Permit me—for I feel it to be a duty—to relate my own experience of this case. I do so for the double purpose of corroborating the absolute and scrupulous accuracy of the facts on which Sir Conan Doyle has based his conclusions, to assure your readers that courtesy and consideration for the reputation of certain people must have induced him to suppress particulars which will probably not be suppressed—which shall not be suppressed— should the hands of Mr. Edalji's advocates be forced, and, lastly, to illustrate the ignoble tactics to which I referred.

About a year and a half ago the distinguished Scottish novelist, Mrs. Pyvie Mayo, directed my attention to the case. She had herself been working at it for months, in sheer pity for a young man who, as she soon discovered, had obviously been the victim of a glaring miscarriage of justice. Having collected all that had appeared about it in print, and being in receipt of a voluminous correspondence, both with the Edalji family and with the innumerable people interested in or connected with the case, she placed these papers in my hands. Needless to say, what had been so obvious to her, to various petitioners, and to the author of the articles in *Truth*, very soon became equally obvious to me. But in pushing my inquiries, both in Birmingham and Walsall, the almost universal cry was, "Have nothing to do with it. No doubt the case was mismanaged; certainly, from a technical point of view, the man was wrongly convicted."

The late Mr. C. E. Matthews was one of the kindest-hearted men who ever breathed, with as chivalrous a sense of right and justice as any man could have. And no one was more emphatic in dissuading interference. He spoke of the case as being embedded in filth and horror, and insisted that any association with it would not only be unfair to myself, but to my official position. Such was the opinion of others who were as incapable as Mr. Matthews of knowingly wronging anyone. I may add that a detective who had no connection with the case and no motive for injuring Mr. Edalji emphatically corroborated what has been hinted. For these abominable accusations thus potent in estranging so many who would otherwise have sympathised with this most unfortunate man I have since learned that there is not a shred of evidence, that they were first broached just after his conviction, and came into vogue when dissatisfaction with his sentence began to spread. This is certain, that where testimony as to his morals can be adduced, as from scores of unimpeachable witnesses, including all his teachers and fellow students at his university, it can, it is emphatic in his favour, but the source or sources of the calumnies referred to are to my certain knowledge absolutely undiscoverable.

Can anyone doubt that what is not imperative is, as Mr. Yelverton—and all honour to him for the part he has played in it—has suggested, the appointment of a Commission for the reopening of the whole case and a rigorous inquiry into what is involved in the case. If Mr. Edalji be—what, in the judgment of any sane man, he is—innocent of the charges on which he was convicted, let his innocence be publicly and formally declared; let him be reinstated in his profession, and compensated, so far as compensation be possible, for the cruel wrong which has been done him. If this inquiry is not instituted the Government may rest assured that a justly-incensed public will know the reason why.—I am, Sir, your obedient servant,

J. Churton Collins
The University, Birmingham.

TO THE EDITOR OF THE *DAILY TELEGRAPH*

Sir—Surely in a case of this kind it is most important to fix public attention on the main issue. Now this, in the present instance, and in the form in which the question of Mr. Edalji's guilt or innocence has now been raised, is not, I venture to think, confined to that. We must remember by whom it has been raised. Sir Arthur Conan Doyle has indeed raised a very serious question. He has a great principle at stake and a great theory to defend. When I say that he has raised this question and maintained this principle and defended his theory for the past twenty years in the most diverting and brilliant fiction, it is clear that what he has in view is not—save by way of example—the guilt or innocence of George Edalji. No, it is whether the police are trustworthy, competent, and successful guardians of public security. Now, throughout the entertaining series of detective stories which have made Sir Conan Doyle's name a household word, the whole police force, including the skilled and trained detective branch of the service, is invariably represented as either hopelessly at fault or altogether wrong in dealing with mysterious crime. That, then, is—clearly—Sir Conan Doyle's view, and he must forgive me if I consider him in the light of an *Advocatus Diaboli*.

As to the case in point, I have an open mind. But after carefully reading Sir Conan Doyle's articles, which have all the fascination of the ever-delightful "Sherlock Holmes," this does occur to me. To put the matter in a nutshell, Sir Conan relies for this defence of Edalji on the incredibility of the charge, and on three distinct grounds—viz., his myopia, his being elsewhere at the time, and his personal character. Now, it does strike me at least as hard to believe that a public official, holding the Sovereign's Commission, presumably a man of honour and integrity, and a member of a distinguished family, should, for no conceivable reason and without a particle of evidence, fix on a mere schoolboy whom he did not know from Adam as the perpetrator of a series of vexatious practical jokes and the writer of abominable anonymous letters, and then, ten years after, when the boy has grown to manhood and is a member of an honourable profession, of a hideous act of cruelty and blood. This, I say, is to me incredible.

And then there is this. I am old enough to remember the Roade murder. From first to last the police never doubted who was the real criminal. They were roundly abused and held up to ridicule. I have a sort of notion that some member of the force suffered in consequence. What people said was that such an idea was "incredible." Yet "the police" had been right all along. By all means, then, let us have an investigation, the fullest that can be made, not only for the sake of Edalji and his family, and of the police, or if these are as a general rule the inept blunderers in every case—certain of them may have been in this or that instance—on behalf of the public. But one thing is most important. Every word of the evidence should be within the reach of that public to whom Sir Conan Doyle has appealed, and I venture to suggest that you, Sir, should publish, either at a moderate cost or as a supplement, a verbatim report of the magisterial inquiry and of the subsequent trial at Quarter Sessions. No one, in my opinion, has any right to form a final judgment, either as regards the police or Edalji, who has not that lying before him.

> CHARLES F. G. TURNER
> Coveney Rectory, Ely, Cambe, Jan. 15.

JANUARY 19, 1907

THE EDALJI CASE
HOME OFFICE DELIBERATING

With regard to the case of Mr. Edalji, the Central News is informed that a consultation took place yesterday afternoon at the chambers of Mr. Yelverton, in the Temple, at which Sir Arthur Conan Doyle and Mr. Yelverton were present. A letter received in the course of the day from the Home Office was considered, and regarded as being of a favourable character. The follow-

ing communication was authorised by the gentlemen present to be made to
the press:

> Our case has been fully stated, and we have every reason to believe that it is
> receiving sympathetic consideration. We have no desire to hustle or force
> the hand of the Home Office, but, of course, we cannot allow Mr. Edalji's
> case to be indefinitely delayed; and, therefore, after a reasonable and neces-
> sarily short time, we propose to turn to the public, and ask their assistance
> in organising public meetings, and using such other means as may be requi-
> site to fully ventilate the very serious national questions which are involved.

TO THE EDITOR OF THE *DAILY TELEGRAPH*

Sir—I should like to supplement Sir Arthur Conan Doyle's excellent letter
in this morning's issue by pointing out that I did not return from Mr. Hand's
by the direct route (nearly a mile from my home), but by way of Watling-
street-road, Walk Mill, and Station-street. I was seen by, and spoke to, two
independent witnesses on the road quite three-quarters of a mile from the
post where the winding path leaves Station-street for the field. This was at
nine p.m., or just after. Hence the time at my disposal was very little indeed.
It was alleged that a policeman walked from the point referred to in Station-
street to the field and back in 21½ minutes, but as this was in daylight, and
no allowance was made for finding and maiming the pony, this proves nothing. As, however, the theory of the crime being done before 9.40 was wholly
abandoned by the prosecution, I need not further argue it. Next, for Mr.
Shapley's letter. He says, "Where was Edalji between 9.40 p.m. and 6.20
a.m? . . . The happenings between this period of time require strong corroboration, and must be supported by better evidence than Sir A. Conan Doyle
adduces."

Now, I ask any reasonable being to say whether, under any conceivable
circumstances, I could have brought stronger evidence than I did to prove my
assertion that I was in the house during the whole of this time? I laid before
the Court the best and only testimony I could obtain, namely, the evidence of

all the inmates of the house. Mr. Shapley is probably thinking of the unfair remark made by the prosecuting council in his reply that it was a "suspicious circumstance that I was not prepared with an independent witness to prove I did not go out after 9.40."

While leaving it to the public to decide whether this was, or was not, "suspicious," I can only suggest it would have appeared fifty times more so had I called a witness to swear that he spent the whole of this rainy night outside my doorstep and that I never came out.—Yours truly,

> G. E. T. EDALJI
> London, Jan. 18.

TO THE EDITOR OF THE *DAILY TELEGRAPH*

Sir—Would you have the kindness to give publicity to the following incident, which may have a very direct bearing upon the Edalji case?

On Oct. 1, 1903, the police received the following letter, bearing the postmark of South-end-on-Sea:

> Seeing in yesterday's issue of *Daily Mail* concerning the cattle-maiming case. You refer to the vicar receiving anonymous letters some years back, and someone sending out goods from various tradesmen for jokes. I think I could inform you who the party was, as I have heard from his own lips that he helped to play the joke upon the vicar. He has been a writer of several annoying letters. Not only has he wrote them himself, but he had got other people. If you think this could help you in any way I will send you address as to where you may find him.—Yours truly,
>
> P.S. Please answer through *Daily Mail*.
>
> A YOUNG HOUSEMAID

No steps were taken by the police.

There is always the possibility of a hoax, but there is, I think, some internal evidence that this letter is genuine. I have endeavoured to pick up the lost thread by advertisement through the *Daily Mail*, but without success. It occurs to me, however, that this woman, if still alive, must retain her interest in the case, and must therefore be following its development in the *Daily Telegraph*. If this should meet her eye I would beg her to communicate with me at this address, and I give her the assurance that she shall be put to no personal loss or inconvenience if she will aid the cause of justice.—Yours faithfully,

ARTHUR CONAN DOYLE
Grand Hotel, London, Jan. 18.

TO THE EDITOR OF THE *DAILY TELEGRAPH*

Sir—Referring to my letter which appeared in your issue of Tuesday last, may I say that "brittly" hairs was a misprint. I wrote "belly" hairs. If Mr. Edalji's friends can succeed in proving that his eyesight was as bad in October, 1903, as it is now, there will be an end of the whole matter. If such is the fact he cannot be the guilty man, and it must be added that if those responsible for his defence had proved it (assuming they could do so) at the trial, then all the subsequent trouble would have been saved. Mr. Edalji and Sir Arthur Conan Doyle both admit that an error, which the former attributes to the over-confidence of his friends, was made here; in other words, they admit that they failed to put in evidence which must have secured an acquittal. I only ask that this may be remembered by those who are so ready to pour abuse upon the gentleman who presided at the trial, and it ought not to be forgotten if the subject of compensation is subsequently mooted. I note that the author abandons his "hair" argument as "a small detail." It appeared to me that he laid great stress on it.

Just a word on the concluding paragraph of Sir Arthur's letter in today's issue. He mentions the fact that the accused man is a total abstainer. How does this help him? Are we to think that such crimes, requiring an iron nerve and a steady hand, are more likely to be committed by a man with a partiality for alcohol? Then, in such deeds, Mr. Edalji could have "no conceivable object in view." I ask what conceivable object could any human being have in the commission of such crimes? And yet they were committed; and a man might in regard to one class of offences be a criminal, while in all other respects "a perfectly sane man."

Now one of the few things that are quite clear in this case is that "an otherwise sane man" must be an accurate description of the actual criminal. It is indisputable that the crimes were committed by a person or persons having a perfect knowledge of the locality, almost certainly by a resident. If there had been a person living in the district whose actions in everyday life proclaimed him to be mad, he must have been suspected. We hear of nothing of the kind, therefore we may infer that the miscreant is a person who passes as a sane individual. I believe this contention to be quite uncontrovertible, and of vast importance.

My only reason, Sir, in devoting myself to "small details" is to illustrate to those who care to read this letter how much depends upon the point of view, and to get these folk to recollect that in this matter Sir Arthur Conan Doyle must be regarded not as a judge, but as an advocate. Already we have demands for Captain Anson's defence "to be published without delay," as though we are to allow our police officials to use State documents for the purpose of newspaper controversy. We hear, for the first time, of gentlemen who "were all along convinced of the man's innocence," of those who are "almost ashamed to be an Englishman." We have hysterical references to "Dreyfus" and "dossiers," the result of it all being a demand for an inquiry into a question upon which all these sticklers for legal etiquette have already made up their minds. By all means, let us have an inquiry—a public inquiry—into this case; such an inquiry will no doubt be ordered by Mr. Gladstone. If not, and in the event of there being an organised agitation to bring it about, I shall be glad if the organisers will add my humble name to the list of helpers in the cause.

Until we have the result of such an inquiry let us defer judgment, and refrain from advocating the scrapping of the great machinery of English law, because upon one job out of a hundred thousand it may not have moved with its wonted smoothness.

A. H. HENDERSON-LIVESEY
5, The Avenue, Bedford Park, W., Jan. 16.

TO THE EDITOR OF THE *DAILY TELEGRAPH*

Sir—I was present throughout the chief part of the now famous, if not also infamous, trial of Mr. Edalji, and should, therefore, like to make a few observations both upon it, and upon the general aspects of the case.

My feeling throughout the trial was that the most amicable, refined, and accomplished chairman was similarly unsuited for the position and that consciousness of this prevented him from the assertion of much-needed authority. He had to deal with an able advocate of considerable experience, and not unnaturally failed to trust his own judgment, which was quite equal to the occasion. He was nervous, apologetic, and allowed the counsel a freedom which would have been promptly checked by one of his Majesty's judges.

What struck me next was the damage inflicted upon the defence by the sudden change of front executed by the prosecution. Their first theory having completely broken down, they were permitted, at a late date in the trial, to start a new theory, viz., that the outrage took place after midnight. This new theory was sprung upon the defence. They were not prepared with evidence on the question of eyesight, which, of course, assumed an importance which it had not previously possessed. There was hardly time for it to be noticed, that the new theory postulated either an almost supernatural adroitness on the part of the accused, or an absolute incapacity on the part of the police, if he was able to run the gauntlet against police supervision both around the house and in the rear neighbourhood of the place where the outrage was committed.

The next point observed at the time was the calm assumption on the part of the Court that a general acquaintance with the case was possessed by all concerned, and thus, while one crime was being nominally investigated, practically Mr. Edalji was being tried for the whole number. In plain fact the jury might, so far as the Court was concerned, have been excused for thinking that if Edalji was not quite proved to have done the crime in question—what about all the rest of them?

So much concerned was I at the time, that, having been asked to sign a protest which was more circumstantial in details than was possible for me to endorse, I drafted a protest on more general lines, which was, I believe, that which later received some 5,000 signatures, and which stated grave dissatisfaction with the form and conduct of the trial, of which I was an impartial observer. As to the more general questions now seen to be involved, and so ably discussed by Sir A. Conan Doyle, I would only make a few remarks. And first as to the letters. These I saw, as they were handed to me by one of the counsel engaged. I certainly thought I saw some degree of resemblance between certain characters in them and the admitted writing of Mr. Edalji. But such a resemblance was only to be expected if the letters were intended as imitations of his handwriting. The expert did not fail in his duty of pointing out such resemblances, but these admitted, we are no nearer a solution.

The obvious question was, and is, granted a likeness—was it due to design on the part of an anonymous writer, or to carelessness and a relapse into his own script on the part of the accused? This it was outside Mr. Gurrin's province to decide. But here comes in the question of probability. Were these letters likely to have been written by Mr. Edalji? The answer is obvious that if he wrote them his proper domicile is a lunatic asylum. People do not in their sane senses write letters with the one object of incriminating themselves and procuring for themselves a dose of penal servitude.

I have next to deal with the question of the hairs stated to have been found upon the coat. I was much impressed with the evidence of the parents, and firmly believe them to have been speaking nothing but what they believed true. How, then, about the presence of the hairs noticed by Dr. Butler? It may have been due to mere carelessness, and to placing coat and skin in juxtaposition. It may have been due to the act of a single policeman. Remember, the temptation was very great. The police had failed in their duty as protectors of society, and had earned, justly or unjustly, public contempt, and even indignation. They certainly believed that Edalji was the criminal, and that if he escaped the ends of justice would be defeated, and their own reputation damaged. Are we prepared to say that among the whole body of policemen there was not one who may not have done evil in order that, what he thought, good might be done.

I am not bringing a wholesale accusation, but these hairs were either due to the police or to someone who had access to the coat, or by the accused. Against the latter supposition there is the evidence of the parents, which I that heard it am certainly prepared to accept. There are also the manifold improbabilities, if not impossibilities, of the nocturnal journey, so convincingly marshalled by Sir A. Conan Doyle. That an enemy did this I am convinced, and also that this enemy was the writer of the anonymous letters would not surprise me. All the evidence seems to show that the actual perpetrator of the outrages was not the writer of the letters, but that the writer intended to fasten the blame on Edalji, and would leave no stone, or, shall we say, no coat, unturned to effect this object—I am, yours sincerely,

A Spectator of the Trial
Hull, Jan. 17.

TO THE EDITOR OF THE *DAILY TELEGRAPH*
Sir—Mr. Edalji thinks I have drawn a misleading inference from the schoolboy incident. I think one of the following must be right: (1) Either Mr. Edalji wrote the "Greatorex" letters; or (2) one of the group of school-boys; or (3) which I think is most improbable, that some other person, who on one of the few occasions on which Mr. Edalji found himself in the same compartment as the boys, saw him. But I do not think he would have connected them with the crime unless he knew that they were acquainted with Mr. Edalji. Again, a porter is accused as well as Mr. Edalji. Now, anyone traveling constantly on this line would be likely to know a porter. Does Mr. Edalji know the porter mentioned, or do any of the schoolboys know him?

In the apology published in 1892–5 Mr. Edalji's correct initials are given, and a person named Brooks is given as an accomplice. Who is the latter?— I remain. Sir, yours faithfully,

W. P. COOK
London, Jan. 18.

CHAPTER FOUR

Public Interest Continues to Grow: The *Daily Telegraph* Publishes a Report on the Trial as the Public Debate Rages On

By mid-January, the public clamor for details about the Edalji case had grown to the point where the editors felt compelled to publish a blow-by-blow account of the trial. (Of course, the fact that circulation was sky-rocketing as a result had little to do with their decision.) On Monday, January 21, 1907, the *Daily Telegraph* began a two-part story on the trial. Part trial transcript, part reportage, the story caused the public furor to grow even more frenzied.

Meanwhile, the constant barrage of letters from readers, Conan Doyle, Edalji and his father, and other interested and impassioned parties continued. On January 26, 1907, the *Daily Telegraph* published a letter by Sir Arthur in which he summed up and seemed to make his final statements about the case. He ends his letter by writing, "I do not know that more can be done until we hear from the authorities."

As it turned out, Conan Doyle—and the rest of Edalji's supporters—would not have long to wait.

JANUARY 21, 1907

EDALJI'S TRIAL
PROSECUTION THEORY
POLICE EVIDENCE

Today we publish the first half of the proceedings at the Staffordshire Quarter Sessions at the end of October, 1903, which resulted in Mr. George Ernest Thompson Edalji being sentenced to seven years penal servitude. The major portion of the report is taken from an excellent account of the trial published in the *Staffordshire Sentinel*, the old established evening paper printed in Hanley. Some of the evidence of Inspector Campbell is reprinted from the *Stafford Advertiser*.

The grand jury empaneled at Staffordshire Quarter Sessions brought in a true bill against George Ernest Thompson Edalji, twenty-eight, solicitor, of Great Wyrley, who was charged with having wounded a horse belonging to the Great Wyrley Colliery Company on Aug. 17, and with having sent a threatening letter to Police-sergeant Robinson, Hednesford. As soon as the grand jury had announced their bill, the case was at once relegated to the Second Court, where Sir Reginald Hardy presided, supported by a dozen other justices; including Mr. W. Kirkham, Mr. W. S. Brough, Mr. T. Bullock, Mr. W. C. T. Mynors, Mr. F. James, Mr. W. Thompsons, and Captain Littleton, R. N. Edalji, who had been in custody at Stafford Gaol since his committal, was ushered into the dock as soon as possible and formally charged. To each indictment he gave a firm denial. His attitude in the dock was charactertised by the same collected demeanour which marked his conduct at the Cannock police-court, his swarthy countenance being almost impassive during the hour which prosecuting counsel took in placing the story before the jury.

Mr. Disturnal and Mr. Harrison prosecuted on behalf of the Treasury (instructed by Mr. Barnes, of Lichfield); and Mr. Vachell and Mr. Gandy defended (retained by Mr. Meek).

OPENING SPEECH

Mr. Disturnal, at the outset, appealed to the jury to shut out from their minds everything they had heard or read in connection with the case, and said the prisoner was to be judged entirely by the evidence which came before the Court. If on that evidence his guilt was established to their reasonable satisfaction, it would be their duty to say he was guilty, no matter the position in life which he occupied. On the other hand if, after such careful consideration of the evidence as they were able to give, it left in their minds a reasonable doubt, it would be their duty to say he was not guilty. Prisoner was admitted to the legal profession in 1898. He had obtained honours under the incorporated Law Society and prizes from the Birmingham Law Society as being the first student of the year. He was the son of the Rev. S. Edalji, vicar of Great Wyrley, near Cannock, who was a Parsee, but his wife was an English lady. Prisoner lived at the Vicarage at the time of the alleged outrage on Aug. 17, and the pony in question was in a field half a mile from the vicarage.

As soon as the outrage was discovered, the police went to the vicarage, but found that the prisoner had gone to his office in Birmingham. The police, however, had an interview with the prisoner's father, and mother, and a pair of trousers, vest, coat, and a pair of boots were produced. Some of the articles were wet, and on the coat were dark stains about the sleeve, which were on analysis, found to be marks of mammalian blood. In addition to the stains there were short hairs upon the coat and vest, which exactly corresponded with the hairs afterwards obtained from the pony's hide. The trousers were wet, the boots were saturated, and the police noticed that the heel of the left boot was worn down very much at the back. The importance of this fact lay in this—that there was a trail of footmarks extending from the shed in the field where the pony was found across several fields leading from the Vicarage. He did not say the trail was unbroken from beginning to end. As a matter of fact, it was interrupted in several places, but it was picked up, and the general direction of the trail was leading from the shed towards the vicarage and ultimately lost on a public footpath going in the direction of the vicarage.

There were peculiarities about those marks on the trail. Counsel detailed the operations of the police in examining the marks and comparing them with the boots of the prisoner. He said the left boot exactly corresponded with the marks found on the trail. It would be for the jury to consider the importance of that evidence. It would be shown that the accused was wearing the clothes the night before, and was out and about. It would be further shown that the prisoner when spoken to gave an account, which he professed to be a full one, of his movements that night, but that the prosecution alleged was by no means the case. After alluding to the visit of the police to prisoner's office at Birmingham, counsel referred to the conversation as to the clothes which accused was wearing on the night of Aug. 17, and to the remark of prisoner that the hairs found upon the coat might have been obtained by leaning on grates against which horses had rubbed.

Passing from what he called direct evidence, Mr. Disturnal said there was a branch of the case to which the prosecution attached great importance. This was contained in a number of documents written in a disguised hand. According to the evidence he would bring forward they were clearly in the handwriting of the prisoner. He intended to call Mr. Gurrin, as expert in handwriting. He was not going to ask the jury to accept the *ipse dixit* of Mr. Gurrin as to handwriting, as it had been said over and over again by great judges that it was for the jury themselves to form an opinion of handwriting after comparing the admitted handwriting of the prisoner with the writing in question. The only use of an expert in matters such as this was to point out to the jury the various features in handwriting for the purposes of comparison. It was well known in regard to disguised handwriting that, although a man might attempt to disguise his writing there would creep into it sooner or later, however careful and clever he might be, little eccentricities or tricks which had manifested in his ordinary writing. Mr. Disturnal submitted that such peculiarities which could be traced in prisoner's admitted handwriting showed themselves in the disguised writing.

The learned counsel remarked that there had been seven outrages of a similar nature as that alleged against the prisoner in the same locality between February and the end of June. Prisoner was in no way charged with those offenses. The anonymous letters suggested that they were the work of some gang of schoolboys. Counsel suggested that the letters clearly showed that the writer was preparing, either by himself or in conjunction with someone else, to carry out outrages at some future time when the opportunity occurred. Some of the letters professed to be written by a lad named Greatorex, who lived with his father near Hadnesford. Greatorex would, however, tell the jury he knew nothing about the letters.

The police saw Edalji about the letters, and the latter did what it was expected he would do if he was the writer. He took advantage of the opportunity of asking the police all about their watches and their methods of detection, and so got information which would be useful to anybody who was desirous of doing the crime. Therefore, the use of Edalji's name in the letters did not go in any way to show that prisoner did not write them. Mr. Disturnal then referred to Edalji advertising a reward of £25 for information leading to the conviction of people who were alleged to have circulated a slander connecting him with the charges.

In commenting on the fact that another outrage was committed on Sept. 21, after prisoner was committed for trial, the learned Counsel said it was quite possible that one person might have committed the outrage on Aug. 17, while quite another person was responsible for that of Sept. 21. One of the anonymous letters said the writer was not acting alone. What, then, was more likely or say, assuming there was a gang operating, that when one of the gang was arrested another member should commit similar outrages in order to create evidence in his favour?

Prisoner was in a good position in life, but when he was offered bail by the magistrates he refused it, and preferred to be in Stafford Gaol from August to October. As he was being placed in the cell at Cannock after committal for trial he made a very singular observation to a policeman, which suggested that in his mind prisoner knew perfectly well what he was about when he refused bail, and that he was not altogether surprised when the offence was committed on Sept. 21. Counsel concludes that prisoner was by anonymous letters and other means preparing the ground for a defense during the committal of the alleged offence.

EVIDENCE FOR THE PROSECUTION

A number of more or less formal witnesses were first examined. Mr. Reginald James Barnes, surveyor and architect, of Lichfield, produced plans, and stated that the distance from Great Wyrley Vicarage to the field where the pony was mutilated was about half a mile.

Constable Rowley proved the receipt of a letter bearing the postmark of July 31.

Joseph Southam in the employ of the Great Wyrley Colliery Company, stated that on June 29 one of the company's horses was injured, and he afterwards received a postcard which he handed to Constable Cooper.

James Walters produced a letter, dated July 7, from the accused to the *Mercury*, Lichfield, asking on the insertion of an advertisement offering a reward.

William Woolten, horsekeeper in the employ of the colliery company, said he saw a pony belonging to the company in a field near the colliery about nine o'clock on the night of Aug. 17. It was then all right. The next morning he found the pony in the field with a wound on its side. The wound was bleeding a little. After the pony had been examined by a veterinary surgeon, witness shot it.

Henry Garrett, a lad, stated that on going to work at a quarter to six on the morning of Aug 18 he saw the pony in a field bleeding from a wound.

William Cooper, the horse slaughterer who examined the pony, declared that the wound was about 14 in. long and extended across the belly. It must have been inflicted by a sharp, short-bladed knife.

Other witnesses spoke to having seen the prisoner in Cheslyn Hay between nine and 9.30 on the night in question.

POLICE EVIDENCE

Inspector Campbell, stationed at Cannock, was the next witness. He spoke to receiving certain documents from Constable Rowley and Sergeant Robinson, and produced a copy of a letter signed "A Lover of Justice." That letter was addressed to "George Edalji, Esq." and in it the writer said:

I do not know you, but I have sometimes seen you on the railway, and I do not expect I would like you much if I did know you, as I don't like natives. But I think everyone ought to have fair treatment, and that is why I write you, because I don't think you have had anything to do with the horrid crimes that everyone talks about. The people all about say it must be you, because they do not think you are the right sort and you would be likely to do them. If another horse is murdered people will say it is you. So why don't you go away for your holidays and be away when the next case happens? Go away and you will not be suspected anymore.

Inspector Campbell, continuing his evidence, said he went to see the prisoner, taking with him the letter which had been received by Sergeant Robinson. He told the accused that his reason for calling was because he thought the prisoner might assist the police. Witness showed him the envelope and the address, and asked if he knew anything about it. Prisoner said he did not. Witness pointed out that the envelope purported to come from Osborn and Son, Birmingham, and Edalji replied, "Oh, yes, it is very easy for anyone to get possession of this."

The prisoner read the postscript on the back of the envelope: "Do not be too hard on me. There was no cruelty in how we killed them. It is really much quicker than the ordinary way, as directly their bowels are out they feel no more." The prisoner said, "What does it matter to anyone who is doing this whether it is cruel or not?" Witness asked if he could recognise the handwriting, but Edalji replied, "No," and then began to talk about the outrages, and asked, "Do you find any traces at all round where they occurred?" Witness said, "No." Prisoner then asked, "Have you ever found a knife or any instrument that it has been done with?" Witness said, "No." Prisoner further said, "Do you think the moon has anything to do with it?" to which witness answered that he did not think it had. Edalji inquired if the police had any idea or suspicion of anybody, and witness said they had not. Prisoner's next question was, "Have you ever thought of employing bloodhounds?" Witness said "no;" he thought it would be impossible to work them. The accused also wanted to know if the police were still watching and witness replied that they were, as well as they could with the few men he had under him. "Do you think it risky work?" was the next query, and witness reply was "No, I do not think it is, Mr. Edalji. You know the country as well as I do round here, and you know how easy it would be for a man to turn out at night without being seen and get into these fields." On July 26 witness received a postcard addressed to the Inspector at Cannock Police-station, signed, "One who knows a bit about it," and bearing the Walsall postmark. On July 27 witness also received a letter from the accused written from his Birmingham Office, and asking the inspector to call upon him. On the same evening witness in company with Police-constable Cooper saw the prisoner at his residence.

Witness told him he had come in answer to his request, and prisoner answered, "Yes, I wanted to see you." He produced a letter he had received, and after witness had read it, prisoner asked him if he had ever seen any writing like it. Witness said he could not say that he had. Prisoner asked, "Do you think it is the writing of a gentleman or a lady?" Witness thought it was a gentleman's writing, and the prisoner thought so, too, and said: "Do you know anything about that letter you came to see me about before?" The inspector replied in the negative and prisoner asked: "Do you think you can trace these anonymous letters? Is it possible to do so?"

Witness said it was a difficult matter to trace letters like that. Showing him the envelope, prisoner said, "Have you ever seen any writing like this before?" Witness answered that he thought he had, adding that the capitals "G" and "B" were very similar to those on the envelope bearing the name of Osborn and Son witness showed him on a previous visit. Prisoner replied, "Do you think so?" and again inquired if the police were watching the district. He also asked witness if there was more than one in it, to which he replied that he could not say, but in his opinion there was not.

EXAMINING EDALJI'S CLOTHES

On Aug. 18, witness continued he, in company with Sergeant Parson and Constable Cooper; went to a field near the Great Wyrley Colliery and there saw a chestnut-coloured pony, on examining which he found a large cut underneath its body extending up to the ribs on the near side and about 14 in. long. He found marks of blood in the field and also in a shed where the pony had been standing. There were foot marks leading into and coming away from the shed. Witness and the other officers proceeded to the prisoner's home at the vicarage, and saw his parents. His mother produced a jacket, vest, and trousers belonging to the accused. On the cuffs of the jacket witness found a dark, reddish stain, the right cuff being much more stained than the left, and on the sleeves were brown and white stains. There were also white marks on the breast of the jacket. Witness found some brownish-coloured hairs, like those of a horse, on the jacket sleeves. The trousers were damp and dirty round the bottom edges.

Witness showed the marks and stains to the prisoner's mother. The boots produced at the trial were very wet right up to the top of the uppers, and were worn down at the heels, the left heel especially so. He (the inspector) then went with Sergeant Parsons to prisoner's office in Newhall-street, Birmingham, and saw Edalji about 10.30 a.m. He said to the prisoner, "We are making some inquiries, Mr. Edalji, about the horse that was maimed at Great Wyrley last night." The accused said, "Yes, I heard something about it when I was coming to business this morning." Witness told him he had been to the vicarage and had been shown certain clothes by Mrs. Edalji, which bore marks and stains. Without asking which clothes witness referred to, the prisoner said, "I did not wear those clothes last night; I did not have them on." Afterwards prisoner said, "The coat is an old one and you may find some grease on it. The white stains may be milk and oatmeal."

Witness also told Edalji that he had examined a pair of boots which were very wet. Prisoner said, "Oh, yes; I had them on last night. They are a pair of old boots that I put on about home at night," and added, "I suppose you have got those boots, then." Witness replied, "Yes." When told that the marks and the hairs had been shown to his parents, prisoner said, "There are no hairs." On witness stating "Oh, yes, there are," Edalji answered, "Well it must be the hair coming through the material." Witness said, "Oh, no," and Edalji rejoined, "Well, if there are any hairs on I may have got them when out at nights leaning on gates and rails of fields where horses run."

The inspector told Edalji he was not satisfied with his explanation, and must take him into custody. He then cautioned and charged the accused, who seemed confused, and said, "Take me into custody?" Witness said, "Yes." Prisoner remarked, "I have got Mr. Lorton to thank for this," and witness replied, "No; I do not think Mr. Lorton knows anything at all about it." The prisoner said, "Where's your evidence, you have got no evidence. What time was this done?" Witness replied that he could not hold a conversation with the prisoner, but at the proper time he would know all about it. The prisoner said, "I can account for all my time last night. I went out about eight o'clock, went down to Bridgetown, took a pair of boots to be repaired, came back to Walkmill, and that way home. I reached home about half-past nine and did not leave home again until this morning when I came to business." After a pause, the prisoner continued, "Where are you going to take me?" Prisoner was taken to the cells in Steel House–lane, Birmingham, and on the way he told a Birmingham constable, "I am not surprised at this. I have been expecting it some time."

The accused was afterwards brought to the police-station at Cannock, and when formally charged he asked, "Is that the only charge you have against me?" Witness said, "Yes, at present." About 2.30 on the same day witness went to the vicarage and received a pair of trousers from the accused's parents. The trousers were not in the same condition as in the morning, having been thoroughly cleaned. In a box in the prisoner's bedroom witness found four razors, all more or less stained. One was wet, and appeared to have been recently used. Witness showed this to prisoner's father, who began to rub the wet off with his thumb. There were also hairs on the razor.

Witness went on to speak of tracing footprints from the field in which the pony was mutilated, across several other fields to a footpath in another field close to the vicarage. The line was sometimes lost, and at other times indistinct, but at places it was very distinct. At different places along the track witness made impressions with the prisoner's boots by the side of those being followed, and found the marks corresponded. The left heel made a peculiar impression on the bare ground. Witness subsequently handed the clothes and razors to Dr. Butler.

INSPECTOR CROSS-EXAMINED

Cross-examined by Mr. Vachell, Inspector Campbell said in consequence of the successive mutilations of cattle, a certain amount of uneasiness prevailed in the district. Edalji was the only person arrested in connection with the crimes, and after his arrest the special constables drafted to Wyrley district to try and fathom the mystery were for a while withdrawn. Another animal was killed on Sept. 21, while the prisoner was in gaol.

Mr. Vachell: Have you discovered who did that?—Witness: No, sir. Oh! I beg your pardon, we have an idea.

Have you made an arrest?—No, sir.

Has anyone admitted to you that he did it?—Yes.

Is that person in court?—He is here.

Brought here by the police?—Yes.

What is his name?—John Harry Green.

He lives at Green's Farm?—Yes, the farmer's son.

Do you know if on the night of Aug. 17 Green was living on that farm?—I could not say that he was at home that night.

Has he been living there for sometime past?—That is his home. I cannot say he is always there.

Have you any reason to believe he was away on that particular night?—No, sir; I have not.

In further cross-examination witness said he had taken no impression of the footprints nor had he had them photographed. A number of anonymous letters had been received in connection with the case. After the committal of the accused further anonymous letters had been received, but they were not in the same handwriting as the earlier letters. Witness admitted that he had heard that the stains on the razor were not bloodstains, and it was not suggested that any of the hairs on the razor were off the dead pony. It was a fact that the only stains of blood on Edalji's coat were two small spots about the size of a three-penny-piece.

Re-examined by Mr. Disturnal, witness said John Harry Green was the owner of the horse which he admitted having mutilated.

Mr. Disturnal: Did he make any admissions as to any previous outrage?—Witness: No.

FURTHER POLICE EVIDENCE

Sergeant Parsons was examined as to the foot marks and as to the visits paid by the police to the prisoner's home.

Mr. Vachell, in cross-examination, pressed witness as to what transpired when Edalji's clothing was produced at the vicarage before Inspector Campbell went to Birmingham to arrest the prisoner. Witness declared that Edalji's father did not say there were no hairs on his son's clothing. He certainly examined the clothing, but he did not say he could not see any hairs. The Rev. Mr. Edalji rubbed his thumb along the wet razor, and would probably remove some of the moisture. Sergeant Parsons went on to say that early in July a report was current in the district that Edalji had been arrested, and this no doubt, led to Edalji offering a reward of £25 for information as to who had circulated defamatory statements about him.

Mr. Vachell asked if people flocked to the field on Aug. 18 on hearing of the outrage, and Sergeant Parsons said that was so, and there were many footprints about when witness began to examine those alleged to be Edalji's. There were other footprints, but of a distinct difference, going in the direction of those tracks which witness believed were Edalji's. The latter were minutely compared alongside impressions made by the left boot of Edalji, which had been obtained from the vicarage. John Harry Green had been subpoenaed to attend the trial that day.

By M. Disturnal: He saw the pony standing in the field about eleven o'clock on Aug. 17, but he did not examine it. He had no lamp, but "he believed it was quite probable" the pony was injured when he saw it.

Police-constable Cooper said he called upon Edalji on Aug. 6 with references to a communication he had received, professing to come from the lad Greatorex, of Littleworth Farm. He considered the letter defamatory and libellous, and said he should have liked to have seen the lad about them.

Edalji made the remark that "the man had stopped killing cattle and taken to writing anonymous letters." "Yes," replied witness, "and woe betide the man if he is caught by some of the farmers as I'm told they are carrying guns." Edalji said, "You don't mean that?" On witness saying, "Yes," Edalji asked "Is Harry Green watching?" Witness said he did not know.

Letters were read which Edalji told the police he had received, bearing the same address of Wilfrid Greatorex. The first one said: "I daresay you think yourself a very sharp fellow, but you are no gentleman, or you would not have put the police on my track. It soon caught on about you murdering the horses, because none of the people think you are the right sort. The police think you did it." The letter went on to refer to two lads in the district in opprobrious terms, and a lady's name was also mentioned. Enclosed in this letter was a postscript written on an old newspaper wrapper bearing the Birmingham post-mark, and the address of Wilfrid Greatorex. In reply to the letters, Edalji wrote to young Greatorex, saying he was sorry if he had suffered any annoyance from anyone, but he (Edalji) had not hinted Greatorex's name to the police. Edalji went on to say he could hardly believe Greatorex had written such letters, and added; "I am sure no boys are concerned in this wretched business. When the truth is known it will be found that it is someone in a very different position."

NO QUESTIONS FROM JURORS

While Cooper was describing his operations in comparing the impressions of Edalji's left boot with the footprints in the field, there occurred an incident which the *Staffordshire Sentinel* reporter rightly calls unusual. One of the jurymen interrupted the witness with the remark, "But you could not get an impression of a man's foot by bearing on it as you say."

The juryman went on: "When a man is fifteen stone in weight he presses all his fifteen stone on one foot when walking. You could not do—"

The court-usher stopped the juryman, and suggested that he should put his questions through the chairman.

Sir Reginald Hardy: Yes, you had better not make any remarks like this. You must not criticise.

Cooper stated that he put all his weight on Edalji's boot when he made the impression in the ground.

In cross-examining, Mr. Vachell said: It is material to know at what time the prisoner returned to the Vicarage on Aug. 17. The prosecution allege he went down to the shed and committed this deed before he returned home.

Mr. Disturnal: I am not alleging that. I did not open my case in that way.

The chairman said it was hardly right to ask the witness what was the theory of the prosecution.

Mr. Vachell hoped no effort would be made to tie his hands in this somewhat difficult defence.

Mr. Disturnal said he did not wish to do anything of the kind.

Cooper stated that a man named Whitehouse had said he saw Edalji enter the Vicarage about 9.30, but Whitehouse had told two or three tales about it.

Mr. Disturnal: Whitehouse was not called for the prosecution.

Mr. Vachell: No, he would not fit in with your case.

Cooper, in describing the method he adopted in making an impression with Edalji's left boot, said he pressed the heel into the ground and eased it towards the toe to get an impression of the whole length of the boot. He got a good shallow impression on the boot. Neither Edalji's father, nor anyone else on Edalji's behalf, was shown the impression and no cast was taken.

Re-examined by Mr. Disturnal, Cooper declared that hairs were on the coat when he first saw it at the Vicarage, and Mrs. Edalji suggested—as her son did when arrested—that they might have adhered to the cloth while Edalji leaned on rails or gates against which horses had rubbed. The coat was wrapped up, with a handkerchief put over the hairs to protect them, and prevent their removal, and the clothing was placed in a brown-paper parcel.

Mr. Disturnal: Did you deliberately put hairs on the coat?—I did not.

Did you come into actual contact with the pony so as to get hairs from it on to your own clothes?—I did not touch the pony. Witness did not see Inspector Campbell or Sergeant Parsons come in contact with the pony. Wilfrid Guy Greatorex, fifteen years of age said he travelled daily by Walsall with school companions. Sometimes Edalji travelled in the same compartment, but his presence did not affect the freedom of their conversation. Witness denied that he had written the letters which bore his name or that he had anything to do with them.

A post office clerk, Frederick George Wootten, also denied that he had written a letter to which his name was attached.

Inspector Campbell and Sergeant Parsons stated that they did not come in contact with the pony so as to get hair upon their clothes.

Mr. Henry Gurrin, called as an expert in handwriting, stated that certain of the anonymous letters were in the same handwriting as letters admittedly written by Edalji, but the writing was disguised.

Dr. John Carr Butler, of Cannock, to whom the police had submitted the clothes taken from the Vicarage, stated that he tested the dark stains on the prisoner's coat and found them to be of mammalian blood. Twenty-nine hairs were found on the coat, and he discovered that these were exactly similar to hairs on a piece of hide taken from the dead pony.

Mr. Vachell cross-examined Dr. Butler as to the nature of the blood. The doctor admitted that the blood might have fallen on the coat from a person's nose, and he could venture no opinion as to the length of time the blood had been on the coat.

Police-constable Meredith said that on Sept. 4, after Edalji had been committed for trial, witness saw him in the cell and asked if he had got bail. Edalji replied, "No, I won't have it; and when the next horse is killed it won't be me."

This closed the case for the prosecution, and in winding up his report for the day, the *Staffordshire Sentinel* reporter said: "The fact that the Crown did not call evidence as to the confession relating to the outrage on Sept. 21 caused evident disappointment to the public in court."

OPENING OF THE DEFENCE

Mr. Vachell commenced his speech in opening the case for Edalji with an appeal to the jury to consider nothing but the evidence, and to shut out from their minds everything they had heard or read. Speaking of the situation in Great Wyrley since the commencement of the outrages, Mr. Vachell said that "alarm" was not the word to describe the state of public feeling. The police were entirely at a loss to discover the culprit. Special officers were watching and patrolling the locality, and still no clue could be found bringing suspicion upon anybody. The public, naturally, expected the police to do something, but they were doing nothing. They must have felt to a certain extent on their trial, and unless shortly they could accomplish something they would fall very much in the estimation of the public.

On Aug. 18—partly on that day—the police, without any evidence at all, and before full inquiries had been made, had come to the conclusion that prisoner was responsible for the crimes. They felt so certain when they arrested the accused that they had got the right man that they withdrew the extra police who had been drafted into the district. He was going to urge that the police, without evidence in the first instance, had made up their minds—he did not say corruptly—that prisoner was the criminal in all these matters, and they had looked at their evidence with a jaundiced and prejudiced eye. They had formed a theory as to the time and manner in which the offence was done, they had tried to force such facts as they had got hold of to fit in with their theory, and facts which they found did not so fit in they had rejected, and abstained from calling witnesses who could have deposed to those conflicting facts. It was no part of his duty to severely criticise the conduct of the police, but he was entitled to say there was a general idea among Englishmen that the duty of the police was not to secure a conviction of the person they chose to accuse at any cost, but to bring all evidence before a jury whether it was for or against the prisoner, and ask the jury to say if under the circumstances conviction was justifiable.

The learned counsel said he should criticise the chain of evidence adduced by the police, and show that some of the links were not reliable and not continuous. They should call the prisoner and his relations and perfectly independent witnesses, some of whom the police had ignored after hearing their story because it did not fit in with their theory. Some of the witnesses would depose as to facts inconsistent with the theory of the Crown. After alluding to the difficulty of a person not acquainted with a horse being able to approach an animal in the dark, Mr. Vachell proceeded to outline the evidence he intended to call to controvert the case of the police as to Edalji's wanderings on the night of Aug. 17. The police did not call Whitehouse because his testimony would utterly ruin their theory, Counsel suggested that the mutilated pony had been wounded within six hours of the time it was found, and that was against the theory of the prosecution.

Edalji had slept for many years in the same room as his father, and the latter would swear that his son never left the vicarage from 9.30 on Aug. 17 until he left for Birmingham on the following day. The police were only human, and had an inclination to fix on everything against an accused person and to see nothing in his favour. How did the police regard Edalji's clothing? What an incriminating cost! One might think they saw it reeking with blood and bespattered with the saliva of the wounded animal. All there was in the evidence was that there were two spots of blood on the coat of the size of three penny pieces, while the "saliva" spots were possibly marks of bread and milk caused by careless feeding. Possibly the blood spots arose from bleeding at the nose. The reason the police did not take away Edalji's clothes from the vicarage when they first called on Aug. 16 was that they found their condition consistent with the prisoner's innocence.

No bloodstains were found on the razors when examined by an analyst, and a razor would be an impossible, or at any rate an awkward weapon to use in maiming a horse in the way described by the police. He did not press the argument that it was possible to get horse hair on a coat by leaning against a gate, because he hoped to establish the fact that Edalji did not wear the coat the police had produced on Aug. 17, but that he wore a blue serge suit he was in the habit of putting on in the evening. The shoemaker to whom Edalji took a pair of boots for repair that night, would come forward and give evidence to that effect. Mr. Vachell asked the jury to reject the police evidence as to footprints as being worthless. He severely criticised the methods adopted by the police, and commented on the neglect to take plaster impressions of the tracks, which was usual in such cases. It would be a strange footprint that would not convince Constable Cooper it was not the footprint he was seeking.

After pointing out that on Aug. 4, when one of the anonymous letters was posted at Walsall and a postcard at Wolverhampton, prisoner and his sister were at Aberyswyth, Mr. Vachell remarked the singular feature was that almost every letter drew attention to Edalji, and asked was it likely he would call attention to and actually accuse himself? Since the police had formed their theory against the prisoner and since his committal another outrage had occurred. The police said the person who did that was John Harry Green. Why was not Green called? If he had been placed in the box he would be rightly warned that he need not answer the question, Did he kill the pony on Aug. 17? But the prosecution could have put Green in the box to say he did not commit that crime. Did the jury believe that there were two people of such fiendish mind in Wyrley going about and destroying horses and cattle at night?

JANUARY 21, 1907

THE EDALJI CASE
LETTER FROM THE FATHER
MR. KENNETH SCOTT'S DIAGNOSIS

Upon page 6 will be found the first installment of a report of the trial of this case, to be followed tomorrow by the conclusion. From a vast number of the letters which we continue to receive on this subject we select the subjoined:

TO THE EDITOR OF THE *DAILY TELEGRAPH*
Sir—Mr. W. T. Shapley asks, "Where was Edalji between 9.40 p.m. and 6.20 a.m.?"

My son was at home at 9.40 p.m. He returned from his walk at about twenty-seven minutes past nine. At half-past nine he took his supper in the dining-room, where I was present. After supper he went into what is called here a "work-room," and was with his mother and sister until he went to bed at about a quarter to eleven. He was in bed all night. This I know as a matter of certainty, for I slept in the same bed-room—my wife and daughter being in an adjoining room. When I went to bed at eleven o'clock I saw my son in bed. I locked the bed-room door, as it has been and still is the custom at our house to lock at night all doors, upstairs and downstairs. My son slept soundly during the whole of the night. I slept badly, and it is, perhaps, hardly necessary to explain why. There have been nights when I could not sleep at all.

On the particular night in question (Aug. 17, 1903) I was suffering from an attack of lumbago. It is a complaint which comes to me like a toothache, and goes like a toothache. I slept very little, and I am sure that if my son had at any time moved out of his bed and unlocked the door I should have known it. But I declare it here, as a most sure and certain fact, and am prepared to declare it on solemn oath, that he never left his bed, and did not leave the bed-room until about twenty minutes to seven next morning.

It was about twenty minutes to six on the morning of August 18, 1903, that the mutilated condition of the horse in question was first discovered by a boy named Garratt. The wound must have been inflicted at some hour before that time. The veterinary surgeon, Mr. R. G. Lewis, who examined the wound on that morning gave it as his opinion that it must have been inflicted at or after 2.30 a.m. on Aug. 18.

If it be alleged that my statement, as given above, is not to be relied upon, I ask what is the reliable statement which the police themselves have made to prove that my son did go out at any hour of the night after 9.30? None whatever. They called no witnesses and produced no evidence in support of their allegation.

Inspector Campbell in his evidence stated that he "was out that night with twenty men in the neighourhood of the occurrence." With so many men ready to stop and interrogate any person passing them or approaching the field in question, it would have been quite impossible for my son to go at night in that direction without falling into the hands of those men.

Again, Sergeant Robinson was asked at the Cannock Police-court whether he was watching Wyrley Vicarage on the night of Aug. 17, 1903, and how many men were there. His reply was: "I was not there on the night of Aug. 17 watching the house. I do not know how many men were there that night." What is the obvious, reasonable, and logical inference to be drawn from these words? Is it not that there were some men watching the house? I appeal to all who are accustomed to weighing words and putting logical constructions upon sentences to consider whether the above-quoted words do not imply the continuance of the watch which the police had commenced some time before the outrage in question. Certainly, if my son had gone out at any hour between 9.30 p.m. and six a.m. those who were watching the house would have been able easily to catch him.

Why is it that the Staffordshire police now affirm that they were not watching the house that night? They know that their original theory of the crime having been committed between nine and ten p.m. was abandoned by their own counsel, and that be substituted for it what may be called a midnight theory, for which he had no evidence except the utterly false allegation that the coat was damp; and if they were to admit that they were watching the house this last straw of a theory would go to pieces, and their case would be completely destroyed.—I am, Sir, your obedient, servant,

S. EDALJI, Vicar of Great Wyrley
Jan. 18.

TO THE EDITOR OF THE *DAILY TELEGRAPH*
Sir—I observe that in your issue today Mr. Livesey says that I abandon my hair argument as a small detail. For this statement there is no foundation at all. My words, after discussing the point, were: "I ask your readers to raise their thoughts from small details and to realise the general hypothesis." If this to abandon an argument Mr. Livesey has repeatedly misstated my argument in this discussion. It would save time and space if he would re-read them before he attacks them.—Yours truly,

ARTHUR CONAN DOYLE
Jan. 19.

TO THE EDITOR OF THE *DAILY TELEGRAPH*

Sir—Although it was originally against my intention to contribute to the series of letters now appearing in your columns with reference to the case of Mr. Edalji, it has become incumbent on me to furnish a few accurate details, in order to avoid the possibility of any misconception as to the nature of the exact defect in Mr. Edalji's vision becoming wrongly impressed upon the mind of the public, whose aid Sir Arthur Conan Doyle has invoked in such an able manner.

At the request of Sir A. Conan Doyle, I made an appointment in December last for Mr. Edalji to call upon me, in order to furnish an exact report of the nature and degree of defect in vision in both eyes, and conducted the examination by such means as to preclude the possibility of simulation by the patient. Until this interview I had not seen Mr. Edalji, nor did I know any of the details of his case, so that I was perfectly unbiased.

The method of examination employed, known as retinoscopy—which was also named in Sir A. Conan Doyle's letter to me—is one which I have constantly used during many years of eye-practice, in all those cases where particular examination of vision is necessary, or where special spectacles are required. The result obtained by this means affords a perfect estimate as to the degree of defect which may exist in the vision, and is absolutely independent of and beyond the control of the patient. By this means the exact degree of myopic error was found in Mr. Edalji's eyes, as subsequently stated by Sir A. Conan Doyle on page 5 of your issue on Friday, the 11th inst., viz.:

Right eye, 8.75 dioptres spherical, with astigmatism superadded on
1.75 dioptres cylindrical, axis 90 deg; and in the
Left eye, 8.25 dioptres spherical.

The fundus, or interior coating of the back of the eye, presented the usual appearance found in nations of darker complexion, and there was nothing abnormal excepting in the left eye only, where there was some slight local bulging backwards at the point of entrance of the optic nerve. This is an ordinary condition in cases of myopia (or short-sightedness).

It cannot be too fully emphasised that Mr. Edalji had never used spectacles at all for distance—that is, in going about—until after his recent release. This fact is not remarkable, as it is by no means uncommon for people, even of high intelligence, who are in actual need of spectacles and who would benefit greatly by using them, to pass through quite a considerable span of life without realising such need and attending to it.

From careful and close observation at the time of Mr. Edalji's visit to me, I was able to form the positive opinion that he was speaking truly in telling me that he had not used spectacles, and I am, moreover, firmly convinced, from similar data, that without the use of such very necessary spectacles to aid him in walking, that it would have been wholly impossible for him, or for anyone else under similar circumstances, to have raced so quickly across an intricate piece of country in order to commit the crime of which he was accused, even in the broadest daylight, without the use of spectacles, and it would be practically impossible of accomplishment when the darkness of night had set in. It cannot be too distinctly borne in mind that this is the sole point at issue in regard to the condition of Mr. Edalji's eyes and the question of his eyesight.

Amongst your correspondence some of the writers have, unhappily, strayed wide of the mark in the nature of several of their remarks, which is the more to be regretted in view of the serious issues which are here at stake. Mr. Edalji's eyes show no appearance of what is known as "progressive myopia," and the very satisfactory results obtained with due correction by spectacles goes far to disprove the suggestion that there has been much advance, if any, in the condition of myopia during the last three years. There is not the slightest ground here to support such an argument; and it should be noted that during the term of Mr. Edalji's incarceration there has been nothing to strain or accentuate the condition of his eyes. Similarly, it is not in accordance with fact to state, as in one of the letters today, 17th inst., that in what has been described as savage races such defects of the eye are unknown.

On the contrary, from the very ample opportunities I have had in this direction my experience proves that it is by no means unusual.

The origin of the myopia with Mr. Edalji may be due to heredity, as I am given to understand that the Rev. S. Edalji, his father, has worn spectacles all his life. In ordinary physical examinations, it should be remembered, every case must be treated on its own particular merits, and there is great variation in the results ascertained by such means; equally must this be so when comparison is made between the exact ratio of vision obtainable from different individuals suffering from defective eyesight. It is, therefore, impossible, and may be regarded as illogically dogmatic, to adduce the powers of vision in one individual in order to positively formulate the comparative capabilities present in another. In proof of this uncertainty of comparison, as it happens, for instance, in this very case of Mr. Edalji, although his degree of myopia treads closely to the dangerous zone of high myopia, and the defect in the right eye is greater than in the left; and, in addition, the former has some astigmatism in conjunction with it, which renders its condition still less favourable; yet it is this same right eye—the more imperfect one—which is unconsciously used by Mr. Edalji in preference for all his work.

It will assist the general mind to more realistically understand the great impairment which such a degree of defective sight causes, when it is known that in order to see anything with tolerable clearness the object must be brought so close to the eyes as to be almost in contact with the face.—I am, Sir, yours faithfully,

KENNETH SCOTT, M.D.
7, Manchester-square,
W., Jan. 17.

THE LAW JOURNAL

Grave doubts were entertained by responsible persons, including many members of the legal profession, when Mr. George Edalji, a young Birmingham solicitor, was convicted of the abominable crime for which he was sentenced to penal servitude for seven years. These doubts concerning his guilt were deepened when the Home Office released him from prison after he had served less than half his sentence. They have assumed a still graver shape from the powerful articles which Sir Arthur Conan Doyle has contributed to the *Daily Telegraph* with the object of convincing the public that Mr. Edalji's conviction was a miscarriage of justice.

Some of the points on which Sir Arthur Conan Doyle relies are that Mr. Edalji's defective eyesight made it physically impossible for him to commit the crime; that no direct evidence of his connection with the maiming of the pony was forthcoming; that cattle were similarly maimed both during his trial and after his conviction; that the Court accepted the evidence of the handwriting expert whose testimony assisted to secure the conviction of Mr. Adolf Beck; and that the attitude of the police towards the prisoner was one of marked prejudice. It is not for us to express an opinion as to the exact value of Sir Arthur Conan Doyle's contentions. The important thing is that, taken in conjunction with the unexplained action of the Home Office in ordering Mr. Edalji's release, they are strong enough to create in the public mind a serious doubt whether justice was properly administered. The question is not merely one of Mr. Edalji's guilt or innocence. It is of the highest importance that the administration of justice should command the full confidence of the public, and the uneasiness which has been created by the Edalji case can be satisfactorily allayed only by the appointment of such a tribunal as inquired into the Beck case. The reasons for such an investigation are certainly not weakened by the fact that Mr. Edalji was tried not at the assizes, but at quarter sessions.

A reference in the following article to an incident involving an anonymous letter writer soon turned the case away from the subject of Edalji's pitiful eyesight to the issue of whether he was a most clever forger of anonymous letters.

STATEMENT BY MR. YELVERTON

On inquiry at the Temple yesterday afternoon our representative was informed by Mr. Yelverton that "no new fact has transpired in connection with this case. It is, however, felt that the question of eyesight is amongst the numerous important points involved in it, and upon this there is a consensus of the best medical opinion in confirmation of Sir Arthur Conan Doyle's views."

Several letters have been forwarded to Mr. Yelverton from members of Parliament, mainly through their constituents, promising to support the movement in favour of Mr. Edalji.

Our representative was also informed: "The General Post Office episode (to which reference is made below) is considered to be an attempt on the part of some person in Staffordshire to induce Mr. Edalji to call at the General Post Office upon a fictitious errand, and this, the perpetrator of the hoax expected, would bring the former in jeopardy, a move which however, happily failed."

In regard to the General Post Office episode, which took place on Wednesday evening last, it appears that on the previous Monday Mr. Edalji received a letter from a Staffordshire correspondent, who stated that he could prove who maimed the pony on Aug. 10, 1903, and requested Mr. Edalji to go to the General Post Office and ask for a letter in the name of the writer. The latter added: "When you have noted my name please destroy this letter, for fear it should fall into wrong hands."

Acting on advice, Mr. Edalji, when he visited the General Post Office, took with him a friend, who inquired for the letter, which he was informed was lying there. The official was then told that an application would be made to the Post-master-General for the letter to be delivered to Sir Arthur Conan Doyle or to Mr. Yelverton. As Mr. Edalji and his friend were leaving the building they were accosted by two men, apparently detectives, who posed as friendly strangers, and asked certain questions concerning the letter. They appeared to be greatly nonplused when Mr. Edalji produced the communication of his Staffordshire correspondent asking him to call for the letter.

JANUARY 22, 1907

EDALJI'S TRIAL

ACCUSED'S EVIDENCE

Today we give the conclusion of the report of the trial of Mr. G. E. T. Edalji for maiming cattle at Great Wyrley. A portion of the report is taken from the *Staffordshire Sentinel,* and extracts have also been obtained from the account of the proceedings published in the *Birmingham Daily Post.* The trial took place in the Second Court of the Staffordshire Quarter Sessions and lasted four days.

Mr. Edalji gave his evidence on the third day of the trial. The *Staffordshire Sentinel* reporter said that Edalji gave his evidence in a very cool and deliberate manner, without the least trace of hesitation. And in the *Birmingham Daily Post* Edalji is said to have faced the Court with perfect composure.

Mr. Edalji, examined by Mr. Vachell, said he received his education at Rugeley Grammar School for six years, and then went to Mason's College, which is now the University of Birmingham. The witness spoke of Inspector Campbell's visiting him in August, and showing him anonymous letters. He emphatically denied that he had had anything to do with the series of anonymous letters which were shown to him, and he declared he had written none of them. He also denied that he had questioned the inspector during the interview in August, in order to obtain information for his own use. Inspector Campbell commenced the conversation about the outrages. It was true that he (Edalji) suggested the use of bloodhounds.

Dealing with his movements on the night of Aug. 17, Mr. Edalji stated that he left the vicarage just before eight p.m. on that evening. He was wearing a blue serge suit, and not the clothes which were seized by the police. He minutely described the route he followed until he returned home, between 9.25 and 9.30, when he had supper and afterwards went to bed. Witness swore that he did not leave the house again until the following morning, when he left to catch the train to Birmingham, where he had his office.

Mr. Edalji next gave his version of the conversation which took place in his office at Birmingham, and which was followed by his arrest. On that occasion Inspector Campbell said to him, "You don't look like a person who would do this"; to which Mr. Edalji replied, "Certainly not; and I did not do it." The prisoner then went on to say that the clothing which the police seized was worn by him only about the house and grounds of the vicarage. The small bloodstains on the sleeve might have been got from a cut finger, a bleeding nose, or in many other ways, and the hair on the coat might have got there by coming into contact with trees or rails against which horses had rubbed themselves. The prisoner finally gave a denial to his having been concerned in any way with the outrages.

Mr. Vachell asked him why he declined to accept bail, and Mr. Edalji replied, "It was refused me on the first occasion, and afterwards I decided not to accept it. I was all right when I was in hospital, quite comfortable, and there was such a commotion everywhere that I could not go on with my business. I had nothing to do with the affair, and I thought it quite possible another outrage might occur."

EDALJI'S CROSS-EXAMINATION

Cross-examined by Mr. Disturnal, Edalji said at neither of the two magisterial inquiries did he give evidence acting on the advice of his advocate.

Inspector Campbell and Police-constable Cooper called upon him on July 8. He was asked if he could throw light on the anonymous letters which had been received. That letter contained a reference to witness, but when he asked to see it the inspector showed him the postscript only.

Mr. Disturnal: Why did you not press Inspector Campbell to let you see the whole letter?

Witness: Because he said it was mere nonsense, like the postscript.

And you were put off with that when you were told that the letter contained a reference to you, and only two days before you had offered a reward for information concerning the person you said had slandered you?

Witness said when he spoke to Inspector Campbell about the maiming, and asked if it were not risky work, he meant hazardous for the police, as the inspector had said the authorities at Stafford were incompetent, and that he had not enough men. Witness admitted the references to bloodhounds and the moon at the interview. He had not had an opportunity of carefully examining the letters, but on the face of them he should say that the handwriting of them was not similar to his own. He did not know whether his solicitor had applied for them. When he wrote to the lad Greatorex, "I am sure no boys are concerned in this wretched business, and that when the truth is known you will find it is somebody in a very different position," he was referring not to the outrages but to the rumours which had been in circulation about him, witness. It was his opinion that boys did not circulate the report.

Mr. Disturnel: Do you agree that the handwriting of these anonymous letters is in several instances similar to yours?

Edalji stated that he had not had much opportunity of inspecting the letters except to satisfy himself that they were not in his handwriting. He did not say to either of the police officers, "Is Harry Green watched?" He had known Green nearly all his life and had not heard of anyone being in communication with him after witness had been committed for trial. He wore the boots the police seized on Aug. 17, and got them wet by splashing in a puddle in the darkness. When he went out on that evening he wore a blue serge suit, but after returning home he changed his clothes.

Asked if he could explain why his mother gave his old suit to the police instead of the blue serge suit, Edalji said probably it was because they were just at hand.

Prisoner was asked if he could explain why it was his father and he occupied the same bed-room. He replied that fifteen or twenty years ago his brother was taken ill, and his mother had to sleep in the same room to nurse him. Ever since that time Edalji and his father had slept in the same bedroom.

Mr. Disturnal asked why that arrangement was continued up to the present time.

Edalji replied that it suited him all right. His brother had now left home, but was often at the vicarage. The bed-room was a large apartment. He and his father occupied different beds. He denied that his father only recently began to occupy the same bed-room, and said the bed-room was locked overnight because it was the custom.

Mr. Disturnal: What! with two men in the room?

Witness: All the doors are locked at night. We have occupied the same room for twenty years.

With regard to the letter from "A Lover of Justice," witness thought it was sent to him by someone who was desirous of keeping him out of the district under circumstances which would cast suspicion on him. He considered the letter was in the handwriting of a lady.

Mr. Disturnal: Do you think the outrages were done by a lady?

Witness: Certainly not; but a lady might have circulated the report about me. Witness further said, when he had the conversation with Constable Cooper, the name of Harry Green was not mentioned. Before the magistrates Cooper did not say anything about Green.

Mr. Vachell (re-examining): Do you know anything of Harry Green in connection with the matter?—Witness: nothing at all.

Harry Loach, of Rosemary House, Cannock, stated that he knew Edalji, and met him on the evening of Aug. 17 on the canal bridge at Bridgetown, about ten minutes to nine. About five minutes later he saw him again near Hawkin's Wharf. From the latter place witness and his companion walked down the road by the side of the prisoner, and when one of the "blowers" went, he, in reply to a question as to the time, pulled out his watch and said it was nine o'clock.

Cross-examined: The next day he made a statement to Police-constables Rowley and Weaver about the time and place at which he had seen the prisoner. It was well known that the "blower" went at nine o'clock, and he could not explain why the prisoner should have asked what the time was.

Re-examined: Although witness told the police about seeing Edalji, they did not call upon him again, nor did they ask him to give evidence.

Fred Cope, a companion of the previous witness, corroborated.

John Hands, bootmaker, of Bridgetown, stated that the prisoner called at his shop on Monday night, Aug. 17, at 8.30, and remained talking about five minutes. So far as witness could see, he was wearing a dark blue suit. The coat produced was not the one. He noticed the time particularly, but could not say why.

VETERINARY SURGEON'S EVIDENCE

Mr. Robert M. Lewis, veterinary surgeon, of Cannock, said he saw the mutilated horse belonging to the Colbery Company about 8.30 on the morning of Aug. 18. He was of opinion that the wound had not been inflicted more than six hours at the most. He believed that the wound was caused by a curved weapon with concaved sides, and attached to a handle, which would afford a person using it a good grip.

THE FATHER'S STATEMENT

The Rev. S. Edalji said he had been vicar of Great Wyrley for twenty-seven years. His son left the house at about eight o'clock on Aug. 17, but witness did not see him go out. He returned about 9.25, and had his supper. Witness went to bed about eleven o'clock, and the accused was then in bed—they had slept in the same room for many years. Before getting into bed witness locked the bedroom door. His son could not have left the room that night without witness being aware of it. He could swear his son did not leave the room. When Inspector Campbell called next morning he told witness another horse had been mutilated, and that he wanted to see the clothes his son wore on the previous evening. Mrs. Edalji handed the clothes to the officer, who showed witness stains on the jacket. Witness said they must be cocoa stains. The inspector then told him there were horse hairs on the jacket, but on examination witness could find none, and told the officer so. Witness denied rubbing any of the razors found in the bedroom. The razors belonged to witness, and had not been used for several years.

Cross-examined, witness swore the jacket was not wet when it was handed to the police. Nothing was said by the police about the razors being wet, and it was untrue that he tried to wipe one of the razors with his thumb.

Mrs. Edalji stated that she produced a bundle of the prisoner's clothes to the police, and they took away the suit which had been produced at the trial. She denied that the coat was wet, and as to the trousers, perhaps her son damped them when sprinkling the garden. She denied she interfered with the clothes between the time the police first saw them and when they took them away.

In cross-examination, Mrs. Edalji asserted that the trousers shown to the police were not muddy.

Miss Maud Evelyn Edalji declared that the prisoner wore a blue suit on the night of Aug. 17.

Dora Earp, domestic at the vicarage, corroborated the evidence given by members of the household that the prisoner was in the house at 9.30 on Aug. 17.

SPEECH FOR THE DEFENCE

Mr. Vachell, in his final statement for the defence, confidently asked the jury if he had not satisfied them that the police, having made up their mind that prisoner had committed the outrage, had only picked out evidence which supported their theory and rejected other witnesses—those whom he (Mr. Vachell) had called—whose testimony showed the police were entirely wrong. Several witnesses for the defence had all given their statements to the police, but the letter had passed over them because they did not support the prosecution theory.

The veterinary surgeon's confident assertion that the wound on the maimed horse had all the appearance of having been done within six hours of the time when the witness saw the animal at 8.30 on Aug. 18 was emphasised, and Mr. Vachell expressed doubt as to whether the prosecution would now suggest Edalji got up in the night, went to the field, and wounded the horse. If that course were adopted, where was there evidence that prisoner did leave the vicarage after retiring to bed, in face of the evidence of the father, who slept in the same room as his son, and who had declared he saw his son in the room all night, and that the door was locked? Counsel submitted that the conduct of Edalji when in the witness box was that of a perfectly innocent person, and of one who showed great candour, and no desire to swear anything to shield himself. He then argued that the two small bloodstains found on Edalji's old coat were old stains, and the jury were cautioned as to the conflicting evidence between the police and Edalji's parents as to the actual presence of hair on the clothing which the police seized.

Beyond that, said counsel, there was the evidence called by him to show that Edalji did not wear the seized clothing outside the house on Aug. 17. After ridiculing the idea that such wounds as the pony received could have been inflicted with a razor, Mr. Vachall turned to the anonymous letters, and said that the question of the handwriting was simply a matter of opinion. Time after time, despite their confident opinions, experts had been proved at fault; therefore, the jury had to satisfy themselves that Edalji really did write the letters, and not condemn him merely on the theories of the expert. No importance need be attached to the incident that prisoner refused bail. Under a cloud, with suspicion upon him, liberty was of no value to the accused. All he wanted was to be in some retreat, away from the prying eyes and the pointing fingers of those coupling him with the hideous crime.

Counsel criticised the prosecution for not having called the young man Green, who was said to have confessed to having perpetrated an outrage on Sept. 21, and inquired if it was to be suggested that there was a gang, and that Green was associated with Edalji. He did not wish to say anything cruel against Green, but the jury knew Green had killed a horse since prisoner had been in gaol; therefore, they knew that there was at large a man who was capable of doing these fiendish acts, and who admitted he had done such an act. In the face of that, and upon such flimsy evidence before them, and the crumbled and shattered theories of the police, why should the jury say that the prisoner was guilty of the earlier offence? It was remarkable that there was a complete absence of any suggestion of motive. Nor was there any hint that the person who committed the crimes was mentally deranged. In con- clusion, he asked if the jury had anything to lead them to believe it was prob- able or possible that a man of Edalji's culture and position was capable of such horrible acts. "As against that," were the closing words of counsel, "never forget there is in that district a man who will do such things, and, indeed, has done it."

THEORY OF THE PROSECUTION

Mr. Disturnal followed for the prosecution. He contended that counsel for the defence had dealt mainly with matters of prejudice. He preferred to deal with the facts of the case, and, after regretting that the prosecution (in real ignorance of what the witness could speak to) had not called the veterinary surgeon, Mr. Disturnal began to criticise the conduct of the chief actor in this matter at critical moments in the history of the case. It was strange, said counsel, that when interviewed in August about an anonymous letter naming him, Edalji should be put off by the statement that the letter contained "nonsense," seeing he was ostensibly seeking those who were slandering him. He made minute inquiries about the work of the police instead of seeking all the information he could about the writer. Did not this show that Edalji knew all about the anonymous letter, and that he desired to learn what was in the knowledge of the police? Edalji's attitude in connection with other letters was touched upon, and counsel remarked upon what he termed the significant fact that the anonymous letters in this particular handwriting stopped after Edalji's arrest. Did the jury think if someone was writing to fool the police the letters would not have been continued? Having dealt at length with the letters, Mr. Disturnal reviewed other features of the case—the blood-stained coat, the identity of the clothing, the horse hairs on the coat, the wet boots, and razor, and the footprints on what he called "the line of betrayal."

He commented on the "extraordinary arrangement" of the father sleeping in the same bedroom as his grown-up son, and argued that piecing all the links of the evidence together the jury must come to a conclusion that Edalji had some connection with the crime. As to the question of motive, spite could not come into this case, nor any suggestion of love for blood, which must be satisfied on the instant. In this case there were skillful plans, opportunities seized, and letters written—all of which were not the act of a man animated by a lust of blood. Counsel did not know how to describe it. Crime seized men in a variety of forms all of which were diseases of the human mind. He was not entitled to any evidence as to who killed the horse on Sept. 21, and although he might have put Green in the box to be questioned, what could he have told to assist them in the case? In the interests of the public he did not think it right to call Green, for the reason that Green could have thrown no light on the matter of Aug. 17, and because he was a tainted person with whom it was not desirable the prosecution should identify themselves. Touching upon the suggestion of defending counsel, Mr. Disturnal remarked that if it was Green who desired to get Edalji arrested, and who circulated the anonymous letters, did the jury think Green would have been such a fool, having accomplished that object, as to subsequently destroy his own horse?

Sir Reginald Hardy, in his summing up, characterized the outrages, which created a "reign of terror" in Great Wyrley, as a blot upon and a disgrace to the fair fame of the county. It was, therefore, he said, difficult to overestimate how important it was to detect the perpetrator of the outrages. The chairman made an exhaustive review of the evidence. He agreed that the prosecution could not call Green. They could not ask a witness incriminating questions. In regard to the absence of any suggested motive, Sir Reginald said the person who committed the outrages was possessed of some peculiar twist of the brain and diabolical cunning. It seemed impossible to arrive at any motive why a man like the prisoner should be guilty of such horrible actions.

The jury retired at two o'clock provided with maps of the district and magnifying glasses with which to examine the letters.

VERDICT AND SENTENCE

The jury returned in fifty minutes with a verdict of guilty, but with a recommendation to mercy.

The Chairman: On what grounds, please?

The Foreman: Because of his personal position.

On hearing the verdict the prisoner, who stood between two wardens, was noticed to turn very pale. The Bench retired to consider the sentence, and on their return the Chairman said: The jury have found you guilty of this very serious charge, and as we think, very properly. Their verdict is a right one. They have also recommended you to mercy, in consideration of the position you hold. We have to consider what punishment to award you. On the one hand we take fully into consideration your position and what this means to you; on the other hand, we have to consider the state of the county of Stafford and the neighbourhood of Great Wyrley, and the disgrace which has been inflicted on us and that neighbourhood by the condition of things. Your sentence is penal servitude for seven years.

The prosecution offered no evidence on the charge of sending a threatening letter to a police officer.

JANUARY 23, 1907

THE EDALJI CASE

TO THE EDITOR OF THE *DAILY TELEGRAPH*

Sir—In your report of Mr. Disturnal's closing speech at my trial the following words occur: "Counsel remarked upon what he termed the significant fact that the anonymous letters in the particular handwriting stopped after Edalji's arrest."

This is but one of the many absolutely false statements made in order to impose upon the jury, and which Sir R. Hardy never noticed in his summing-up. Mr. Disturnal no doubt took advantage of the chairman's inexperience, and also knew that my counsel had no right to make a further speech, and that therefore, any unfair allegations would pass practically unchallenged.

The true facts (which I defy Mr. Disturnal or anyone else to disprove) are that the day after the police alleged they commenced to watch my home the first letter was posted, and further missives were sent every day or two up to Aug. 4, on which day they wholly ceased. I was not arrested till Aug. 18, so how any man with a conscience can assert they stopped after my arrest passes my comprehension. But had they ceased on my being taken into custody this would not have proved I was the writer, for they were so wholly opposed to my interests, so obviously written to secure my arrest and conviction, and so cunningly concocted to prevent my benefiting by further outrages, that it is absurd to suppose my enemy would nullify his labours by writing while I was in prison.—Yours truly,

G. E. T. EDALJI
Jan. 22.

TO THE EDITOR OF THE *DAILY TELEGRAPH*

Sir—From the letters that are appearing in your columns, one would imagine that nine out of ten of your readers had been convinced of the innocence of the convicted Edalji by the articles of Sir A. Conan Doyle. I regret being unable to range myself with the majority.

The chief points of the defence are as follow:

(1) That Edalji's eyesight rendered it impossible for him to have committed the outrage.

(2) That it is inconceivable that he wrote the letters.

(3) That after his conviction the outrages still continued.

(1) In answer to this point, I would venture to suggest that a man with even as defective an eyesight as Edalji, in a country he knew well, would walk with almost as much confidence as one having the full use of his eyes. Sir A. Conan Doyle's challenge in this matter appears to me to be puerile. As well ask a man suddenly blindfolded to do what a blind man does as ask a man blessed with perfect sight to walk on a dark night wearing glasses that reduced his powers of vision to those of Edalji. Should it be possible to prove that a man knowing the country well cannot cover the distance within the time in which Edalji must have covered it, it would be a strong point in favour of the defence. It would be interesting to know how well lighted is the road over which it is admitted Edalji walked on the evening of the crime.

(2) As regards the letters, I would suggest that the plea advanced by Sir A. Conan Doyle, that it is inconceivable that Edalji could have written such letters about himself, is exactly the idea which (supposing him to have been the author) would have naturally occurred to a man of Edalji's training as a good defence. Nothing can prove the truth of this reasoning more strongly than the line now taken by Sir Conan Doyle.

(3) Sir A. Conan Doyle states that the outrages continued after Edalji's arrest. Did they? I was living near Cannock at the time, and I say confidently that from the time of Edalji's arrest the terror (for such it was) abated. There were certainly two outrages on cattle at a later date, the perpetrators of which were laid by the heels at once. In one case a father's son mutilated his own horse, in the other a miner was convicted of killing some sheep. I was in court at the hearing of this latter case, and though the evidence was only circumstantial, I can hardly imagine that a single person who heard it had the least doubt as to the prisoner's guilt. "Betrayed by a breeches' button" may have made a useful headline for the local Press, but the fact that a button similar to those worn by the prisoner, one of which was missing, was found near the slaughtered animals was only one important—very important, perhaps—detail of the evidence. Sir A. Conan Doyle advances as the theory of the police the idea that there was a gang of which Edalji and the miner were both members. It seems more probable that the theory of the police was that the miner was persuaded or bribed to commit the crime to counteract the damning evidence afforded by the cessation of the outrages. Did Sir A. Conan Doyle investigate a statement which was, I believe, given in evidence, and which was certainly widely discussed at the time, to the effect that Mr. Edalji, sen., had been seen in conversation with the convicted man either directly before or directly after the outrage?

Might I suggest that the attacks on the Chief Constable, which are extremely wanting in good taste, do nothing to strengthen the cause of the convicted man, and that letters similar to that written by J. Churton Collins serve no good purpose? "Outraged Justice," lame though she be, is well able to look after herself without the aid of hysterical supporters.

I share the hope of all your readers that an inquiry may be held.

FIDELITER
Woking, Jan. 18.

MORE MYSTERIOUS LETTERS

It will be remembered that Mr. George Edalji recently received at his lodging in London a letter from an address in Birmingham, signed "Martin Molton," in which the writer declared that he could prove who maimed the pony on Aug. 10, 1903, and requesting the recipient to go on the following Wednesday to the General Post Office and ask for a letter in the name of the writer. Yesterday morning Mr. Edalji received another letter, apparently from the same correspondent. Unlike the letter received on Monday, the 14th inst., it bore no address, and was unsigned. The handwriting, however, was identical, and the postmark was again that of Birmingham. Mr. Yelverton informed a representative of the *Daily Telegraph* that the writer declares he is the author of the letters of 1893, and that it can be easily discovered that he is the writer, as he always uses the Greek "e." He goes on to say that Mr. Edalji is entirely innocent of the crimes ascribed to him, and that he (the writer) was extremely sorry for the trouble he had caused the family, and that as he was now leaving for Melbourne "he did not mind what he said."

It is, of course, conceivable that this letter received yesterday, like that received on Monday week, is a hoax, but a coincidence which lends some colour to the belief that the writer of both these letters really does know something about the case and may, as he declares, have been the writer of the letters in 1893, is the curious fact that the letter signed "Martin Molton," received on Monday week, is written on the back and front of a sealed envelope, enclosed in another envelope. Two of the mysterious letters received in 1893 were also written on the front and back of a sealed envelope! The texture of the writing paper is also almost identical.

We reproduce a facsimile of the envelope and letter delivered to Mr. Edalji at his London address on Monday, the 14th, asking him to call at the General Post Office on the following Wednesday for a letter which would then be awaiting him (see following page).

Anyone who can definitely identify the handwriting is requested by Mr. Yelverton to communicate with Sir Arthur Conan Doyle at the Grand Hotel, Charing-cross, London.

Commenting on the letter which he received on Monday week, Mr. George Edalji, in an interview with a representative of the *Daily Telegraph* yesterday at Mr. Yelverton's chambers in the Temple, said that he wrote in response to the letter at the address given, but that his letter had been returned from the Dead Letter Office. It would appear that no such person as "Martin Molton" is known at the address given.

JANUARY 26, 1907

THE EDALJI CASE
SUMMING UP
BY
SIR A. CONAN DOYLE

TO THE EDITOR OF THE *DAILY TELEGRAPH*

Sir—I am unable now to find any points which have not been already dealt with in my original articles or in the long correspondence which has ensued. I claim that every point has been fairly met, and that an impartial man must

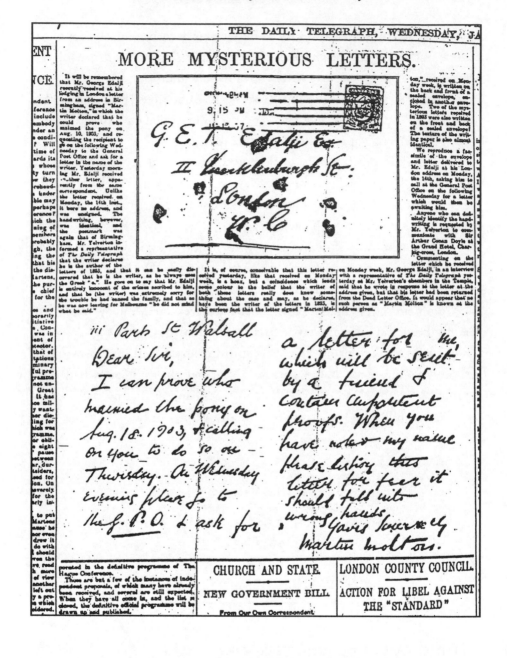

do violence to his reason in having any doubts as to the propriety of a public inquiry into all the circumstances of the case.

Council has been somewhat darkened by the multitude of opinions, conjectures, and false statements which have been made. May I be permitted for the last time to remind your readers of those points of defence, briefly stated, which combine to make up the case:

1. The inherent improbability of a man of Edalji's virtuous, studious, and retiring habits committing these brutal crimes.

2. The proofs that a long conspiracy, extending back for fifteen years, had existed against the Edalji family.

3. The fact that Edalji's evening up to 9.30 is fully accounted for, save for fifty minutes between 8.35 and 9.25. That in this time it was not possible for him to have walked first a mile along the road and then half a mile each way over difficult country, including the finding of the pony and its mutilation. The evidence of the veterinary surgeon proved the wound to have been inflicted in the early morning.

4. The impossibility of Edalji having done it after 9.30. His father, sleeping in the same room, his mother, his sister, and the maid, all agree that no one left the house. There is the strong probability that the house was watched outside, and the certainty that twenty watchers were scattered round. There was heavy rain all night, and every garment must have been soaking wet.

5. The fact that the evidence was nearly all police evidence, open, as I have shown, to the gravest suspicion, and contradicted at every point by reputable witnesses.

6. The fact that the writing expert was shown to have blundered in the Beck case.

7. The physical disability produced by the myopia from which Mr. Edalji suffered.

Those are the main headings which I have previously elaborated, and they are all immensely strengthened by the continuance of the letters and the outrages after Mr. Edalji's arrest, and by the connivance at the flight of Green, who had confessed to a similar offense. This is the case which I present in favour of a miscarriage of justice having occurred. I claim that it is a very strong one, and has in no respect been shaken by subsequent inquiry or debate.

Dealing with point 7, I would say that I would by no means wish that this technical professional point should take undue prominence over all the other considerations which I have alleged. Perhaps, having myself some special ophthalmic knowledge, and having been over the ground, I was inclined to make too much of it, forgetting that others could not appreciate obstacles which they had not seen. To me the idea of a myope of eight dioptres doing in so short a time, upon a pitch-dark night, what I, a fairly active man, did not do so quickly in daylight, is inexpressibly absurd. I have really suffered somewhat by understating my case, for I might well have taken the broader ground that a normal man could not have done it in the time. My argument really was that, *a fortiori*, a myope could not have done it. Many correspondents have ignored this, however, and taking for granted that the normal man could have done it, have contented themselves with drawing comparisons between the powers of the normal and myopic eye, and how far deftness of touch can make up for dimness of vision. I am sending in the opinions to the Home Office to-day. The great majority are to the effect that such a crime, with such eyes, under such circumstances, is either "quite impossible" or "highly improbable." Both Sir Anderson Critchett and Mr. Nettleship have favoured me with opinions.

I have now done what I could, drawing largely upon the stores which Mr. Yelverton had ready for me, to present this case to the British public and also to the Home Office. I do not know that more can be done until we hear from the authorities.—Yours faithfully,

ARTHUR CONAN DOYLE
Grand Hotel, Jan. 25.

CHAPTER FIVE

THE HOME OFFICE RESPONDS; SIR ARTHUR FIRES BACK; THE CONTROVERSY CONTINUES; EDALJI IS PARDONED (BUT WITH A CATCH)

Public pressure on the government to reexamine the Edalji case grew until Home Office Secretary Herbert Gladstone—son of the late four-time Prime Minister, William Gladstone—agreed to appoint a committee to inquire into the case. Unfortunately for Gladstone, once the three prominent Englishmen who made up the committee got a close look at the trial findings, they sensed they were getting into a situation that was, at best, lose-lose. The committee, headed by the Right Honorable Sir Robert Romer, G.C.B., quit.

However, Gladstone—ever his father's son—managed to broker a deal. The committee agreed to look over the evidence and trial transcripts and make a recommendation. On March 2, 1907, the *Daily Telegraph* broke the news of Gladstone's efforts. Just over a week later, Sir Arthur was back in print publicly supporting the committee (as well as advising them on their options), but reminding everyone who had contributed to the Edalji legal fund to leave their money in, just in case.

Letters continued to pour in on the Edalji case, many critical of the committee's decision to work in private. Work in private they did, however, and on April 23, the committee rendered a recommendation that no one had expected and few could believe: Edalji was innocent of the animal maimings and should therefore receive a full pardon, but since he probably wrote the damaging letters, he had brought his troubles on himself and therefore deserved no compensation for his ill treatment at the hands of the government.

When contacted by reporters for his reaction, Edalji said he was "profoundly dissatisfied." In contrast to Edalji's understated response, Sir Arthur was furious. "All these results," he wrote, "have been brought about by the extraordinary conduct of the police, and the stupidity of a court. . . ."

MARCH 2, 1907

───────────────────

THE EDALJI CASE
HOME OFFICE STATEMENT

───────────────────

COMMITTEE OF INQUIRY

The following official communication is issued from the Home Office:

The Home Secretary invited the Right Hon. Sir Robert Romer, G.C.B., the Right Hon. Sir Arthur Wilson, and the Right Hon. J. Lloyd Wharton to form a committee to inquire into and report upon the case of Mr. George Edalji. They consented to meet, and subsequently the following letter was received by the Home Secretary from Sir R. Romer:

Dear Mr. Gladstone—When you first mentioned to me that you contemplated the appointment of a committee of three, with myself as chairman, to inquire into the Edalji case, and I intimated my willingness to assist you, I did not fully realise what the duties of the committee would be or the difficulties in their way. After further consideration of the matter with you and with Sir Arthur Wilson and Mr. Wharton, I find it impossible for me to act for the following reasons:

I had not fully recognised that anything more was contemplated than my assistance in advising you whether a free pardon should be granted to Mr. Edalji, having regard to the materials in the possession of the Home Office, upon which in the ordinary course the Home Secretary would come to a decision. That assistance I was quite willing to give, but on going into the matter more fully with you I see that something more is contemplated, namely, a general inquiry into the case, and indeed possibly a public investigation.

Now it appears to me that if such an inquiry is embarked on, it ought, in order to be satisfactory, to be done according to the ordinary rules of procedure governing a criminal trial. In my view, an inquiry of that kind ought to be in public, or not at all, and I am not willing to undertake it. May I point out to you some of the difficulties in the way of it? Apart from the objection of a re-trial of a criminal charge so long after the conviction without a jury, there is the question of evidence; such a committee as you were desirous of appointing would have no power to call witnesses or administer an oath. To make the inquiry effective, witnesses ought to be properly examined and cross-examined.

I think that the committee ought not to take upon itself the duty of cross-examination, and if counsel be employed, the question arises who would act as counsel for the prosecution, and by whom would he be instructed? It appears to be thought that the inquiry in the Beck case was analogous to the present; but in that case the innocence of the convict was assumed, and no question of a re-trial for a criminal offence arose. At any rate, speaking for myself, I do not see my way to set, as it were, in judge and jury in trying the particular question of the guilt or innocence of Mr. Edalji, and that without any proper legal power of summoning witnesses.—I am yours very faithfully,

ROBERT ROMER

P.S.—I may say that Sir Arthur Wilson and Mr. Wharton have seen this letter, and authorise me to state that they entirely concur in it.

Sir R. Romer and his colleagues, however, intimated that they were prepared to examine the material in possession of the Home Office, and to give their advice on the case to the Home Secretary. In the circumstances, the Home Secretary decided to accept this offer. Some delay was caused owing to the withdrawal of Sir R. Romer on account of private matters, which had unexpectedly arisen. Sir A. De Rutzen, the Chief Magistrate of London, having consented to fill the vacancy that created, the examination of the papers is now proceeding. [De Rutzen was a second cousin of Chief Constable George Anson of the Staffordshire police!]

MARCH 11, 1907

THE EDALJI CASE

TO THE EDITOR OF THE *DAILY TELEGRAPH*

Sir—I observe from this week's *Truth*, and also from the *Police Review*, that both Mr. Voules and Mr. Kempster, two of the warmest champions of the Edalji cause, take a pessimistic view of the chances of any good result springing from the present Committee of Inquiry. I may say at the outset that neither Mr. Edalji nor, so far as I know, any one of his friends or advisers knew anything of the formation of this Committee, nor of its terms of reference, until they read of it in the newspapers. Taking it as it stands, however, I am more hopeful of good results coming from it than these two gentlemen appear to be.

I think that their conclusions are largely founded upon the idea that the papers to be examined by the Committee consist merely of those official reports which have been the principal material at all previous reconsiderations of the case. This, however, will not be so. Pains have been taken that Mr. Edalji's case should be very fully represented. Among the evidence which will be laid before the three distinguished and independent gentlemen who form the Committee there will be,

1. The full statement of the case as it appeared in the *Daily Telegraph*.

2. The opinion of some twenty experts upon the question of eyesight and its relation to the crime.

3. An alternative theory of the outrages, with evidence in its support.

4. A considerable amount of further evidence throwing a light upon the affair.

It will be seen, therefore, that this inquiry differs very much from all preceding ones, in that it is independent and that it contains much new matter.

There are four courses, as it seems to me, any one of which the Committee may choose. They may leave things as they are, though that is, I trust, most improbable. They may advise a re-trial; they may advise a Royal Commission; or, finally, they may advise a "free pardon" with compensation. We do not stand to lose in any case. A re-trial or Commission is what we desire. The last supposition (a free pardon) would give us at least a large instalment of that for which we are working. Therefore, on the whole, I am hopeful as to our prospects from the Advisory Committee.

We may still need all the funds subscribed, so I trust that those who have so generously supported the cause of fair play and justice will be content to leave their money in the fund until we see what turn things may take.—Yours faithfully,

ARTHUR CONAN DOYLE
Monkstown,
Crowborough, March 4.

MAY 18, 1907

EDALJI CASE
HOME SECRETARY'S DECISION

A FREE PARDON

The report of the committee that has been inquiring into the case of George Edalji was issued as a Parliamentary paper last night, and with it an intimation by the Home Secretary that he would advise the King to grant Mr. Edalji a free pardon, but that no compensation would be given. The committee sent its report to the Home Office on April 23, and Mr. Gladstone informed the chairman of his decision rather more than three weeks later, in the following letter:

Home Office, Whitehall, S. W.,
May 16, 1907

Dear Sir Arthur Wilson—I have to thank you and your colleagues for your careful and exhaustive report upon the case of Mr. G. Edalji, following the examination of all the documents which, at my request, you were good enough to undertake.

That report, however, has presented questions of great difficulty for my decision. On the one hand, you have clearly stated the reasons for thinking that Mr. Edalji's conviction was unsatisfactory on the evidence at the trial, and for differing from the verdict of the jury. You find that too much evidentiary weight was attributed to the letters of 1903, that their authorship does not necessarily involve participation in the outrages, and that, apart from them, the other evidence was insufficient to establish Mr. Edalji's guilt; and you have expressed the opinion "that the case may properly be considered in an exceptional manner."

On the other hand, you make it plain that, on the principles which have for many years governed the exercise of the Royal prerogative of mercy, and which have been approved in express terms in the report of the

181

Beck committee, Mr. Edalji, as regards the establishment of innocence, is not entitled to a free pardon; and, agreeing with what you take to be the finding of the jury, namely, that Mr. Edalji was the author of the letters of 1903, you are of the opinion that, even on the assumption of innocence of the outrage, Mr. Edalji, to some extent, brought his troubles upon himself.

I accept the conclusions at which you have arrived; but I can give effect to your view only by departing from the general principles which govern the action of the Home Secretary, and under which he advises the grant of a free pardon only when a prisoner's innocence has been established to his satisfaction. I feel, however, that this case, as you point out, is a very exceptional one, and that I ought to give weight to your opinion that the permanent disqualifications which are not part of the sentence, but follow necessarily from the conviction, might now be removed. After the fullest and most anxious consideration I have decided to advise his Majesty, as an act of Royal clemency, to grant Mr. Edalji a free pardon. But I have also come to the conclusion that the case is not one in which any grant of compensation can be made.—I am yours very truly,

H. J. GLADSTONE

Associated with Sir Arthur Wilson on the committee of inquiry were Mr. John Lloyd Wharton, chairman of Quarter Sessions for the county of Durham, and Sir Albert De Rutzen, chief magistrate in London. In the report on which Mr. Gladstone has based his decision the committee reviewed the peculiar circumstances surrounding the trial of Mr. Edalji, in view of the strong feeling with regard to the cattle-maiming outrages that prevailed at Great Wyrley, and point out that "the police commenced and carried on their investigations, not for the purpose of finding out who was the guilty party, but for the purpose of finding evidence against Edalji, who they were already sure was the guilty man."

After dealing with the circumstantial evidence brought against Mr. Edalji and the discrepancies in the statements of different police officers, the committee express their opinion that the Bench could not have withdrawn the case from the jury, and they add that, "judging from the printed evidence, we think it doubtful whether the jury would have convicted upon the circumstantial evidence alone, if they had not been influenced by the case put to them regarding the anonymous or pseudonymous letters," known as the Greatorex.

On this subject of the mysterious letters, the committee points out that the jury must be taken to have held that Edalji was their author, and having carefully examined the letters, and compared them with the admitted handwriting of Edalji, they are not prepared to dissent from that finding. The report continues:

> But the value of those letters as evidence that Edalji committed the crime with which he was charged is quite another question. It seems to have been assumed almost throughout that the writer of those letters had himself committed the outrages prior to that of Aug. 17 or 18, and it seems to have been inferred from that that he was, or was likely to be, the perpetrator of the latter outrage. We do not think those letters have anything like the evidentiary weight which has been attributed to them. Their value depends on the content of the letters themselves. They contain, or purport to contain statements relating to the outrages, and they make allegations of guilt against a variety of persons, including Edalji himself. We do not think that it is at all safe to infer that they are the letters of a guilty man, accusing himself in order the more easily to accuse others, or for any other motive which has been suggested. We think it quite as likely that they are the letters of an innocent man, but a wrong-headed and malicious man, indulging in a piece of impish mischief, pretending to know what he may know nothing of, in order to puzzle the police and increase their difficulties in a very difficult investigation.

While Edalji was in prison awaiting trial another maiming outrage occurred, and a man named Harry Green admitted having committed it. With respect to the plea that it was his own horse, the committee observe that a man who in good faith wants to kill his horse does not go out and rip up its belly, and they declare that this occurrence very much weakened the case against Edalji. As for the theory which the prosecution brought forward at this stage, that there was a gang at work, of whom Edalji was one, Sir Arthur Wilson and his colleagues find no evidence to support it. Moreover, "since the conviction two more outrages, very similar in character to the earlier ones, have been committed in the same neighbourhood, and this tends to weaken the case connecting Edalji with the outrages."

With reference to the contention that the condition of his eyesight would have made it impossible for Edalji to traverse on a dark night the route he must have followed if he were guilty, the report says:

> Whether the question of eyesight was brought before the jury at the trial we do not positively know, but we can find no indication that it was. If the prisoner's advisers had attached importance to it, it certainly would have been relied upon. We have carefully considered the report of the eminent expert who examined Edalji in prison and the opinions of oculists that have been laid before us; and the materials now collected appear to us entirely insufficient to establish the alleged impossibility.

Summing up the conclusions to which their investigations have led them, the Committee say:

> In our opinion, the conviction was unsatisfactory, and, after a most careful consideration of all the facts and printed evidence placed before us, we cannot agree with the verdict of the jury. The view of the case, however, which we have taken is one which would not have warranted the Home Office in interfering with the conviction, in view of the memorandum prepared by Sir Kenelm Digby as to the practice of the Home Office, which was submitted to the Committee in the Beck case, and mentioned with approval by that Committee in their report in the following words: "In a valuable report handed in by Sir K. Digby, the limits which the Home Office regards as in practice defining their jurisdiction are stated, and, speaking broadly, we think that the reasons urged for observing those limitations are sound."

Nevertheless, the Committee regard the case as one for exceptional treatment:

> We understand it to be the wish of the Secretary of State that we should offer any suggestions which may assist him in deciding whether to advise the exercise of the prerogative of mercy by the grant of a free pardon to Edalji. We therefore indicate the following matters as in our opinion worthy of consideration. On the one hand, we think the conviction ought not to have taken place for the reasons we have stated; that conviction, in addition to the sentence of the Court, necessarily brought upon Edalji the total ruin of his professional position and prospects; and as long as things continue as they are he must remain under police supervision, a condition in which it would be extremely difficult, if not impossible, for him to recover anything like the position he has lost. On the other hand, being unable to disagree with what we take to be the finding of the jury, that Edalji was the writer of the letters of 1903, we cannot but see that, assuming him to be an innocent man, he has to some extent brought his troubles upon himself.

In conclusion, the Committee testify to the care that the Home Office authorities have given to the case from time to time:

> We are anxious that it should be clearly understood that what we have said implies no criticism of the decision of the late and the present Home Secretaries not to interfere with Edalji's conviction. That decision was obviously in accordance with the principles acted upon by the Home Office, in cases in which it is alleged there has been a wrongful conviction. But under the reference to us we have felt ourselves free to consider the case from a less restricted point of view. We have regarded it as a very exceptional case, which may properly be considered in an exceptional manner.
>
> We are most sensible of the very careful and patient endeavours which have been made, at every stage of the case, by the officials of the Home Office (which we have become aware of during our inquiry) to ascertain the true facts of this extraordinary case. Having regard to the very vague asper-

sions which have already been made as to the conduct of officials, we think it only fair to give our testimony to the conduct of those who have from first to last done all that was possible in the interests of justice.

STATEMENT BY MR. EDALJI

Seen last night by a Press representative, Mr. Edalji said he was profoundly dissatisfied with the result of the commissioners' inquiry, adding:

It is at least a step in the right direction, but the statement that I contributed to my conviction by writing some of the letters which played so prominent a part in the case is a slander—an insult. It is so far satisfactory to know that they are granting me a free pardon, but that statement about the letters is a baseless insinuation, and I shall not rest content until it is withdrawn and an apology tendered. Further, I am disappointed to find that no compensation is offered. They have offered me a free pardon, they admit that I was wrongly convicted, and it is only just that I should be compensated for the three years penal servitude that I suffered. I shall not let matters rest as they are. I want compensation for my wrongs.

MAY 20, 1907

EDALJI CASE
LETTER FROM SIR CONAN DOYLE

TO THE EDITOR OF THE *DAILY TELEGRAPH*
Sir—While the friends of Mr. George Edalji rejoice that his innocence has at last been admitted (though in the most grudging and ungracious fashion), they feel that their work is only half done so long as compensation is refused

him. It is clearly stated in the report of the Committee that: "The police commenced and carried on their investigations, not for the purpose of finding out who was the guilty party, but for the purpose of finding evidence against Edalji, who they were already sure was the guilty man."

The result has proved that he was not the guilty man, and this inversion of all sane methods upon the part of the police has given untold mental agony to himself and to his family, has caused him to undergo the ordeal of the double trial, the three years of incarceration, and an extra year of police supervision. Apart from the misery which has been unjustly inflicted upon him, he has been unable to exercise his profession during that time, and has been put to many heavy expenses, which only the self-sacrifice of his relations had enabled him to meet. And now, though all these results have been brought about by the extraordinary conduct of the police, and the stupidity of a Court of Quarter Sessions, the unfortunate victim is told that no compensation will be made him.

The position is absolutely illogical and untenable. Either the man is guilty or else there is no compensation which is adequate for the great wrong which this country, through its officials, has inflicted upon him. It is hard, indeed, that such compensation should be drawn from the pockets of the taxpayer. It might well be levied in equal parts from the Staffordshire police, the Quarter Sessions Court, and the officials of the Home Office, since it is these three groups of men who are guilty among them of this fiasco. But since there is no means by which those who are responsible can be forced to pay, it lies upon the conscience of this country to do what is just in an endeavour to right this grievous wrong. Could anything be imagined meaner or more un-English than that the mistake should be admitted but reparation refused?

The Committee, while setting right the other faults both of the police and of the court, have, unhappily, stated "that they are not prepared to dissent from the finding of the jury," that the letters of 1903 were in the writing of George Edalji. Their cautious phrase means, I take it, not that they are by any means convinced that it is so, but that they have not sufficient evidence to enable them to contradict it. I do not know how the matter was laid before them, but I will undertake in half an hour, with the documents before him, to convince any reasonable and impartial man, that George Edalji did not write, and could not possibly have written, those letters. Of that I am absolutely certain, and there is no room for doubt whatever. Not only the character of the writing, but the internal evidence of the allusions to people and things, which were beyond his knowledge, show that he was not the author. Since the letters accused him of the crimes it is impossible to imagine how, save on the supposition of insanity (of which there has been no evidence in his life), he could possibly be imagined to have written them. On this subject of the letters I should like, with your permission, to deal further at some length on a future occasion.

As soon as possible after the holidays a meeting will be called of the committee appointed to administer the *Daily Telegraph* Fund. As this money was subscribed for legal expenses, and none have been incurred, the committee has not felt justified in spending it on any other object, and it is still intact. After the meeting the course of action advised by the committee, which consists at present of Sir George Lewis, Mr. Horace Voules, Professor Churton Collins, Mr. Jerome, Mr. J. Hall Richardson, and myself, will be laid before your readers.—I am, Sir, yours truly,

ARTHUR CONAN DOYLE

THE REV. S. EDALJI

TO THE EDITOR OF THE *DAILY TELEGRAPH*
Sir—Sir Arthur Wilson and his colleagues, in their report to the Home Secretary, say that they were "unable to disagree with what" they take "to be the finding of the jury that Edalji was the writer of the letters in 1903." Allow me to say that the jury were not asked to give their verdict as to whether my son wrote the letters or not. I have it on the authority of the late Clerk of the Peace at Stafford that the jury returned their verdict on one count only— namely, the maiming and wounding of a horse. The letters were produced

only as collateral evidence in support of the charge. How much of that evidence they believed, or even understood, nobody can tell.

If the jury believed that my son wrote the letters it was only on the authority of Mr. Gurrin and of Sir Reginald Hardy, who was rash and illogical enough to tell them that "he who wrote the letters also committed the crime." It was the summing up of this assistant chairman that misled the jury. A distinguished barrister, who was present at the trial, has described the summing up as "a regrettable performance."

Both the report and the letter written by Mr. Herbert Gladstone are open to criticism. A very carefully devised attempt is made in them to shield the "officials" on one hand and to save the compensation money on the other hand; but it is not a very successful and praiseworthy attempt. There is something most shocking and heartless in the manner in which my son has been treated both by the Staffordshire police and the Home Office authorities. The former charged him falsely and sent him to prison, and the latter assisted them by keeping him there for three years. Sir Arthur Wilson and his colleagues, as well as Mr. Herbert Gladstone, regard with perfect indifference the insults and the injuries which have been heaped upon him and my family for nearly four years. They grant him a free pardon grudgingly, and leave him in ruin for life. This may be diplomacy, statecraft, but it is not what they would have done if he had been the son of an English squire or an English nobleman.—Yours obediently,

S. EDALJI,
Vicar of Great Wyrley

CHAPTER SIX

SIR ARTHUR TACKLES THE PROBLEM OF THE ANONYMOUS LETTERS

Never one to let go of a perceived injustice, Sir Arthur Conan Doyle now attempted to disprove the Gladstone committee's findings that Edalji probably wrote the threatening anonymous letters that accompanied the Great Wyrley horse maimings. On May 23, 1907, he published the first of three letters outlining the results of a second investigation he undertook to prove Edalji innocent.

In the first installment, Sir Arthur assumed an expertise in handwriting analysis that was perhaps a bit of a stretch. He depended on facsimile reproductions of Edalji's handwriting samples and the Great Wyrley letters to make his case and gets very specific, even obsessive, about some of his points. He also gives a capsule history of the letters and some of their shocking content.

That same day, the Chief Constable of Staffordshire, Captain G. A. Anson, gave an interview in which he, not surprisingly, vehemently denied the Gladstone committee's—and Conan Doyle's—allegations that his police department unfairly had targeted Edalji as the guilty man. Captain Anson also confessed to the reporter, again not surprisingly, that "he felt very indignant at criticisms of the police. . . ."

In the second and third installments of Conan Doyle's handwriting investigation, he turns to the content of the letters to refute the jury and the Gladstone committee's contention that Edalji wrote the threatening and abusive letters. He also makes a persuasive case that the letter writer was, in fact, in league with at least one other person and probably two. He also hypothesizes that the three boys were probably brothers, that one of them was exceedingly "rude and foul-mouthed," and that he attended the Walsall Grammar School as a boy.

Sir Arthur's inferences are so concrete and specific that one is tempted to think he knows more than he's telling. In fact, that is probably the case. Conan Doyle had not simply read the trial transcripts in order to form his opinions. He had traveled to Great Wyrley and interviewed many of the residents. It was here that he learned of two local hooligans: Royden and Wallace Sharp. Royden, especially, had a reputation as a liar, a forger, and a sadist who was quick with a knife. He made his living as a butcher's apprentice and, coincidentally, when Royden shipped out to sea on a cattle boat, the letters stopped. When he returned, the sick letter writing campaign began again.

Conan Doyle took his findings to the local police. For reasons that one can only speculate, the local constables not only ignored Conan Doyle's evidence, they told him if he published his findings, he'd be guilty of libeling Royden Sharp. Strangely, Sir Arthur backed off. His *Statement of the Case Against Royden Sharp* was not published until the mid-1980s. It remains to this day one of the last articles about this case and one of the few pieces of Conan Doyle's writing left under copyright protection. As such, it is jealously guarded by the Conan Doyle estate.

CASE OF GEORGE EDALJI
LETTER FROM SIR A. CONAN DOYLE

FACSIMILE DOCUMENTS—NO. 1

Some six weeks ago a correspondent in the Midlands wrote to me to the effect that the police, when driven out of the position that George Edalji committed the crime for which he was sentenced to seven years penal servitude, would endeavour to defend a second line—namely, that he had written the anonymous letters, and was therefore responsible for the mistake to which he fell a victim. The insight or the information of the writer has seemed to be correct, and this is, indeed, the defence which has been set up, with such success that it has prevented the injured man from receiving that compensation which is his due. In this article I ask your permission to examine this contention, and I hope I shall satisfy your readers, or enable them to satisfy themselves, that the supposition is against all reason or probability, and that a fresh injustice and scandal will arise if it should retard the fullest possible amends being made to this most shamefully-treated man.

During an investigation of this case, which has now extended over five months, I have examined a very large number of documents, and tested a long series of real and alleged facts. During all that time I have kept my mind open, but I can unreservedly say that in the whole research I have never come across any considerations which would make it, I will not say probable, but in any way credible, that George Edalji had anything to do, either directly or indirectly, with the outrages or with the anonymous letters. As the latter question seems to be at the bottom of the ungenerous decision not to give Edalji compensation, I will, with your permission, place some of the documents before your readers, so that they may form their own opinion as to how far the contention that Edalji wrote them can be sustained. First, I will take the mere question of the handwriting of the letters, and secondly, I will take the internal evidence of their contents.

The exhibits, which I will call 1 and 2, are specimens of Edalji's ordinary writing, which is remarkably consistent in the many samples which I have observed. He says, and I believe with truth, that he has little power of varying his script. No proof has ever been adduced that he has such power. The specimens here given may be open to the objection that they are four years later than the time of the outrages, but Edalji was twenty-seven years of age then, and is now thirty-one, and no marked development of writing is likely to occur in the interval. I give two separate specimens that the consistency of their peculiarities may be observed:

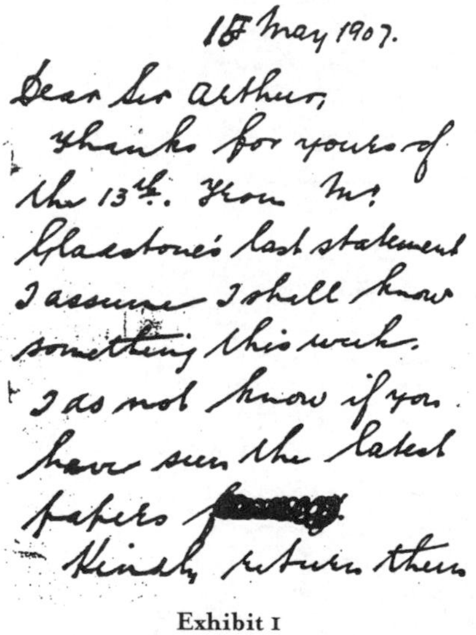

Exhibit 1

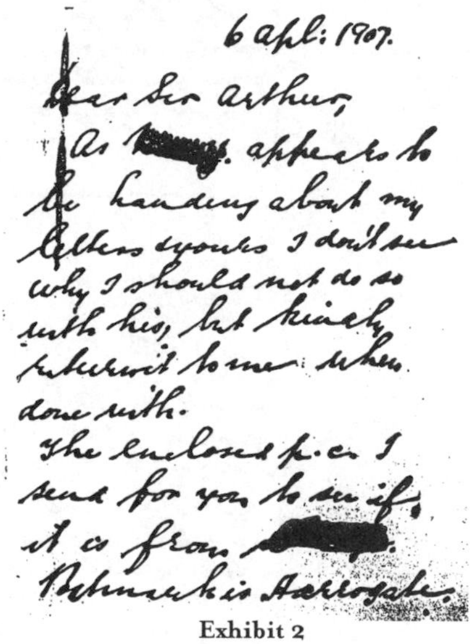

Exhibit 2

I now, for purposes of comparison, give two samples of those letters in 1903 which Mr. Gurrin, the expert who was at fault in the Beck case, declared to be, to be best of his belief, in the writing of George Edalji. To the ruin of the young man he persuaded the jury to adopt his view, and now the committee chosen by the Home Office has endorsed the opinion of the jury, with the result that compensation has been withheld. Exhibits 3 and 4 give specimens of the anonymous letters of 1903:

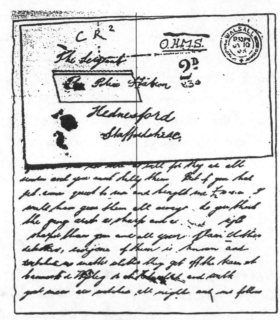

Exhibit 3

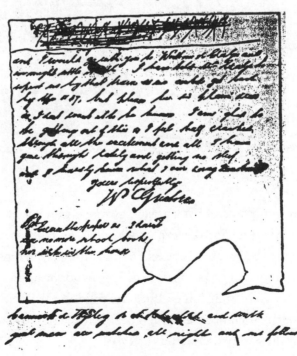

Exhibit 4

Now, on comparing the two specimens of Edalji with the two anonymous letters, the first general observation, before going into any details, is that the former is the writing of an educated man, and that the latter is certainly not so. A forger may imitate certain details in writing. A curious fashion of forming a letter is within the powers of even a clumsy imitator. But character is more difficult, and more subtle. Compare the real Edalji writing with the addressed envelope of three, or with the postscript of four, and ask yourself whether they do not belong to an entirely different class. Apart from the question of educated as against uneducated writing, the most superficial observer of character, as expressed in writing, would say that one and two were open and free, while three and four were cramped and mean. Yet Mr. Gurrin, the jury, and the Home Office Committee contend that they are the same, and a man's career has been ruined on the resemblance.

Now let us examine the details. There are one or two points of resemblance which are sufficiently close to make me believe that it is not entirely coincidence, and that there may have been some conscious, though very imperfect imitation, of Edalji's writing. One of these is a very small twirl made occasionally in finishing a letter. It is visible in the "c" in the fourth line from the bottom of exhibit 2, and in the "c" of the word "clothes" fifth line from the bottom of 3. A close inspection might detect it in several letters of both exhibits, and I am told that it was more common in Edalji's writing of that date. Another resemblance is the long upward stroke in beginning such words as "kindly" in two, and "known" four lines from the bottom of three. This formation, however, is not unusual. Lastly, there is the "r," which might occasionally almost be an "e," as in "return" in two, and in "sharp" in three. These peculiarities, especially the last, are so marked that they are, one would imagine, the first points which anyone disguising his hand would suppress, and anyone imitating would reproduce.

But now consider the points of difference. See the peculiar huddling of the letters together appearing in such words as "brought," "sharper," and "would," in 3, or in "don't," "write," and "known," in 4. Where is there any trace of this in Edalji's own writing? Compare the rounded "g" of the anonymous letters with the straight "g" of Edalji. Compare the final "r" of Edalji as seen in "Dear Sir Arthur," with the final "r" of "matter" and "your" in 3, or of "paper" and "nor" in the postscript of 4. Finally, take a very delicate test, beyond the power of observation of a clumsy forger. If you take the letter "u" in Edalji's letters you will find that he has a very curious and consistent habit of dropping the second curve of the "u" to a lower level than the first one. There is hardly an exception. But the anonymous writer, in three cases out of four, has the second curve as high as, or higher than, the first. Can any impartial and fair-minded man, examining these exhibits, declare that there is such an undoubted resemblance that a man's career might be staked upon it, or that the public is exonerated by it from making reparation for an admitted wrong?

So much for the actual writing. The matter becomes perfectly grotesque when we examine the internal evidence of the letters. In the first place, they are written for the evident purpose of exciting the suspicions of the police against two persons—the one being Edalji himself, and the other being young Greatorex, whose name was forged at the end of them. Why should Edalji, an eminently sane young lawyer, with a promising career before him, write to the police accusing himself of a crime of which he was really innocent? The committee speak of a spirit of impish mischief. What evidence of such a spirit has ever been shown in the life of this shy, retiring man? Such an action would appear to me to be inconsistent with sanity, and yet Edalji has always been eminently sane. What possible evidence is there to support so incredible a supposition? And suppose such a thing were true, how then would the introduction of young Greatorex be explained? Young Greatorex and Edalji were practically strangers. They had at most met without conversation when chance threw them into the same railway carriage on the Walsall line. There was no connection between them, no cause of quarrel, no possible reason why Edalji should involve Greatorex in a terrible suspicion, and then voluntarily come to share his danger. The whole supposition is monstrous. But it all becomes clear when we regard the letters as the work of a third person, who was the enemy both of Edalji and of Greatorex, and who hoped by this device to bring down both his birds with one stone. That Edalji had enemies, who had brought ingenious mystifications in letter writing to a fine point, is shown by the persecution to which he and his family were subjected from 1892 to 1895. One has only to show that one of those persecutors had also reason to wish evil to young Greatorex, and then it needs no fanciful theories of people writing scurrilous letters about themselves to make the whole situation perfectly credible and clear.

A priori, then, the likelihood of the letters being by Edalji is so slight that nothing but the most marked resemblance in the script could for a moment justify such a supposition. How far such an overpowering resemblance exists the reader can now judge for himself. But apart from the inherent improbability of such a theory, look at all the other points which should have laughed it out of court. Edalji was a well-educated young man, brought up in a clerical atmosphere, with no record of coarse speech or evil life. From his school days at Rugeley, where his headmaster gave him the highest character, until the time when he won the best prizes within his reach at the Legal College of Birmingham, there is nothing against his conduct or his language. Yet these letters are written by a foul-mouthed boor, a blackguard who has a smattering of education, but neither grammar nor decency. They do not, as the Committee have said, actually prove that the writer was the man who did the outrages, but they at least show that he had a cruel and bloodthirsty mind, which loved to dwell upon revolting details. "I caught each under the belly, but they did not spurt much blood." "We will do twenty wenches like the horses." "He pulls the hook smart across 'em and out the entrails fly." This is the writing of a hardened ruffian. Where in Edalji's studious life has he ever given the slightest indications of such a nature? His whole career and the testimony of all who have known him cry out against such a supposition.

Finally, there are certain allusions in the letters which are altogether outside Edalji's possible knowledge. In one of them some seven or eight people are mentioned, all of whom live in a group two stations down the line from Wyrley, and entirely removed from Edalji's very limited circle. They were a group immediately surrounding young Greatorex, and they were put in with a view to substantiating the pretence that he was the writer, for the entanglement of Greatorex was evidently the plotter's chief aim, and the ruin of Edalji was a mere by-product in the operation. One of the people mentioned was the village dressmaker, a second the doctor, a third the butcher, all in the neighbourhood of Greatorex and out of the ken of Edalji. In his attempt to entangle Greatorex the writer actually gave himself away, as it is clear to any intelligence above that of a prejudiced official that he must be one of the very limited number of people who was himself acquainted with this particular group.

There is one other peculiarity in the first Greatorex letter which cannot fail to arrest attention. It is the reiterated allusions to the sea. Edalji had no connection with the sea, and there was no reason why he should write of it. But in this one letter there are three or four references to it. How is this to be accounted for? When one considers that there had been a former persecution, that this had ended abruptly at the beginning of 1896, that peace had reigned for six years, and that now a new series of letters is commenced by someone whose mind is running upon the sea, one would like to make inquiry as to the possibility of some sailor having returned to the neighbourhood. Should such a man exist, as is likely enough upon a crowded countryside, the fact alone would be of small weight, but, at least, it might be worth an investigator's while to trace the matter further and see if any other points of contact could be established.

I have now dealt with the so-called "Greatorex" letters, and have enabled the reader to judge for himself as to how far the script is identical with that of Edalji. I have also shown that the *a-priori* reasoning and the internal evidence are absolutely opposed to the idea that the young lawyer wrote them. I am suppressing nothing in order to make a case, for I cannot find any single point in the letters which can be used as an argument that Edalji did write them. It is amazing to me that three men of position like Sir Albert De Rutzen, Sir Arthur Wilson, and the Hon. Mr. Wharton should express themselves as being in agreement with the senseless opinion of the Stafford jury. What possible facts can they allege to support such a contention? Where is the evidence of this "impish spirit" which they have themselves conjured up? It has added three more names to that long line of policemen, officials, and politicians who owe a very abject apology to this ill-used man. Until this apology is offered and reparation made no mutual daubings of complimentary white-wash will ever get them clean.

There are many other documents connected with this case which I should wish to discuss and reproduce in a later article. I should be glad, therefore, if your readers would retain the present specimens for future comparison.

ARTHUR CONAN DOYLE
Undershaw,
Hindhead, May 18.

MAY 23, 1907

POLICE AND MR. EDALJI
CAPTAIN ANSON'S STATEMENT

The Chief Constable of Staffordshire (Captain the Hon. G. A. Anson) granted a *Staffordshire Sentinel* representative an interview yesterday, in reference to the case of Mr. George Edalji. Captain Anson said he had no desire to make any observation upon the general facts of the case, but there was one feature of the report of the committee who had inquired into the matter upon which he thought he need not keep silent. He referred to the criticisms which, he considered, involved the honour of the police. The committee had said: "The police commenced and carried on their investigations, not for the purpose of finding out who was the guilty party, but for the purpose of finding evidence against Edalji, who they were already sure was the guilty man."

"That is absolutely untrue," said Captain Anson. The committee's report proceeded: "This is shown not only by the continuous watch kept upon the vicarage, but also by the fact that the police officers went straight to Edalji's house from the field where they saw the injured animal." As a matter of fact, said the chief constable, Edalji was not suspected at all until some months after the outrages commenced. Various persons were indicated as being conceivably implicated in the offences, but as time went on any grounds for suspecting them disappeared one by one. Suspicion finally became excited against Edalji, owing

199

to his commonly-talked-of habits of wandering abroad late at night, and a watch was kept on Wyrley Vicarage, with the object of verifying absolutely what were the facts on this point. It was obvious that if a further offence had occurred while the watching was going on, and Edalji had been known not to have left the vicarage, he would have been absolutely cleared of complicity.

The chief constable went on to say that the watching was abandoned some time before the offence of Aug. 18, because it was found impossible—owing to the nature of the surroundings—to make absolutely certain that no one could come in or out of the house without being observed. Captain Anson added: "It appears strange that exception should be taken to the police going straight to Edalji's house after the offence was discovered. If they had done nothing at the time, and gone to the house a week afterwards, they would certainly have been accused of inaction, and very properly so." Speaking on another matter in the report, he said: "The committee has accused the police of inconsistency and of making contradictory statements in respect of the watching of the vicarage on the night of Aug. 17. The house had not been particularly watched for some time previous to this date. In a general sense it was, of course, under observation. Sergeant Robinson, in cross-examination, said that the house was under observation, but he did not pretend to any personal knowledge on the subject, as he was on duty some distance away on the other side of the Walsall-road. Inspector Campbell, who gave general directions, and Sergeant Parsons, who actually detailed the men for duty on the vicarage side of the road, both stated positively that no one was watching the vicarage, but the committee has by an extraordinary blunder, converted Inspector Campbell's words, 'I gave general directions; no one watching the vicarage that night' into 'I gave general directions to one watching the vicarage.' On this blunder of their own the committee found the charge of inconsistency, and they comment on the fact that no such person was called as a witness. If there had been any actual discrepancy of evidence, the discrepancy would, of course, have been brought out at the trial by the able counsel who defended."

Captain Anson confessed that he felt very indignant at criticisms of the police founded on such grounds, and he added, in reply to a further remark, that there were no horse-hairs adhering to the razor, and Sergeant Parsons did not say there were. It would have been perfectly easy, he said, for the committee to have verified these points before condemning the police unheard. He regretted that the inquiry had not been a public one, which he thought would have been more satisfactory to all concerned. "As to the writing," Captain Anson concluded, "the committee could not have come to any other conclusion, so there is nothing new in the decision that Edalji had written the letters."

MAY 24, 1907

CASE OF GEORGE EDALJI
LETTER FROM SIR A. CONAN DOYLE

WHO WROTE THE LETTERS?—NO. 2

In my last article I laid before the reader copies of the actual writings of George Edalji, together with specimens of the anonymous letters of 1903, so that each might form his own opinion as to the degree of resemblance in the script. I also showed by the internal evidence of the letters themselves how grotesque is the theory that they were from the pen of the young lawyer, and how mean the refusal to compensate him for his unjust punishment by pretending that he had contributed to his own ruin. I will now lay some further documents before the public in order to illustrate the peculiar nature of the long persecution to which the Edalji family has been subjected, and to prove the fact that the anonymous letters now received by Edalji and by his friends come from the same hand which wrote some of the letters in the series of 1892–95.

If anyone conceives the wild theory that Edalji has been persecuting himself during all these years, I will undertake to show that such a supposition cannot be fitted into the facts. I admit that no one can put a limit to the strange aberrations of human nature, and that it is possible to conceive of a man otherwise sane who had some kink in his brain which compelled him from time to time to write abusive and scurrilous documents to himself and to

201

his people. In this case, however, it is not only possible to show that Edalji did not write the letters, but also to draw some fairly reliable inferences as to the people who did. This, I venture to do in the hope that some remark of mine may possibly prove suggestive to good citizens upon the spot, and help them to find some of the missing links in this long and tangled chain of events.

Those who have interested themselves in the case will remember that the main persecution of the Edalji family began in the year 1892, and lasted until the beginning of 1896. During that time hundreds of letters of an extraordinary nature were sent to them; hoaxes of the most ingenious description were played upon them; bogus advertisements of an offensive character were put in their names into the papers; objects were thrown into the vicarage grounds, and many other pranks played upon them. Any one of these might be described as trivial, but the continued, ingenious persecution, lasting over three years, became cruelty of a most diabolical kind, under which the minds of the victims might well have broken down. To the lasting disgrace of the Staffordshire police this man-baiting was allowed to continue for this long period without any serious effort upon their part to shield the unfortunate family from their brutal tormentors. Their complaints were unheeded, or else it was hinted to them, exactly as it is now said to the son, that their sufferings were in some way due to themselves. It is a story which any unofficial Englishman must read with shame and indignation.

I have carefully examined a considerable number of the letters and postcards written by the conspirators, and I have been able to come to some definite conclusions about them. In the first place, there appear to have been three of them, two adults and a boy. I must admit that the writings of the two adults are so fluid, and run so frequently into the same characteristics, that I am prepared to find that they both came from one individual. Such a supposition is possible, but I think that it is very improbable. I seem to trace three lines of thought and character, as well as three peculiarities of script. We will take it, then, that there is adult writing and that there is boy writing, the adult writing being separable into two. Of the boy, it may be definitely stated that he could not have been less than twelve or more than sixteen. I find no exact evidence as to the age of the others, save that the mischief which characterises the whole proceeding, and the fact that they could devote so very much time and attention to it—some of the letters are of great length—would seem to indicate that they were still youths, and that they had no settled occupation. It is fairly certain that they must have lived within a radius of a mile or two of the vicarage, since many of the missives were left by hand.

Let me now consider what relation these three plotters bore to each other. Had there been a cramming establishment, or any other centre where mischievous young men could congregate, I should say that very likely they were no relations, but mere partners in a cruel practical joke. I have been unable to find, however, that anything of the sort exists in that neighbourhood. Yet these three individuals, the two young adults and the boy, undoubtedly lived under the same roof. Their epistles are continually on the same paper, and in the same envelopes. In some cases the rude scrawl of the boy comes in upon the very page which is taken up by the educated writing of the adult. A sheet may exhibit on one side an elaborate forgery of the signatures of the Edaljis, the Brookes, or some other neighbouring family, while on the other is a rude drawing (rude in every sense), which could only have been done by a lad. The adults appeared to pride themselves upon forgery, and the results, so far as I have been able to test them, show that they had remarkable powers in that direction. "Do you think that we could not imitate your kid's writing?" they say exultantly in one of the 1892 letters. They most certainly could—and did.

What are we to say, then, of three youths, all living under one roof, and engaged over several years in long succession of heartless practical jokes. It is possible that they were three clerks in an office, or three assistants in a business, but in such a case, how are we to account for the presence among them of a boy? On the whole, the balance of probability is greatly in favour of there being three relatives, brothers for choice, who are working together in the matter. The fact that the rude writing of the youngest developed at a later date some of the peculiarities of his elders, would seem to indicate a family habit.

In this way we have built up, as a rough working hypothesis, the idea of two young men and an exceedingly foul-mouthed boy, who are brothers or close relations, and fellow-conspirators in this persecution. Let us see now if an inspection of the letters can give us any information of the habits of those young blackguards. The first thing which is perfectly evident is the connection of the younger one with Walsall Grammar School. Walsall Grammar School is an excellent educational establishment, and a great boon to all the country round, but, like every other school, it has an occasional black sheep, and it needs no far-fetched inference to make it certain that this youngster was among them. Let me explain here that it was not merely the Edalji family who were persecuted by scurrilous letters, but that several other families in the neighbourhood, notably the Brookes and the Wynnes, were troubled in the same fashion. Now, both the Brookes and the Wynnes had a son at that time at Walsall School, and the headmaster of Walsall was also a recipient of anonymous letters, written in the same rough boyish hand, so that the focus of trouble seems certainly to lie there. I may explain in passing that George Edalji was at Rugeley Grammar School, and had no connection whatever with Walsall.

My point is, then, that the youngest of these three brothers, the ill-conditioned boy, had some connection with Walsall School. To illustrate it I append an exhibit, which, for purposes of future reference, I will call No. 1. Here the writer, dragging in as usual the butt, Edalji, whose very name he cannot at that time spell, utters the most scurrilous threats against the headmaster.

This writing is, beyond all doubt, as will afterwards be demonstrated, the same as that of the younger conspirator.

Here now we are getting at something tangible. The writer of 1 was a boy who entertained a malignant hatred of the headmaster of Walsall School. Why? It does not seem to be stretching the argument to suppose that it is a boy who has often felt the headmaster's cane, or possibly has been expelled for his evil conduct. Without over-elaborating the point it can at least be stated as a probability, indeed almost a certainty, that the boy brother was a scholar at Walsall (and a very backward unruly one) in the year 1892. The argument up to this point must certainly approximate to the truth. It is possible, therefore, that an examination of the records of Walsall Grammar School at that date would give a starting point for an investigation.

Not only can we say with some certainty that this young rascal was at Walsall, but there is a strong probability that one of the others was at the same

No. I

school, though his age, as indicated by his writing, would show that he had either left before the other joined, or that he was in the higher when his younger brother was in the lower classes. He joins his young brother in writing anonymously to the Brookes and the Wynnes, showing a certain community of interest where school matters are concerned. His scholastic record must have been a very different one, for both his script and the contents of his letters show a very alert and ingenious mind. In one of his letters there is a long quotation from Milton. I believe that I am correct in stating that this particular book of Milton had been the school exercise some little time before. I repeat, therefore, that the balance of evidence is in favour of one at least of the elder

205

brothers having been a senior scholar at Walsall at or about the time when his brother was a junior. This should narrow down the field of an inquiry.

In this connection we must consider the incident of the Walsall Grammar School key. This key was discovered by the village constable on Dec. 12, 1892, upon the window-sill of the vicarage, and George Edalji, upon the unvarying principle of laying everything mysterious to his charge, was at once accused of having put it there. How he could have got it from the six-mile-off school, or what end could be served by so foolish a prank, was never explained. Yet it was over this incident that the chief constable wrote: "If the persons concerned in the removal of the key refuse to make any explanation of the subject, I must necessarily treat the matter as a theft. I may say at once, that I shall not pretend to believe any protestations of ignorance which your son may make about this key. My information on the subject does not come from the police." When one takes this incident with the preceding evidence as to Walsall Grammar School being the focus of the mischief, is it not exceedingly probable that the key was brought over by the same mischievous scholars who wrote the letters, and that the chief constable's information was conveyed in one of their ingenious epistles? There is, at least, nothing unnatural or far-fetched in such a supposition, while the suggestion that George Edalji would travel twelve miles in order to lay on his own father's window-sill a key which nobody wanted is grotesque in its improbability. I only recall the incident at present as a corroboration of the theory which I am demonstrating that the storm-centre at that time lay in Walsall School.

I will now present specimens of the script of the two elders of the trio, with the proviso that it is within the bounds of possibility that the two may eventually prove to have been one. For the present, at least, I will differentiate them. One of them, who seems to me to be the elder, as his thought and express are the more developed, is the creature who writes extraordinary religious rant over the signature of "God-Satan." There are remarkable qualities in these mad effusions, grim humour, wild imagination, and a maniacal turn of mind, which alternates between hysterical religion and outrageous blasphemy. It was no ordinary man who wrote the following characteristic effusion:

"I must live partly in Heaven and partly in hell, so if that ever-accursed monster Satan tries to detain me in hell I will fight with him and throw myself into the gulf which is fixed between hell and Heaven, and then I shall be able to climb out of the gulf into Heaven. And moreover, if God tries to push me back into hell I will defy God and struggle with Him, and if I cannot prevail I will hold on to God and fall with Him over the precipice of hell."

"If you wish to escape having your house blown up by dynamite you are to do this thus, namely, order the postman to take Mrs. M.'s body out of her grave and bring it to your house. You are then to break open her head, take out her brains, and boil them in a cauldron of port wine for three hours. Next you are to order Mr. ———— to come to your house, make him open his mouth and drink the contents of the cauldron whilst boiling. If you do this to my satisfaction I will ask God not to give you such a hot place in hell."

There are countless pages of this strange, pernicious stuff, alternating with such lighter passages as this: "You vindictive wretch, I dare you to do to me whatever your vengeance prompts you, but spare, oh, spare, the honest police!" I append as a specimen of the script the page, which I shall number 2, upon which the latter gem appears.

The writing in all these effusions is fluent and easy, with every mark of an educated hand. I can find no evidence that any particular care has been taken to disguise it, but it is naturally unformed, and does not set rigidly into definite characteristics.

From 1896 onwards this individual disappears entirely, and I was at some loss to form an opinion as to whether the mania was real or simulated. It bore every aspect of being real, but on the other hand it was difficult to conceive that such a person could so conceal his mental eccentricity as to escape general comment. Some weeks ago, however, an incident occurred which convinced me that the man still lives, and that he is now a

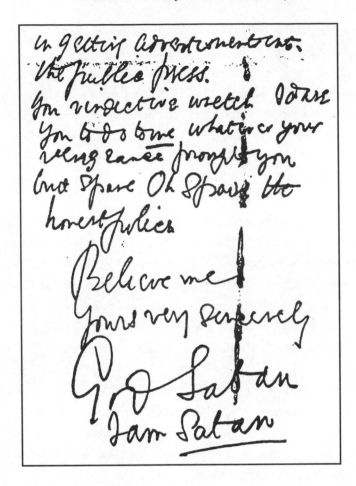

No. 2

marked religious maniac. A newspaper containing some account of the Edalji affair had found its way to Long Beach, California, in the United States. A page of it was sent back to Mr. George Edalji, with religious and blasphemous comments scribbled in pencil all round the margins. The general character of this script, the knowledge shown of the case, and the singular mental conditions, have all convinced me that, whatever be his name, God-Satan is now to be found on the Pacific Coast, and that he is an undoubted madman.

So much for the elder of the three hypothetical individuals. He now

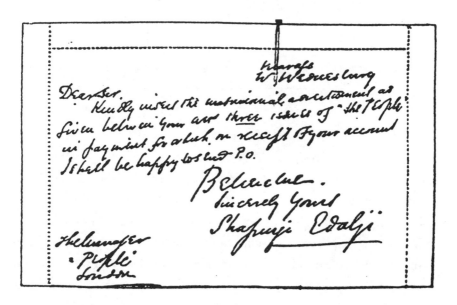

No. 3

drops out of the narrative and we come to the second. This man writes a closer, smaller hand, with many of his senior's peculiarities. There is no fancy and no madness in his productions. On the contrary, they are particularly practical. They are usually postcards of an abusive character, sent to someone at a distance, and signed with a forged name. At his ingenious bidding deluded tradesmen have brought huge consignments of goods to the vicarage, brother clergymen have hastened to Wyrley upon all sorts of urgent summonses, and editors have inserted the most monstrous advertisements as to the extraordinary needs of the vicar. The exhibit No. 3 gives a specimen of the script. Of this man's future I know nothing, and it may well prove, when the veil comes to be lifted, that he is simply another manifestation of the ingenuity of "God-Satan."

I will pursue the subject in a concluding letter.

ARTHUR CONAN DOYLE
Undershaw,
May 20.

CAPT. ANSON AND MR. EDALJI

TO THE EDITOR OF THE *DAILY TELEGRAPH*

Sir—As reported in to-day's *Telegraph*, Captain Anson says: "Suspicion finally became excited against Edalji, owing to his commonly talked of habits of wandering abroad late at night." It is plain now on what a flimsy foundation the charge was trumped up against me. But, as a fact, I never once did "wander abroad late at night," and unless returning by a late train from Birmingham, or from some evening entertainment in the district, I was invariably in by about 9.30—as on the night of the outrage. I should imagine no person in the district was less in the habit of being out at night than I was, and apparently the police took seriously something meant only as a joke at my habit of always being home so early. Obviously, had I been often out late, the fact would have been known to the large body of police who were patrolling the parish.

There is another matter referred to by Captain Anson, which shows the Committee of Inquiry do not stand alone in making misstatements. He says: "There were no horse-hairs adhering to the razor, and Sergeant Parsons did not say there were." Now, it was conclusively established that no hairs were on the razor, but yet Parsons did swear there were some. I have his evidence before me as I write. In conclusion, let me emphatically state that I wrote none of the anonymous letters. They only came to hand after the police began to watch my home, so it was not the letters which led them to suspect me. The letters were written in a clumsy imitation of my handwriting, in order to fabricate evidence against me.

I desire to thank the Press and all those through whose exertions my innocence has at last been acknowledged, and trust in time to obtain also an apology and compensation.—Yours truly,

G. E T. EDALJI

POLICE AND MR. EDALJI

The Chief Constable of Staffordshire, says the *Manchester Guardian*, recognizes the gravity of the charges made against him and the force under him in the Edalji report, but everybody who reads the account given today of an interview with him will realise how unsatisfactory both to the police and the committee is the situation which that report has created. Captain Anson is naturally greatly perturbed, and as the committee's judgment was pronounced without an exhaustive public inquiry affording adequate opportunities for defense, he permits himself the liberty of declaring "absolutely untrue" the charge that the police carried on their investigations "not for the purposes of finding out who was the guilty party, but for the purpose of finding evidence against Edalji, who, they were already sure, was the guilty man." The committee, of course, is not in a position to reply, and, in any case, the best way to clear up the truth of a matter so vital to the administration of justice is not to interchange more or less polite negations in the columns of the Press. What is wanted is a formal inquiry by a competent tribunal, and apparently Captain Anson would have no objection to one; indeed, he could hardly have any. Meanwhile one contradiction in Captain Anson's statement is worth pointing out. He says that the watching of the vicarage was abandoned some time before Aug. 18—this is a point upon which the committee found the statements of police in their depositions "inconsistent, and, indeed, contradictory"—because it was found impossible, owing to the nature of surroundings, to make absolutely certain that no one could come in or out of the house without being observed. Yet he declares "it is obvious that if a further offence had occurred while the watching was going on, and Edalji had been known not to have left the vicarage he would have been absolutely cleared of complicity." If no system of watching could make absolutely certain, how could Edalji have been known not to have left the vicarage? Captain Anson's declaration throws little light, but it constitutes yet another argument for a public inquiry into the whole of the case.

MAY 27, 1907

CASE OF GEORGE EDALJI

LETTER FROM SIR A. CONAN DOYLE

THE "MARTIN MOLTON" LETTERS—NO. 3

We now come to the third individual whom we have constructed, foul-mouthed boy. He is far the more interesting and important of the three, for whereas the others drop out he carries on the persecution. As I will presently show, I have myself received a letter from him within the last few weeks, one of a considerable series which have been signed by various pseudonyms, but which I will call in future the Martin Molton letters, since that was the name which was attached to the first specimen. That Martin Molton, of 1907, and the bad boy of 1892 are the same individual is, as I will show, beyond all reasonable doubt.

Let me pause here for one instant to consider the theory which I believe still lingers at the Home Office, that the bad boy of 1892–95 was actually George Edalji reviling his own people, and writing furious letters to those who had never offended him. If the officials could only make good that proposition, then they could point to him also as being Martin Molton, and all would be well. But to any unprejudiced mind, with no official theory to sustain, the thing is beyond argument. Look at the writing of 1 and also of 4. It is rude, coarse, and unformed to the last degree. Such as it is it appears unchanged in the persecuting letters up to the end of 1895. Now, at that date George Edalji was nineteen years of age, an excellent scholar, who had finished his grammar-school education, and had already started that course of legal study in Birmingham at which he was to win such distinction. Can anyone believe that he is responsible for this barbarous writing and more barbarous spelling and grammar. It is impossible to suppose such a thing, and by saying so we dispose for ever of the wild idea that Martin Molton was George Edalji, for whoever wrote the schoolboy scrawl of 1892–95 wrote the letters of 1907.

Let me now make that point clear before I go any further. I present side by side two exhibits, which I call 4 and 5. 4 is a specimen of the bad boy's writing, dating back to 1893. Alienists will be interested in the circular dots to the i's, which are recognised as a symptom of lunacy. 5 is a short extract from a long abusive anonymous letter which reached me on April 17 of this year, posted on that date in the N.W. or Euston quarter of London.

Compare the character of the writing. Compare the words "run" and the words "murder" in each. Compare the peculiar r's shaped like x. Is there any reasonable man who can doubt that the thing is beyond coincidence, and that the same hand fashioned each? It may be fairly inferred, also, that the writer has been employed during the fourteen years which have elapsed in some trade which has not required much clerical work, as it is difficult to believe otherwise that he would not have developed his calligraphy.

No. 4

No. 5

Having, as I hope, satisfied the reader that the young rascal of 1893 is the writer of the anonymous letter quoted above, I must complete my point by showing that the latter is also Martin Molton. The handwriting of all these 1907 letters is identical, save that in some cases the Greek e is used with an ordinary r, while in others the ordinary e is used with the peculiar r. I append an extract from my letter, 6, and one from the Martin Molton series, 7, which will, I hope, satisfy the reader that they are the same script, and that they are therefore both the handiwork of the bad boy of Walsall School. I may add

No. 6

No. 7

that of the Martin Molton series five were posted in London and two in Birmingham.

Now we have secured the two ends of our chain, and it only remains to examine those central links which are formed by the letters of 1903—those letters which the committee, and also the jury, have most unreasonably ascribed to Edalji. I claim that I have shown these two ends to be from another hand, and if I can show that there is any correspondence or connection between them and the 1908 letters, then the latter also are from another hand. I have in my previous article shown, both by the script and by the internal evidence, that it is in the highest degree improbable that they could have been by Edalji. I now propose to show that it is, on the other hand, in the highest degree probable that they are by the same author as the others. Who that may be it is for those upon the spot to determine.

First of all I reproduce part of the envelope of one of the Martin Molton letters (8), and I place below it the forged signature of Wilfred Greatorex in

214

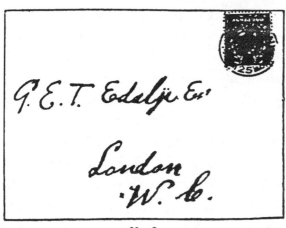

No. 8

No. 9

1903. Let the reader look at the two capital W's. Each is curiously fashioned, and yet there is an absolute similarity between them.

Is this within the range of coincidence? I have shown that there is a history of forgery in the family from the beginning, and the actual writing is cleverly concealed, but every here and there, as in this conspicuous W, there is a glaring lapse. Even the same phrases recur in the different series of letters. I have one of the 1908 letters before me as I write, and I read in it, "None of the people think you a right sort," addressed to George Edalji. Turn to exhibit 6, and you will find the same phrase applied to the same man in the letters of 1907. Is this also coincidence? See the continued ill will towards the Edaljis breaking out in 1893, 1903, and again in 1907. Is this also coincidence, and is the central mystification distinct from the first and the last? It is not for me to state who actually wrote the letters of 1903, but I claim that, while in my last article I proved that all the evidence is against them having been done by George Edalji, in the present I have shown that there are very sound reasons to believe that they are from the same hand as those of 1893 and of 1907. I have also given some indications by which that hand may be traced.

Just one word at this point as to the object of all this elaborate mystification. Of that I have no doubt at all. The culprit is a lunatic, and his destination when his pranks have all been brought home to him should be, not a prison, but an asylum. The religious mania of the elder conspirator is the

215

index of a family weakness which becomes a diabolically mischievous madness in the junior. He will be found, when exposed, to be a man of eccentric life and character, with periodical accessions of actual madness, during which he loses all prudence and control. Had the persecution been confined to the Edaljis, one might well have imagined that some secret reason could explain it, but it has broken out in so many directions, and been accompanied by such senseless deeds, that nothing but a disordered brain can be behind it. Such a man is a danger to the community in which he lives, as no one can say what turn his destructive propensities may take. That he still lives in the Midlands, and possibly in the very district of the crimes, is made feasible by the postmarks of two of the Martin Molton letters. I trust that it will not be long before he is under medical supervision.

I have purposely said nothing of the outrages themselves and confined my remarks to the letters, since these are the only things for which Edalji is now held responsible, and it is on account of that alleged responsibility that compensation is refused him. The writing of the letters does not appear to be a criminal offence, or at worst a minor one, so that if the assertion were true that Edalji wrote them, the country would none the less owe him compensation for his three years of gaol. I trust, however, that I have convinced every impartial man that the balance of evidence is enormously against Edalji having had anything to do with the letters. Redress for one unjust accusation has been refused by the simple process of making a second equally unjust. Nowhere in the state document is there one word of sorrow or repentance for the blunder so tardily found out. All honest, manly admission and moderate redress would have been met in a conciliatory spirit, and the matter would have ended. As it is, the sore still runs. Fortunately, behind the mutual whitewashers and the ring of interested officials, there is always the great public to whom an injured man may appeal.

Those who have followed my argument, and who agree with those conclusions, which seem to me to be inevitable, may well ask why all these documents and this reasoning have not been laid before the committee and the Home Office. My answer is that they were so. I wish I could say with assurance that the committee ever considered them. "Facts and printed matter" is their guarded description of what they have examined, and my documents could not be included in the latter. In their report there is not a word which leads me to think that my evidence was considered, and there are several passages—notably about Green, and about the eyesight—which make it difficult for me to believe that it was so. In the matter of the eyesight, the opinion of some unnamed prison doctor is endorsed, while there is no comment on the views of fifteen experts, some of them the first oculists in the country, which I sent in. As to the Home Office, I have shown them documents and demonstrated the points here set forth until I was weary. I was treated always with courtesy, but I was met also with a chilly want of sympathy. Instead of recognising that I had no possible object save the ends of justice, and that it was their function in this country to see that justice was done, they took an obvious side in favour of impeached officialdom, and made me feel at every point that there was a hostile atmosphere around me. However, in spite of every obstacle, nine-tenths of the victory is won, and I have not a doubt that the fair-minded men of this country, apart from every consideration of persons or politics, will see that it is made complete by public apology and redress for a public wrong.

ARTHUR CONAN DOYLE
Undershaw,
May 20.

Some Mysteries Are Never Solved

The strange case of George Edalji is not a mystery that wraps up neatly. Conan Doyle never got the satisfaction of seeing any officials punished or anyone else convicted for the crimes Edalji was supposed to have committed. Furthermore, although Home Secretary Herbert Gladstone comes off looking like a pettifogging public official, his private diaries show he inquired deeply into the case.

What troubled Gladstone was that Mr. Vachell, Edalji's own solicitor, believed Edalji guilty of writing at least some of the anonymous letters! It seems that George's own brother Horace turned in, as a sample of George's handwriting, a dirty, obscene letter much like those received around the district. Of course, if Horace had wanted to put a noose around his brother's neck, he couldn't have done a better job, and his motives for supplying the incriminating evidence have never been explained. Nor has it ever been explained why Mr. Vachell accepted the evidence at face value rather than questioning it.

What we do know is that neither the cattle maiming nor the anonymous letter writing ceased. For some months various individuals received threatening letters, and a young butcher named Hollis Morgan was arrested on suspicion of maiming animals. The case was thrown out of court when police failed to produce convincing evidence that Morgan had been anywhere near the injured animals.

A letter-writer to the *Daily Telegraph* had warned readers that the maiming of animals was not unknown in rural counties. Perhaps, in the end, the crimes had been nothing more than the activity of neighborhood hooligans—who got away with it.

PART TWO

THE CASE OF
OSCAR SLATER

CHAPTER ONE

"A Disreputable, Rolling-Stone of a Man"

"It is impossible to read and weigh the facts in connection with the conviction of Oscar Slater in May, 1909, at the High Court in Edinburgh, without feeling deeply dissatisfied with the proceedings, and morally certain that justice was not done."

With this bold and direct statement, Sir Arthur Conan Doyle began his treatise on one of the most outrageous examples of the failure of justice in the history of British jurisprudence. Oscar Slater was railroaded into taking the rap for a murder he had nothing to do with. He didn't know the victim, Marion Gilchrist, and there was nothing to connect him with her murder besides the weak and flawed testimony of a couple of eyewitnesses, one of whom may not have been entirely innocent herself. Reading Conan Doyle's analysis of the case makes one wonder how something like this could have ever happened in the first place, and yet it did. Oscar Slater escaped the gallows by the barest thread and spent eighteen years in prison, all the while protesting his innocence (and usually in a fashion that got him into trouble).

Unlike the Edalji case, however, Sir Arthur took a different approach to helping Oscar Slater. There was little sympathy for Slater in Conan Doyle's words. At one point, he compares the Slater case to that of George Edalji:

"I must admit they are not of the same class. George Edalji was a youth of exemplary character. Oscar Slater was a blackguard. . . . Thus, one cannot feel the same burning injustice over the matter."

To Conan Doyle, the outrage that was committed was not against Slater so much as the vaunted British justice system. As far as Slater was concerned, Conan Doyle thought he had at least some of his punishment coming to him, and hoped that "the judgment may in some way be reconsidered and the man's present punishment allowed to atone for those irregularities of life which helped to make his conviction possible."

As always, Sir Arthur Conan Doyle didn't mince words. In *The Case of Oscar Slater*, we see him at his best, as he skewers not only Slater, but the police, the prosecutors, the judge, and even Slater's defense team. This is a wonderful example of a world-class writer at his impassioned best.

THE CASE OF
OSCAR SLATER

It is impossible to read and weigh the facts in connection with the conviction of Oscar Slater in May, 1909, at the High Court in Edinburgh, without feeling deeply dissatisfied with the proceedings, and morally certain that justice was not done. Under the circumstances of Scotch law I am not clear how far any remedy exists, but it will, in my opinion, be a serious scandal if the man be allowed upon such evidence to spend his life in a convict prison. The verdict which led to his condemnation to death, was given by a jury of fifteen, who voted: Nine for "Guilty," five for "Non-proven," and one for "Not Guilty." Under English law, this division of opinion would naturally have given cause for a new trial. [The Scottish verdict of "not proven" is an eminently sensible judgment not generally used by other countries. An English verdict, and by extension, an American verdict requires a jury to find an accused guilty or not guilty, which leaves the conclusion of a case very definitive, and sometimes unsatisfactorily so. The verdict of "not proven" allows a jury to say it has taken note of the evidence brought against the defendent but isn't convinced a clear-cut decision can be given, and that must very often be the case when jurors are charged to find a defendent guilty if the evidence is beyond "reasonable doubt." "Not proven" allows a jury to simply say the evidence is not sufficient to convict. Guilt or innocence is not assured based on the evidence put before them. Incidentally, the death penalty is no longer exacted throughout the United Kingdom, no matter how sure the verdict of guilty.] In Scotland the man was condemned to death, he was only reprieved two days before his execution, and he is now working out a life sentence in Peterhead convict establishment. How far the verdict was a just one, the reader may judge for himself when he has perused a connected story of the case.

There lived in Glasgow in the year 1908, an old maiden lady named Miss Marion Gilchrist. She had lived for thirty years in the one flat, which was on the first floor in 15, Queen's Terrace. The flat above hers was vacant, and the only immediate neighbours were a family named Adams, living on the ground floor below, their house having a separate door which was close alongside the flat entrance. The old lady had one servant, named Helen Lambie, who was a girl twenty-one years of age. This girl had been with Miss Gilchrist for three or four years. By all accounts Miss Gilchrist was a most estimable person, leading a quiet and uneventful life. [Conan Doyle was woefully misinformed on this point. Actually, Miss Gilchrist did not get along with her relatives, had birthed a child out of wedlock, and took extraordinary precautions with regard to her personal safety. In light of her death, we assume she had good reasons for such actions.] She was comfortably off, and she had one singular characteristic for a lady of her age and surroundings, in that she had made a collection of jewelry of considerable value. These jewels, which took the form of brooches, rings, pendants, etc., were bought at different times, extending over a considerable number of years, from a reputable jeweller. I lay stress upon the fact, as some wild rumour was circulated at the time that the old lady might herself be a criminal receiver. Such an idea could not be entertained. She seldom wore her jewelry save in single pieces, and as her life was a retired one, it is difficult to see how anyone outside a very small circle could have known of her hoard. The value of this treasure was about three thousand pounds. It was a fearful joy which she snatched from its possession, for she more than once expressed apprehension that she might be attacked and robbed. Her fears had the practical result that she attached two patent locks to her front door, and that she arranged with the Adams family underneath that in case of alarm she would signal to them by knocking upon the floor.

It was the household practice that Lambie, the maid, should go out and get an evening paper for her mistress about seven o'clock each day. After bringing the paper she then usually went out again upon the necessary shopping. This routine was followed upon the night of December 21st. She left her mistress seated by the fire in the dining-room reading a magazine. Lambie took the keys with her, shut the flat door, closed the hall door downstairs, and was gone about ten minutes upon her errand. It is the events of those ten minutes which form the tragedy and the mystery which were so soon to engage the attention of the public.

According to the girl's evidence, it was a minute or two before seven when she went out. At about seven, Mr. Arthur Adams and his two sisters were in their dining-room immediately below the room in which the old lady had been left. Suddenly they heard "a noise from above, then a very heavy fall, and then three sharp knocks." They were alarmed at the sound, and the young man at once set off to see if all was right. He ran out of his hall door, through the hall door of the flats, which was open, and so up to the first floor, where he found Miss Gilchrist's door shut. He rang three times without an answer. From within, however, he heard a sound which he compared to the breaking of sticks. He imagined therefore that the servant girl was within, and that she was engaged in her household duties. After waiting for a minute or two, he seems to have convinced himself that all was right. He therefore descended again and returned to his sisters, who persuaded him to go up once more to the flat. This he did and rang for the fourth time. As he was standing with his hand upon the bell, straining his ears and hearing nothing, someone approached up the stairs from below. It was the young servant-maid, Helen Lambie, returning from her errand. The two held council for a moment. Young Adams described the noise which had been heard. Lambie said that the pulleys of the clothes-lines in the kitchen must have given way. It was a singular explanation, since the kitchen was not above the dining-room of the Adams, and one would not expect any great noise from the fall of a cord which suspended sheets or towels. However, it was a moment of agitation, and the girl may have said the first explanation which came into her head. She then put her keys into the two safety locks and opened the door.

At this point there is a curious little discrepancy of evidence. Lambie is prepared to swear that she remained upon the mat beside young Adams. Adams is equally positive that she walked several paces down the hall. This inside hall was lit by a gas, which turned half up, and shining through a coloured shade, gave a sufficient, but not a brilliant light. Says Adams: "I stood at the door on the threshold, half in and half out, and just when the girl had got past the clock to go into the kitchen, a well-dressed man appeared. I did not suspect him, and she said nothing; and he came up to me quite pleasantly. I did not suspect anything wrong for the minute. I thought the man was going to speak to me, till he got past me, and then I suspected something wrong, and by that time the girl ran into the kitchen and put the gas up and said it was all right, meaning her pulleys. I said: 'Where is your mistress?' and she went into the dining-room. She said: 'Oh! come here!' I just went in and saw this horrible spectacle."

The spectacle in question was the poor old lady lying upon the floor close by the chair in which the servant had last seen her. Her feet were towards the door, her head towards the fireplace. She lay upon a hearth-rug, but a skin rug had been thrown across her head. Her injuries were frightful, nearly every bone of her face and skull being smashed. In spite of her dreadful wounds she lingered for a few minutes, but died without showing any sign of consciousness.

The murderer when he had first appeared had emerged from one of the two bedrooms at the back of the hall, the larger, or spare bedroom, not the old lady's room. On passing Adams upon the doormat, which he had done with the utmost coolness, he had at once rushed down the stair. [Conan Doyle **assumed, as have most others, that the man who passed Lambie and Adams in the hallway was the murderer. For a different and most suggestive view of who Lambie saw, read Thomas Toughill's book** *Oscar Slater: The Mystery Solved* **(London: Canongate Press, 1993).**] It was a dark and drizzly evening, and it seems that he made his way along one or two quiet streets until he was lost in the more crowded thoroughfares. He had left no weapon nor possession of any sort in the old lady's flat, save a box of matches with which he had lit the gas in the bedroom from which he had come. In this bedroom a number of articles of value, including a watch, lay upon the dressing-table, but none of them had been touched. A box containing papers had been forced open, and these papers were found scattered upon the floor. If he were really in search of the jewels, he was badly informed, for these were kept among the dresses in the old lady's wardrobe. Later, a single crescent diamond brooch, an article worth perhaps forty or fifty pounds, was found to be missing. Nothing else was taken from the flat. It is remarkable that though the furniture round where the body lay was spattered with blood, and one would have imagined that the murderer's hands must have been stained, no mark was seen upon the half-consumed match with which he had lit the gas, nor upon the match box, the box containing papers, nor any other thing which he may have touched in the bedroom.

We come now to the all-important question of the description of the man seen at such close quarters by Adams and Lambie. Adams was short-sighted and had not his spectacles with him. His evidence at the trial ran thus:

"He was a man a little taller and a little broader than I am, not a well-built man but well featured and clean-shaven, and I cannot exactly swear to his moustache, but if he had any it was very little. He was rather a commercial traveller type, or perhaps a clerk, and I did not know but what he might be one of her friends. He had on dark trousers and a light overcoat. I could not say if it were fawn or grey. I do not recollect what sort of hat he had. He seemed gentlemanly and well-dressed. He had nothing in his hand so far as I could tell. I did not notice anything about his way of walking."

Helen Lambie, the other spectator, could give no information about the face (which rather bears out Adams's view as to her position), and could only say that he wore a round cloth hat, a three-quarter length overcoat of a grey colour, and that he had some peculiarity in his walk. As the distance traversed by the murderer within sight of Lambie could be crossed in four steps, and as these steps were taken under circumstances of peculiar agitation, it is difficult to think that any importance could be attached to this last item in the description.

It is impossible to avoid some comment upon the actions of Helen Lambie during the incidents just narrated, which can only be explained by supposing that from the time she saw Adams waiting outside her door, her whole reasoning faculty had deserted her. First, she explained the great noise heard below: "The ceiling was like to crack," said Adams, by the fall of a clothes-line and its pulleys of attachment, which could not possibly, one would imagine, have produced any such effect. She then declares that she remained upon the mat, while Adams is convinced that she went right down the hall. On the appearance of the stranger she did not gasp out: "Who are you?" or any other sign of amazement, but allowed Adams to suppose by her silence that the man might be someone who had a right to be there. Finally, instead of rushing at once to see if her mistress was safe, she went into the kitchen, still apparently under the obsession of the pulleys. She informed Adams that they were all right, as if it mattered to any human being; thence she went into the spare bedroom, where she must have seen that robbery had been committed, since an open box lay in the middle of the floor. She gave no alarm however, and it was only when Adams called out: "Where is your mistress?" that she finally went into the room of the murder. It must be admitted that this seems strange conduct, and only explicable, if it can be said to be explicable, by great want of intelligence and grasp of the situation.

[There is another far more sinister explanation for Helen Lambie's seemingly confused and disoriented testimony, as Doyle subsequently learned. In 1927, the year Oscar Slater was finally pardoned, journalist William Park, who had dedicated himself to finding out the facts about the Slater case, published a book titled *The Truth About Oscar Slater*. In it Park made the following startling points:

Only two days after the murder, the Glasgow police sent one of their best officers, King's Medallist Lt. John T. Trench, bodyguard to the royal family upon their visits to Scotland, to interview Margaret Birrell, a niece of the murdered woman, for a precognition [statement]. In part Miss Birrell's statement reads:

"My mother was a sister of the deceased. Miss Gilchrist was not on good terms with her relations. Few, if any, visited her. . . . I can never forget the night of the murder. Miss Gilchrist's servant, Nellie Lambie, came to my door about 7.15. She was excited. She pulled the bell violently. On the door being opened she rushed into the house and exclaimed: 'Oh, Miss Birrell, Miss Gilchrist has been murdered, she is laying dead in the dining-room, and oh Miss Birrell, I saw the man who did it!' I replied: 'My God, Nellie, this is awful. Who was it? Do you know him?' Nellie replied: 'Oh, Miss Birrell, I think it was Dr. Charteris. I am sure it was Dr. Charteris.' I said to her: 'My God, Nellie, don't say that. . . . Unless you are very sure of it, Nellie, don't say that.' She again repeated to me that she was sure it was Francis Charteris."

Now Dr. Francis Charteris was a young medical man in his early thirties. Only remotely connected with Marion Gilchrist, he was questioned about his whereabouts by the Glasgow police on the information provided by Detective Trench.

This whole line of inquiry was kept secret from the public at the time of Slater's trial, and his own defense attorney was never made aware that there had ever been another suspect.

When questioned by the police, Dr. Charteris deposed that he only found himself at the crime scene, after the fact, because the police had asked him to tell his mother of Marion Gilchrist's death. For some reason, which he did not explain, he stopped by the location of the murder to look in. Dr. Charteris deposed that there he found the police questioning Helen Lambie, who is supposed to have said, in effect, that the murderer looked similar to or "like" Dr. Charteris.

In any case, it was not long before the police dropped all inquiries about Francis Charteris, whose father had been professor of medicine at the University of Glasgow and whose two brothers distinguished themselves in the law and the military.

As for John Trench's work on the case, it ruined his police career: He would not back off from his story that Helen Lambie, some fifteen minutes after the murder, had rushed to Margaret Birrell and told her that it was Francis Charteris who had walked past her in the hall only moments after Miss Gilchrist has been killed. It remained for Conan Doyle to write Trench's epitaph:

"[But] most outstanding of all was the heroic detective, Trench, who ruined his career in the defence of right. Trench is more like one of Charles Reade's wonderful heroes, than a man of this workaday world. . . . He rose to distinction in the Glasgow police force, and gained such a reputation that he was borrowed by other towns when difficult cases arose. From the first, he seems to have been on the right line in the Slater case, but was unable to influence his superiors. His conscience was clearly not at rest and, finally, he felt constrained to risk his whole career and his pension in an effort to get his views before the public. In order to do so, it would be necessary for him to reveal matters learned by him in the course of his professional duties, and this was against the local laws of the police force, however much it might be in the interest of public justice. Knowing this, Trench asked for an indemnity from the Scottish Office against the probable anger of his superiors, and it was with the assurance that he had obtained this indemnity that he bore witness. The sequel, however, shocking to relate, was that he was immediately afterwards turned out of the force and deprived of his pension on the very charge which he had foreseen and, as he thought, provided against.

"There was worse to come, however, and the Trench case provides a scandal only second to that out of which it arose. Trench and Cook, the lawyer who had acted with him, were presently arrested upon a criminal charge, which was so absurd that the judge at once laughed it out of court. Cook, however, took the matter greatly to heart, and it is said to have contributed to his death a short time afterwards. Trench did some good service in connection with the War, and, before the outbreak, was instrumental in securing the arrest of Dr. Karl Graves, a most important foreign spy, who had designs on the Forth Bridge. He was, however, a stricken man from the time of his disgrace, and he sank into a decline from which he never rallied."]

On Tuesday, December 22nd, the morning after the murder, the Glasgow police circulated a description of the murderer, founded upon the joint impressions of Adams and of Lambie. It ran thus:

"A man between 25 and 30 years of age, five foot eight or nine inches in height, slim build, dark hair, clean-shaven, dressed in light grey overcoat and dark cloth cap."

Four days later, however, upon Christmas Day, the police found themselves in a position to give a more detailed description:

"The man wanted is about 28 or 30 years of age, tall and thin, with his face shaved clear of all hair, while a distinctive feature is that his nose is slightly turned to one side. The witness thinks the twist is to the right side. He wore one of the popular tweed hats known as Donegal hats, and a fawn coloured overcoat which might have been a waterproof, also dark trousers and brown boots."

The material from which these further points were gathered, came from a young girl of fifteen, in humble life, named Mary Barrowman. According to this new evidence, the witness was passing the scene of the murder shortly after seven o'clock upon the fatal night. She saw a man run hurriedly down the steps, and he passed her under a lamp-post. The incandescent light shone clearly upon him. He ran on, knocking against the witness in his haste, and disappeared round a corner. On hearing later of the murder, she connected this incident with it. Her general recollections of the man were as given in the description, and the grey coat and cloth cap of the first two witnesses were given up in favour of the fawn coat and round Donegal hat of the young girl. Since she had seen no peculiarity in his walk, and they had seen none in his nose, there is really nothing the same in the two descriptions save the "clean-shaven," the "slim build" and the approximate age.

It was on the evening of Christmas Day that the police came at last upon a definite clue. It was brought to their notice that a German Jew of the assumed name of Oscar Slater had been endeavouring to dispose of the pawn ticket of a crescent diamond brooch of about the same value as the missing one. Also, that in a general way, he bore a resemblance to the published description. Still more hopeful did this clue appear when, upon raiding the lodgings in which this man and his mistress lived it was found that they had left Glasgow that very night by the nine o'clock train, with tickets (over this point there was some clash of evidence) either for Liverpool or London.

Three days later, the Glasgow police learned that the couple had actually sailed upon December 26th upon the Lusitania for New York under the name of Mr. and Mrs. Otto Sando. It must be admitted that in all these proceedings the Glasgow police showed considerable deliberation. The original information had been given at the Central Police Office shortly after six o'clock, and a detective was actually making enquiries at Slater's flat at seven-thirty, yet no watch was kept upon his movements, and he was allowed to leave between eight and nine, untraced and unquestioned. Even stranger was the Liverpool departure. He was known to have got away in the southbound train upon the Friday evening. A great liner sails from Liverpool upon the Saturday. One would have imagined that early on the Saturday morning steps would have been taken to block his method of escape. However, as a fact, it was not done, and as it proved it is as well for the cause of justice, since it had the effect that two judicial processes were needed, an American and a Scottish, which enables an interesting comparison to be made between the evidence of the principal witnesses.

Oscar Slater was at once arrested upon arriving at New York, and his seven trunks of baggage were impounded and sealed. On the face of it there was a good case against him, for he had undoubtedly pawned a diamond brooch, and he had subsequently fled under a false name for America. The Glasgow police had reason to think that they had got their man. Two officers, accompanied by the witnesses to identity—Adams, Lambie and Barrowman—set off at once to carry through the extradition proceedings and bring the suspect back to be tried for his offence. In the New York Court they first set eyes upon the prisoner, and each of them, in terms which will be afterwards described, expressed the opinion that he was at any rate exceedingly like the person they had seen in Glasgow. Their actual identification of him was vitiated by the fact that Adams and Barrowman had been shown his photographs before attending the Court, and also that he was led past them, an obvious prisoner, whilst they were waiting in the corridor. Still, however much one may discount the actual identification, it cannot be denied that each witness saw a close resemblance between the man before them and the man whom they had seen in Glasgow. So far at every stage the case against the accused was becoming more menacing. Any doubt as to extradition was speedily set at rest by the prisoner's announcement that he was prepared, without compulsion, to return to Scotland and to stand his trial. One may well refuse to give him any excessive credit for this surrender, since he may have been persuaded that things were going against him, but still the fact remains (and it was never, so far as I can trace, mentioned at his subsequent trial) that he gave himself up of his own free will to justice. On February 21st Oscar Slater was back in Glasgow once more, and on May 3rd his trial took place at the High Court in Edinburgh.

But already the very bottom of the case had dropped out. The starting link of what had seemed an imposing chain had suddenly broken. It will be remembered that the original suspicion of Slater was founded upon the fact that he had pawned a crescent diamond brooch. The ticket was found upon him, and the brooch recovered. It was not the one which was missing from the room of the murdered woman, and it had belonged for years to Slater, who had repeatedly pawned it before. This was shown beyond all cavil or dispute. The case of the police might well seem desperate after this, since if Slater were indeed guilty, it would mean that by pure chance they had pursued the right man. The coincidence involved in such a supposition would seem to pass the limits of all probability.

Apart from this crushing fact, several of the other points of the prosecution had already shown themselves to be worthless. It had seemed at first that Slater's departure had been sudden and unpremeditated—the flight of a guilty man. It was quickly proved that this was not so. In the Bohemian clubs which he frequented—he was by profession a peddling jeweller and a man of disreputable, though not criminal habits—it had for weeks before the date of the crime been known that he purported to go to some business associates in America. A correspondence, which was produced, showed the arrangements which had been made, long before the crime, for his emigration, though it should be added that the actual determination of the date and taking of the ticket were subsequent to the tragedy.

This hurrying-up of the departure certainly deserves close scrutiny. According to the evidence of his mistress and of the servant, Slater had received two letters upon the morning of December 21st. Neither of these were produced at the trial. One was said to be from a Mr. Rogers, a friend of Slater's in London, telling him that Slater's wife was bothering him for money. The second was said to be from one De Voto, a former partner of Slater's asking him to join him in San Francisco. Even if the letters had been destroyed, one would imagine that these statements as to the letters could be disproved or corroborated by either the Crown or the defence. They are of considerable importance, as giving the alleged reasons why Slater hurried up a departure which had been previously announced as for January. I cannot find, however, that in the actual trial anything definite was ascertained upon the matter.

Another point had already been scored against the prosecution in that the seven trunks which contained the whole effects of the prisoner, yielded nothing of real importance. There were a felt hat and two cloth ones, but none which correspond with the Donegal of the original description. A light-coloured waterproof coat was among the outfit. If the weapon with which the deed was done was carried off in the pocket of the assassin's over-coat—and it is difficult to say how else he could have carried it, then the pocket must, one would suppose, be crusted with blood, since the crime was a most sanguinary one. No such marks were discovered, nor were the police fortunate as to the weapon. It is true that a hammer was found in the trunk, but it was clearly shown to have been purchased in one of those cheap half-crown sets of tools which are tied upon a card, was an extremely light and fragile instrument, and utterly incapable in the eyes of commonsense of inflicting those terrific injuries which had shattered the old lady's skull. It is said by the prosecution to bear some marks of having been scraped or cleaned, but this was vigorously denied by the defence, and the police do not appear to have pushed the matter to the obvious test of removing the metal work, when they must, had this been indeed the weapon, have certainly found some soakage of blood into the wood under the edges of the iron cheeks or head. But a glance at a facsimile of this puny weapon would convince an impartial person that any task beyond fixing a tin-tack, or cracking a small bit of coal, would be above its strength. It may fairly be said that before the trial had begun, the three important points of the pawned jewel, the supposed flight, and the evidence from clothing and weapon had each either broken down completely, or become exceedingly attenuated.

Let us see now what there was upon the other side. The evidence for the prosecution really resolved itself into two sets of witnesses for identification. The first set were those who had actually seen the murderer, and included Adams, Helen Lambie, and the girl Barrowman. The second set consisted of twelve people who had, at various dates, seen a man frequenting the street in which Miss Gilchrist lived, and loitering in a suspicious manner before the house. All of these, some with confidence, but most of them with reserve, were prepared to identify the prisoner with this unknown man. What the police never could produce, however, was the essential thing, and that was the least connecting link between Slater and Miss Gilchrist, or any explanation how a foreigner in Glasgow could even know of the existence, to say nothing of the wealth, of a retired old lady, who had few acquaintances and seldom left her guarded flat.

It is notorious that nothing is more tricky than evidence of identification. In the Beck case there were, if I remember right, some ten witnesses who had seen the real criminal under normal circumstances, and yet they were all prepared to swear to the wrong man. [The witnesses in the Beck case had at least some excuse for their mistaken identifications. They had been defrauded years before, and the police themselves supposed they were presenting for identification the same John Smith who was up to his old tricks. Beck's protestations that he had been out of the country at the time of the earlier deeds were to no effect against powerful prejudice.] In the case of Oscar Slater, the first three witnesses saw their man under conditions of excitement, while the second group saw the loiterer in the street under various lights, and in a fashion which was always more or less casual. It is right, therefore, that in assigning its due weight to this evidence, one should examine it with some care. We shall first take the three people who actually saw the murderer.

There seems to have been some discrepancy between them from the first, since, as has already been pointed out, the description published from the data of Adams and Lambie, was modified after Barrowman had given her information. Adams and Lambie said:

"A man between twenty-five and thirty years of age, 5 feet 8 or 9 inches in height, slim build, dark hair, clean shaven, dressed in light grey overcoat and dark cloth cap."

After collaboration with Barrowman the description became:

"Twenty-eight or thirty years of age, tall and thin, clean shaven, his nose slightly turned to one side. Wore one of the popular round tweed hats known as Donegal hats, and a fawn-coloured overcoat which might have been a waterproof, also dark trousers and brown boots."

Apart from the additions in the second description there are, it will be observed, two actual discrepancies in the shape of the hat and the colour of the coat.

As to how far either of these descriptions tallies with Slater, it may be stated here that the accused was thirty-seven years of age, that he was above the medium height, that his nose was not twisted, but was depressed at the end, as if it had at some time been broken, and finally that eight witnesses were called upon to prove that, on the date of the murder, the accused wore a short but noticeable moustache.

I have before me a verbatim stenographic report of the proceedings in New York and also in Edinburgh, furnished by the kindness of Shaughnessy & Co., solicitors, of Glasgow, who are still contending for the interests of their unfortunate client. I will here compare the terms of the identification in the two Courts:

Helen Lambie, New York, January 26th, 1909.

Q. "Do you see the man here you saw there?"

A. "One is very suspicious, if anything."

Q. "Describe him."

A. "The clothes he had on that night he hasn't got on to-day—but his face I could not tell. I never saw his face."

(Having described a peculiarity of walk, she was asked):

Q. "Is that man in the room?"

A. "Yes, he is, sir."

Q. "Point him out."

A. "I would not like to say—"

(After some pressure and argument she pointed to Slater, who had been led past her in the corridor between two officers, when both she and Barrowman had exclaimed: "That is the man," or "I could nearly swear that is the man.")

Q. "Didn't you say you did not see the man's face?"

A. "Neither I did. I saw the walk."

The reader must bear in mind that Lambie's only chance of seeing the man's walk was in the four steps or so down the passage. It was never at any time shown that there was any marked peculiarity about Slater's walk.

Now take Helen Lambie's identification in Edinburgh, May 9th, 1909.

Q. "How did you identify him in America?"

A. "By his walk and height, his dark hair and the side of his face."

Q. "You were not quite sure of him at first in America?"

A. "Yes, I was quite sure."

Q. "Why did you say you were only suspicious?"

A. "It was a mistake."

Q. "What did you mean in America by saying that you never saw his face if, in point of fact, you did see it so as to help you to recognize it? What did you mean?"

A. "Nothing."

On further cross-examination she declared that when she said that she had never seen the man's face she meant that she had never seen the "broad of it" but had seen it sideways.

Here it will be observed that Helen Lambie's evidence had greatly stiffened during the three months between the New York and the Edinburgh proceedings. In so aggressively positive a frame of mind was she on the later occasion, that, on being shown Slater's overcoat and asked if it resembled the murderer's, she answered twice over: "That is the coat," although it had not yet been unrolled, and though it was not light grey, which was the colour in her own original description. It should not be forgotten in dealing with the evidence of Lambie and Adams that they are utterly disagreed as to so easily fixed a thing as their own proceedings after the hall door was opened, Adams swearing that Lambie walked to nearly the end of the hall, and Lambie that she remained upon the doormat. Without deciding which was right, it is clear that the incident must shake one's confidence in one or other of them as a witness.

In the case of Adams the evidence was given with moderation, and was substantially the same in America and in Scotland.

"I couldn't say positively. This man (indicating Slater) is not at all unlike him."

Q. "Did you notice a crooked nose?"

A. "No."

Q. "Anything remarkable about his walk?"

A. "No."

Q. "You don't swear this is the man you saw."

A. "No, sir. He resembles the man, that is all that I can say."

In reply to the same general questions in Edinburgh, he said:

"I would not like to swear he is the man. I am a little near-sighted. He resembles the man closely."

Barrowman, the girl of fifteen, had met the man presumed to be the murderer in the street, and taken one passing glance at him under a gas lamp on a wet December's night—difficult circumstances for an identification. She used these words in New York:

"That man here is something like him," which she afterwards amended to "very like him." She admitted that a picture of the man she was expected to identify had been shown to her before she came into the Court. Her one point by which she claimed to recognise the man was the crooked nose. This crooked nose was not much more apparent to others than the peculiarity of walk which so greatly impressed Helen Lambie that, after seeing half a dozen steps of it, she could identify it with confidence. In Edinburgh Barrowman, like Lambie, was very much more certain than in New York. The further they got from the event, the easier apparently did recognition become. "Yes, that is the man who knocked against me that night," she said. It is remarkable that

239

both these females, Lambie and Barrowman, swore that though they were thrown together in this journey out to New York, and actually shared the same cabin, they never once talked of the object of their mission or compared notes as to the man they were about to identify. For girls of the respective ages of fifteen and twenty-one this certainly furnishes a unique example of self-restraint.

These, then, are the three identifications by the only people who saw the murderer. Had the diamond brooch clue been authentic, and these identifications come upon the top of it, they would undoubtedly have been strongly corroborative. But when the brooch has been shown to be a complete mistake, I really do not understand how anyone could accept such half-hearted recognitions as being enough to establish the identity and guilt of the prisoner.

There remains the so-called identification by twelve witnesses who had seen a man loitering in the street during the weeks before the crime had been committed. I have said a "so-called" identification, for the proceedings were farcical as a real test of recognition. The witnesses had seen portraits of the accused. They were well aware that he was a foreigner, and then they were asked to pick out his swarthy Jewish physiognomy from among nine Glasgow policemen to two railway officials. Naturally they did it without hesitation, since this man was more like the dark individual whom they had seen and described than the others could be.

Read their own descriptions, however, of the man they had seen, with the details of his clothing, and they will be found in many respects to differ from each other on one hand, and in many from Slater on the other. Here is a synopsis of their impressions:

Mrs. McHaffie.—"Dark. Moustached, light overcoat, not waterproof, check trousers, spats. Black bowler hat. Nose normal."

Miss M. McHaffie.—"Seen at same time and same description. Was only prepared at first to say there was some resemblance, but 'had been thinking it over, and concluded that he was the man.'"

Miss A. M. McHaffie.—"Same as before. Had heard the man speak and noticed nothing in his accent." (Prisoner has a strong German accent.)

Madge McHaffie (belongs to the same family).—"Dark, moustached, nose normal. Check trousers, fawn overcoat and spats. Black bowler hat. 'The prisoner was fairly like the man.' "

In connection with the identification of these four witnesses it is to be observed that neither check trousers, nor spats were found in the prisoner's luggage. As the murderer was described as being dressed in dark trousers, there was no possible reason why these clothes, if Slater owned them, should have been destroyed.

Constable Brien.—"Claimed to know the prisoner by sight. Says he was the man he saw loitering. Light coat and a hat. It was a week before the crime, and he was loitering eighty yards from the scene of it. He picked him out among five constables as the man he had seen."

Constable Walker.—"Had seen the loiterer across the street, never nearer, and after dark in December. Thought at first he was someone else whom he knew. Had heard that the man he had to identify was of foreign appearance. Picked him out from a number of detectives. The man seen had a moustache."

Euphemia Cunningham.—"Very dark, sallow, heavy featured. Clean shaven. Nose normal. Dark tweed coat. Green cap with peak."

W. Campbell.—"Had been with the previous witness. Corroborated. 'There was a general resemblance between the prisoner and the man, but he could not positively identify him.' "

Alex Gillies.—"Sallow, dark haired and clean shaven. Fawn coat. Cap. 'The prisoner resembled him, but witness could not say he was the same man.' "

R. B. Bryson.—"Black coat and vest. Black bowler hat. No overcoat. Black moustache with droop. Sallow, foreign. (This witness had seen the man the night before the murder. He appeared to be looking up at Miss Gilchrist's windows.)"

A. Nairn.—"Broad shoulders, long neck. Dark hair. Motor cap. Light overcoat to knees. Never saw the man's face. 'Oh! I will not swear in fact, but I am certain he is the man I saw—but I will not swear.' "

Mrs. Liddell.—"Peculiar nose. Clear complexion, not sallow. Dark, clean shaven, brown tweed cap. Brown tweed coat with hemmed edge. Delicate man 'rather drawn together.' She believed that prisoner was the man. Saw him in the street immediately before the murder."

These are the twelve witnesses as to the identity of the mysterious stranger. In the first place there is no evidence whatever that this lounger in the street had really anything to do with the murder. It is just as probable that he had some vulgar amour, and was waiting for his girl to run out to him. What could a man who was planning murder hope to gain by standing nights beforehand eighty and a hundred yards away from the place in the darkness? But supposing that we waive this point and examine the plain question as to whether Slater was the same man as the loiterer, we find ourselves faced by a mass of difficulties and contradictions. Two of the most precise witnesses were Nairn and Bryson who saw the stranger upon the Sunday night preceding the murder. Upon that night Slater had an unshaken alibi, vouched for not only by the girl, Antoine, with whom he lived, and their servant, Schmalz, but by an acquaintance, Samuel Reid, who had been with him from six to ten-thirty. This positive evidence, which was quite unshaken in cross examination, must completely destroy the surmises of the stranger and Slater. Then come the four witnesses of the McHaffie family who are all strong upon check trousers and spats, articles of dress which were never traced to the prisoner. Finally, apart from the discrepancies about the moustache, there is a mixture of bowler hats, green caps, brown caps, and motor caps which leave a most confused and indefinite impression in the mind. Evidence of this kind might be of some value if supplementary to some strong ascertained fact, but to attempt to build upon such an identification alone is to construct the whole case upon shifting sand.

The reader has already a grasp of the facts, but some fresh details came out at the trial which may be enumerated here. They have to be lightly touched upon within the limits of such an argument as this, but those who desire a fuller summary will find it in an account of the trial published by Hodge of Edinburgh, and ably edited by William Roughead, W.S. [Roughead nicely summarized his work on the Oscar Slater case in his 1951 book *Classic Crimes*, published by Cassell Publishers of London.] On this book and on the verbatim precognitions and shorthand account of the American proceedings, I base my own examination of case. First, as to Slater's movements upon the day of the crime. He began the day, according to the account of himself and the women, by the receipt of the two letters already referred to, which caused him to hasten his journey to America. The whole day seems to have been occupied by preparations for his impending departure. He gave his servant Schmalz notice as from next Saturday. Before five (as was shown by the postmark upon the envelope), he wrote to a post office in London, where he had some money on deposit. At 6.12 a telegram was sent in his name and presumably by him from the Central Station to Dent, London, for his watch, which was being repaired.

According to the evidence of two witnesses he was seen in a billiard room at 6.20. The murder, it will be remembered, was done at seven. He remained about ten minutes in the billiard room, and left some time between 6.30 and 6.40. Rathman, one of these witnesses, deposed that he had at the time a moustache about a quarter of an inch long, which was so noticeable that no one could take him for a clean-shaven man. Antoine, his mistress, and Schmalz, the servant, both deposed that Slater dined at home at 7 o'clock. The evidence of the girl is no doubt suspect, but there was no possible reason why the dismissed servant Schmalz should perjure herself for the sake of her ex-employer. The distance between Slater's flat and that of Miss Gilchrist is about a quarter of a mile. From the billiard room to Slater's flat is about a mile. He had to go for the hammer and bring it back, unless he had it jutting out of his pocket all day. But unless the evidence of the two women is entirely set aside, enough has been said to show that there was no time for the commission by him of such a crime and the hiding of the traces which it would leave behind it. At 9.45 that night, Slater was engaged in his usual occupation of trying to raise the wind at some small gambling club. The club-master saw no discomposure about his dress (which was the same as, according to the Crown, he had done this bloody crime in), and swore that he was then wearing a short moustache "like stubble," thus corroborating Rathman. It will be remembered that Lambie and Barrowman both swore that the murderer was clean shaven.

On December 24th, three days after the murder, Slater was shown at Cook's Office, bargaining for a berth in the "Lusitania" for his so-called wife and himself. He made no secret that he was going by that ship, but gave his real name and address and declared finally that he would take his berth in Liverpool, which he did. Among other confidants as to the ship was a barber, the last person one would think to whom secrets would be confided. Certainly, if this were a flight, it is hard to say what an open departure would be. In Liverpool he took his passage under the assumed name of Otto Sando. This he did, according to his own account, because he had reason to fear pursuit from his real wife, and wished to cover his traces. This may or may not be the truth, but it is undoubtedly the fact that Slater, who was a disreputable, rolling-stone of a man, had already assumed several aliases in the course of his career. It is to be noted that there was nothing at all secret about his departure from Glasgow, and that he carried off all his luggage with him in a perfectly open manner.

The reader is now in possession of the main facts, save those which are either unessential, or redundant. It will be observed that save for the identifications, the value of which can be estimated, there is really no single point of connection between the crime and the alleged criminal. It may be argued that the existence of the hammer is such a point; but what household in the land is devoid of a hammer? It is to be remembered that if Slater committed the murder with this hammer, he must have taken it with him in order to commit the crime, since it could be no use to him in forcing an entrance. But what man in his senses, planning a deliberate murder, would take with him a weapon which was light, frail, and so long that it must project from any pocket? The nearest lump of stone upon the road would serve his purpose better than that. Again, it must in its blood-soaked condition have been in his pocket when he came away from the crime. The Crown never attempted to prove either blood-stains in a pocket, or the fact that any clothes had been burned. If Slater destroyed clothes, he would naturally have destroyed the hammer, too. Even one of the two medical witnesses of the prosecution was driven to say that he should not have expected such a weapon to cause such wounds.

It may well be that in this summary of the evidence, I may seem to have stated the case entirely from the point of view of the defence. In reply, I would only ask the reader to take the trouble to read the extended evidence. ("Trial of Oscar Slater" Hodge & Co., Edinburgh.) If he will do so, he will realise that without a conscious mental effort towards special pleading, there is no other way in which the story can be told. The facts are on one side. The conjectures, the unsatisfactory identifications, the damaging flaws, and the very strong prejudices upon the other.

Now for the trial itself. The case was opened for the Crown by the Lord-Advocate, in a speech which faithfully represented the excited feeling of the time. It was vigorous to the point of being passionate, and its effect upon the jury was reflected in their ultimate verdict. The Lord-Advocate spoke, as I understand, without notes, a procedure which may well add to eloquence while subtracting from accuracy. It is to this fact that one must attribute a most fatal mis-statement which could not fail, coming under such circumstances from so high an authority, to make a deep impression upon his hearers. For some reason, this mis-statement does not appear to have been corrected at the moment by either the Judge or the defending counsel. It was the one really damaging allegation—so damaging that had I myself been upon the jury and believed it to be true, I should have recorded my verdict against the prisoner, and yet this one fatal point had no substance at all in fact. In this incident alone, there seems to me to lie good ground for a revision of the sentence, or a reference of the facts to some Court or Committee of Appeal. Here is the extract from the Lord-Advocate's speech to which I allude:

"At this time he had given his name to Cook's people in Glasgow as Oscar Slater. On December 25th, the day he was to go back to Cook's Office—his name and his description and all the rest of it appear in the Glasgow papers, and he sees that the last thing in the world that he ought to do, if he studies his own safety, is to go back to Cook's Office as Oscar Slater. He accordingly proceeds to pack up all his goods and effects upon the 25th. So far as we know, he never leaves the house from the time he sees the paper, until a little after six o'clock, when he goes down to the Central Station."

Here the allegation is clearly made and it is repeated later that Oscar Slater's name was in the paper, and that, subsequently to that, he fled. Such a flight would clearly be an admission of guilt. The point is of enormous, even vital importance. And yet on examination of the dates, it will be found that there is absolutely no foundation for it. It was not until the evening of the 25th that even the police heard of the existence of Slater, and it was nearly a week later that his name appeared in the papers, he being already far out upon the Atlantic. What did appear upon the 25th was the description of the murderer, already quoted: "with his face shaved clean of all hair," &c., Slater at that time having a marked moustache. Why should he take such a description to himself, or why should he forbear to carry out a journey which he had already prepared for? The point goes for absolutely nothing when examined, and yet if the minds of the jury were at all befogged as to the dates, the definite assertion of the Lord-Advocate, twice repeated, that Slater's name had been published before his flight, was bound to have a most grave and prejudiced effect.

Some of the Lord-Advocate's other statements are certainly surprising. Thus he says: "The prisoner is hopelessly unable to produce a single witness who says that he was anywhere else than at the scene of the murder that night." Let us test this assertion. Here is the evidence of Schmalz, the servant, verbatim. I may repeat that this woman was under no known obligations to Slater and had just received notice from him. The evidence of the mistress that Slater dined in the flat at seven on the night of the murder I pass, but I do not understand why Schmalz's positive corroboration should be treated by the Lord-Advocate as non-existent. The prisoner might well be "hopeless" if his witnesses were to be treated so. Could anything be more positive than this?

Q. "Did he usually come home to dinner?"

A. "Yes, always. Seven o'clock was the usual hour."

Q. "Was it sometimes nearly eight?"

A. "It was my fault. Mr. Slater was in."

Q. "But owing to your fault was it about eight before it was served?"

A. "No. Mr. Slater was in after seven, and was waiting for dinner."

This seems very definite. The murder was committed about seven. The murderer may have regained the street about ten minutes or quarter past seven. It was some distance to Slater's flat. If he had done the murder he could hardly have reached it before half-past seven at the earliest. Yet Schmalz says he was in at seven, and so does Antoine. The evidence of the woman may be good or bad, but it is difficult to understand how anyone could state that the prisoner was "hopelessly unable to produce, etc." What evidence could he give, save that of everyone who lived with him?

For the rest, the Lord-Advocate had an easy task in showing that Slater was a worthless fellow, that he lived with and possibly on a woman of easy virtue, that he had several times changed his name, and that generally he was an unsatisfactory Bohemian. No actual criminal record was shown against him. Early in his speech, the Lord-Advocate remarked that he would show later how Slater may have come to know that Miss Gilchrist owned the jewels. No further reference appears to have been made to the matter, and his promise was therefore never fulfilled, though it is clearly of the utmost importance. Later, he stated that from the appearance of the wounds, they must have been done by a small hammer. There is no "must" in the matter, for it is clear that many other weapons, a burglar's jemmy, for example, would have produced the same effect. He then makes the good point that the prisoner dealt in precious stones, and could therefore dispose of the proceeds of such a robbery. The criminal, he added, was clearly someone who had no acquaintance with the inside of the house, and did not know where the jewels were kept. "That answers to the prisoner." It also, of course, answers to practically every man in Scotland. The Lord-Advocate then gave a summary of the evidence as to the man seen by various witnesses in the street. "Gentlemen, if that was the prisoner, how do you account for his presence there?" Of course, the whole point lies in the italicised phrase [sic]. There was, it must be admitted, a consensus of opinion among the witnesses that the prisoner was the man. But what was it compared to the consensus of opinion which wrongfully condemned Beck to penal servitude? The counsel laid considerable stress upon the fact that Mrs. Liddell (one of the Adams family) had seen a man only a few minutes before the murder, loitering in the street, and identified him as Slater. The dress of the man seen in the street was very different from that given as the murderer's. He had a heavy tweed mixture coat of a brownish hue, and a brown peaked cap. The original identification by Mrs. Liddell was conveyed in the words: "One, slightly," when she was asked if any of a group at the police station resembled the man she had seen. Afterwards, like every other female witness, she became more positive. She declared that she had the clearest recollection of the man's face, and yet refused to commit herself as to whether he was shaven or moustached.

We have then the recognitions of Lambie, Adams and Barrowman, with their limitations and developments, which have been already discussed. Then comes the question of the so-called "flight" and the change of name upon the steamer. Had the prisoner been a man who had never before changed his name, this incident would be more striking. But the short glimpse we obtain of his previous life show several changes of name, and it has not been suggested that each of them was the consequence of a crime. He seems to have been in debt in Glasgow and he also appears to have had reasons for getting away from the pursuit of an ill-used wife. The Lord-Advocate said that the change of name "could not be explained consistently with innocence." That may be true enough, but the change can surely be explained on some cause less grave than murder. Finally, after showing very truly that Slater was a great liar and that not a word he said need be believed unless there were corroboration, the Lord-Advocate wound up with the words: "My submission to you is that this guilt has been brought fairly home to him, that no shadow of doubt exists, that there is no reasonable doubt that he was the perpetrator of this foul murder." The verdict showed that the jury, under the spell of the Lord-Advocate's eloquence, shared this view, but, viewing it in colder blood, it is difficult to see upon what grounds he made so confident an assertion.

Mr. M'Clure, who conducted the defence, spoke truly when, in opening his speech, he declared that "he had to fight a most unfair fight against public prejudice, roused with a fury I do not remember to have seen in any other case." Still he fought this fight bravely and with scrupulous moderation. His appeals were all to reason and never to emotion. He showed how clearly the prisoner had expressed his intention of going to America, weeks before the murder, and how every preparation had been made. On the day after the murder he had told witnesses that he was going to America and had discussed the advantages of various lines, finally telling one of them the particular boat in which he did eventually travel, curious proceedings for a fugitive from justice. Mr. M'Clure described the movements of the prisoner on the night of the murder, after the crime had been committed, showing that he was wearing the very clothes in which the theory of the prosecution made him do the deed, as if such a deed could be done without leaving its traces. He showed incidentally (it is a small point, but a human one) that one of the last actions of Slater in Glasgow was to take great trouble to get an English five-pound note in order to send it as a Christmas present to his parents in Germany. A man who could do this was not all bad. Finally, Mr. M'Clure exposed very clearly the many discrepancies as to identification and warned the jury solemnly as to the dangers which have been so often proved to lurk in this class of evidence. Altogether, it was a broad, comprehensive reply, though where so many points were involved, it is natural that some few may have been overlooked. One does not, for example, find the counsel as insistent as one might expect upon such points as, the failure of the Crown to show how Slater could have known anything at all about the existence of Miss Gilchrist and her jewels, how he got into the flat, and what became of the brooch which, according to their theory, he had carried off. It is ungracious to suggest any additions to so earnest a defence, and no doubt one who is dependent upon printed accounts of the matter may miss points which were actually made, but not placed upon record.

Only on one point must Mr. M'Clure's judgment be questioned, and that is on the most difficult one, which a criminal counsel has ever to decide. He did not place his man in the box. This should very properly be taken as a sign of weakness. I have no means of saying what considerations led Mr. M'Clure to this determination. It certainly told against his client. In the masterly memorial for reprieve drawn up by Slater's solicitor, the late Mr. Spiers, it is stated with the full inner knowledge which that solicitor had, that Slater was all along anxious to give evidence on his own behalf. "He was advised by his counsel not to do so, but not from any knowledge of guilt. He had undergone the strain of a four days' trial. He speaks rather broken English, although quite intelligible—with a foreign accent, and he had been in custody since January." It must be admitted that these reasons are very unconvincing. It is much more probable that the counsel decided that the purely negative evidence which his client could give upon the crime would be dearly paid for by the long recital of sordid amours and blackguard experiences which would be drawn from him on cross-examination and have the most damning effect upon the minds of a respectable Edinburgh jury. And yet, perhaps, counsel did not sufficiently consider the prejudice which is excited—and rightly excited—against the prisoner who shuns the box. Some of this prejudice might have been removed if it had been made more clear that Slater had volunteered to come over and stand his trial of his own free will, without waiting for the verdict of the extradition proceedings.

There remains the summing up of Lord Guthrie. His Lordship threw out the surmise that the assassin may well have gone to the flat without any intention of murder. This is certainly possible, but in the highest degree improbable. He commented with great severity upon Slater's general character. In his summing-up of the case, he recapitulated the familiar facts in an impartial fashion, concluding with the words, "I suppose that you all think that the prisoner possibly is the murderer. You may very likely all think that he probably is the murderer. That, however, will not entitle you to convict him. The Crown have undertaken to prove that he is the murderer. That is the question you have to consider. If you think there is no reasonable doubt about it, you will convict him; if you think there is, you will acquit him."

In an hour and ten minutes the jury had made up their mind. By a majority they found the prisoner guilty. Out of fifteen, nine, as was afterwards shown, were for guilty, five for non-proven, and one for not guilty. By English law, a new trial would have been needed, ending, possibly, as in the Gardiner case, in the complete acquittal of the prisoner. By Scotch law the majority verdict held good.

"I know nothing about the affair, absolutely nothing," cried the prisoner in a frenzy of despair. "I never heard the name. I know nothing about the affair. I do not know how I could be connected with the affair. I know nothing about it. I came from America on my own account. I can say no more."

Sentence of death was then passed.

The verdict was, it is said, a complete surprise to most of those in the Court, and certainly is surprising when examined after the event. I do not see how any reasonable man can carefully weigh the evidence and not admit that when the unfortunate prisoner cried, "I know nothing about it," he was possibly, and even probably, speaking the literal truth. Consider the monstrous coincidence which is involved in his guilt, the coincidence that the police owing to their mistake over the brooch, by pure chance started out in pursuit of the right man. Which is *a priori* the more probable: That such an unheard-of million-to-one coincidence should have occurred, or, that the police, having committed themselves to the theory that he was the murderer, refused to admit that they were wrong when the bottom fell out of the original case, and persevered in the hope that vague identifications of a queer-looking foreigner would justify their original action? Outside these identifications, I must repeat once again there is nothing to couple Slater with the murder, or to show that he ever knew, or could have known that such a person as Miss Gilchrist existed.

The admirable memorial for a reprieve drawn up by the solicitors for the defence, and reproduced at the end of this pamphlet, was signed by 20,000 members of the public, and had the effect of changing the death sentence to one of penal servitude for life. The sentence was passed on May 6th. For twenty days the man was left in doubt, and the written reprieve only arrived on May 26th within twenty-four hours of the time for the execution. On July 8th Slater was conveyed to the Peterhead Convict prison. There he has now been for three years, and there he still remains.

I cannot help in my own mind comparing the case of Oscar Slater with another, which I had occasion to examine—that of George Edalji. I must admit that they are not of the same class. George Edalji was a youth of exemplary character. Oscar Slater was a blackguard. George Edalji was physically incapable of the crime for which he suffered three years imprisonment (years for which he has not received, after his innocence was established, one shilling of compensation from the nation). Oscar Slater might conceivably have committed the murder, but the balance of proof and probability seems entirely against it. Thus, one cannot feel the same burning sense of injustice over the matter. And yet I trust for the sake of our character not only for justice, but for intelligence, that the judgment may in some way be reconsidered and the man's present punishment allowed to atone for those irregularities of life which helped to make his conviction possible. [**Conan Doyle's reference to Slater's "irregularities of life" seems strangely hypocritical for an author who courted his future second wife for ten years before his consumptive first wife passed away.**]

Before leaving the case it is interesting to see how far this curious crime may be reconstructed and whether any possible light can be thrown upon it. Using second-hand material one cannot hope to do more than indicate certain possibilities which may already have been considered and tested by the police. The trouble, however, with all police prosecutions is that, having once got what they imagine to be their man, they are not very open to any line of investigation which might lead to other conclusions. Everything which will not fit into the official theory is liable to be excluded. One might make a few isolated comments on the case which may at least give rise to some interesting trains of thought.

One question which has to be asked was whether the assassin was after the jewels at all. It might be urged that the type of man described by the spectators was by no means that of the ordinary thief. When he reached the bedroom and lit the gas, he did not at once seize the watch and rings which were lying openly exposed upon the dressing-table. He did not pick up a half-sovereign which was lying on the dining-room table. His attention was given to a wooden box, the lid of which he wrenched open. (This, I think, was "the breaking of sticks" heard by Adams.) The papers in it were strewed on the ground. Were the papers his object, and the final abstraction of one diamond brooch a mere blind? Personally, I can only point out the possibility of such a solution. On the other hand, it might be urged, if the thief's action seems inconsequential, that Adams had rung and that he already found himself in a desperate situation. It might be said also that save a will, it would be difficult to imagine any paper which would account for such an enterprise, while the jewels, on the other hand, were an obvious mark for whoever knew of their existence.

Presuming that the assassin was indeed after the jewels, it is very instructive to note his knowledge of their location, and also its limitations. Why did he go straight into the spare bedroom where the jewels were actually kept? The same question may be asked with equal force if we consider that he was after the papers. Why the spare bedroom? Any knowledge gathered from outside (by a watcher in the back-yard for example) would go to the length of ascertaining which was the old lady's room. One would expect a robber who had gained his information thus, to go straight to that chamber. But this man did not do so. He went straight to the unlikely room in which both jewels and papers actually were. Is not this remarkably suggestive? Does it not presuppose a previous acquaintance with the inside of the flat and the ways of its owner?

But now note the limitations of the knowledge. If it were the jewels he was after, he knew what room they were in, but not in what part of the room. A fuller knowledge would have told him they were kept in the wardrobe. And yet he searched a box. If he was after papers, his information was complete; but if he was indeed after the jewels, then we can say that he had the knowledge of one who is conversant, but not intimately conversant, with the household arrangements. To this we may add that he would seem to have shown ignorance of the habits of the inmates, or he would surely have chosen Lambie's afternoon or evening out for his attempt, and not have done it at a time when the girl was bound to be back within a very few minutes. What men had ever visited the house? The number must have been very limited. What friends? what tradesmen? what plumbers? Who brought back the jewels after they had been stored with the jewellers when the old lady went every year to the country? One is averse to throw out vague suspicions which may give pain to innocent people, and yet it is clear that there are lines of inquiry here which should be followed up, however negative the results.

How did the murderer get in if Lambie is correct in thinking that she shut the doors? I cannot get away from the conclusion that he had duplicate keys. In that case all becomes comprehensible, for the old lady—whose faculties were quite normal—would hear the lock go and would not be alarmed, thinking that Lambie had returned before her time. Thus, she would only know her danger when the murderer rushed into the room, and would hardly have time to rise, receive the first blow, and fall, as she was found, beside the chair, upon which she had been sitting. [In 1912 when this book was written, Conan Doyle did not know that the first physician on the scene, a Dr. John Adams, had given a deposition to the police in which he stated he believed the mahogany chair beside which Marion Gilchrist lay when she breathed her last was the instrument by which she had been bludgeoned to death. In fact, none of Dr. Adams's initial findings were included at the trial, perhaps for the simple reason that practically none of his conclusions would have benefited the police case. They wanted the jury to believe that Slater had bent over the woman, with his knee on her chest, and beat her to death with twenty to forty blows from a tack hammer. (Yet no one who claimed to have seen Slater after the crime testified to seeing him covered with blood, which he surely would have been if he had committed the crime as the police presented it.)] That is intelligible. But if he had not the keys, consider the difficulties. If the old lady had opened the flat door her body would have been found in the passage. Therefore, the police were driven to the hypothesis that the old lady heard the ring, opened the lower stair door from above (as can be done in all Scotch flats), opened the flat door, never looked over the lighted stair to see who was coming up, but returned to her chair and her magazine, leaving the door open, and a free entrance to the murderer. This is possible, but is it not in the highest degree improbable? Miss Gilchrist was nervous of robbery and would not neglect obvious precautions. The ring came immediately after the maid's departure. She could hardly have thought that it was her returning, the less so as the girl had the keys and would not need to ring. If she went as far as the hall door to open it, she only had to take another step to see who was ascending the stair. Would she not have taken it if it were only to say: "What, have you forgotten your keys?" That a nervous old lady should throw open both doors, never look to see who her visitor was, and return to her dining-room is very hard to believe.

And look at it from the murderer's point of view. He had planned out his proceedings. It is notorious that it is the easiest thing in the world to open the lower door of a Scotch flat. The blade of any penknife will do that. If he was to depend upon ringing to get at his victim, it was evidently better for him to ring at the upper door, as otherwise the chance would seem very great that she would look down, see him coming up the stair, and shut herself in. On the other hand, if he were at the upper door and she answered it, he had only to push his way in. Therefore, the latter would be his course if he rang at all. And yet the police theory is that though he rang, he rang from below. It is not what he would do, and if he did do it, it would be most unlikely that he would get in. How could he suppose that the old lady would do so incredible a thing as leave her door open and return to her reading? If she waited, she might even up to the last instant have shut the door in his face. If one weighs all these reasons, one can hardly fail, I think, to come to the conclusion that the murderer had keys, and that the old lady never rose from her chair until the last instant, because, hearing the keys in the door, she took it for granted that the maid had come back. But if he had keys, how did he get the mould, and how did he get them made? There is a line of inquiry there. The only conceivable alternatives are, that the murderer was actually concealed in the flat when Lambie came out, and of that there is no evidence whatever, or that the visitor was some one whom the old lady knew, in which case he would naturally have been admitted.

There are still one or two singular points which invite comment. One of these, which I have incidentally mentioned, is that neither the match, the match-box, nor the box opened in the bedroom showed any marks of blood. Yet the crime had been an extraordinarily bloody one. This is certainly very singular. An explanation given by Dr. Adams who was the first medical man to view the body is worthy of attention. He considered that the wounds might have been inflicted by prods downwards from the leg of a chair, in which case the seat of the chair would preserve the clothes and to some extent the hands of the murderer from bloodstains. [**Again, Conan Doyle shows he was unfamiliar with Adams's detailed testimony.**] The condition of one of the chairs seemed to him to favour this supposition. The explanation is ingenious, but I must confess that I cannot understand how such wounds could be inflicted by such an instrument. There were in particular a number of spindle-shaped cuts with a bridge of skin between them which are very suggestive. My first choice as to the weapon which inflicted these would be a burglar's jemmy, which is bifurcated at one end, while the blow which pushed the poor woman's eye into her brain would represent a thrust from the other end. Failing a jemmy, I should choose a hammer, but a very different one from the toy thing from a half-crown card of tools which was exhibited in Court. Surely commonsense would say that such an instrument could burst an eye-ball, but could not possibly drive it deep into the brain, since the short head could not penetrate nearly so far. The hammer, which I would reconstruct from the injuries would be what they call, I believe, a plasterer's hammer, short in the handle, long and strong in the head, with a broad fork behind. But how such a weapon could be used without the user bearing marks of it, is more than I can say. It has never been explained why a rug was laid over the murdered woman. The murderer, as his conduct before Lambie and Adams showed, was a perfectly cool person. It is at least possible that he used the rug as a shield between him and his victim while he battered her with his weapon. His clothes, if not his hands, would in this way be preserved.

I have said that it is of the first importance to trace who knew of the existence of the jewels, since this might greatly help the solution of the problem. In connection with this there is a passage in Lambie's evidence in New York which is of some importance. I give it from the stenographer's report, condensing in places:

Q. "Do you know in Glasgow a man named ———?"

A. "Yes, sir."

Q. "What is his business?"

A. "A book-maker."

Q. "When did you first meet him?"

A. "At a dance."

Q. "What sort of dance?"

A. "A New Year's dance." (That would be New Year of 1908.)

Q. "When did you meet him after that?"

A. "In the beginning of June."

Q. "Where?"

A. "In Glasgow."

Q. "At a street corner?"

A. "No, he came up to the house at Prince's Street."

Q. "Miss Gilchrist's house?"

A. "Yes, sir."

Q. "That was the first time since the dance?"

A. "Yes, sir."

Q. "Do you deny that you had a meeting with him by a letter received from him at a corner of a street in Glasgow?"

A. "I got a letter."

Q. "To meet him at a street corner?"

A. "Yes."

Q. "The first meeting after the dance?"

A. "Yes."

Q. "And you met him there?"

A. "Yes."

Q. "And you went out with him?"

A. "No, I did not go out with him."

Q. "You went somewhere with him, didn't you?"

A. "Yes, I made an appointment for Sunday."

Q. "Did you know anything about the man?"

A. "Yes, I did, sir."

Q. "What did you know about him?"

A. "I didn't know much."

Q. "How many times did he visit you at Miss Gilchrist's house?"

A. "Once."

Q. "Quite sure of that?"

A. "Quite sure."

Q. "Didn't he come and take tea with you there in her apartment?"

A. "That was at the Coast."

Q. "Then he came to see you at Miss Gilchrist's summer place?"

A. "Yes."

Q. "How many times?"

A. "Once."

Q. "Did he meet Miss Gilchrist then?"

A. "Yes, sir."

Q. "You introduced him?"

A. "Yes, sir."

Q. "Did she wear this diamond brooch?"

A. "I don't remember."

Q. "When did you next see him?"

A. "The first week in September."

Q. "In Glasgow?"

A. "Yes, sir."

Q. "By appointment?"

A. "Yes."

Q. "When next?"

A. "I have not met him since."

Q. "And you say he only called once at the country place?"

A. "Once, sir."

Q. "In your Glasgow deposition you say: 'He visited me at Girvan and was entertained at tea with me on Saturday night, and at dinner on Sunday with Miss Gilchrist and me.'"

A. "Yes, sir."

Q. "Then you did see him more than once in the country."

A. "Once."

He read the extract again as above.

Q. "Was that true?"

A. "Yes."

Q. "Then you invited this man to tea at Miss Gilchrist's summer house?"

A. "Yes."

Q. "On Saturday night?"

A. "Yes."

Q. "And on Sunday night?"

A. "He wasn't there."

Q. "On Sunday you invited him there to dinner with Miss Gilchrist and yourself, didn't you?"

A. "Yes, sir. I didn't invite him."

Q. "Who invited him?"

A. "Miss Gilchrist."

Q. "Had you introduced him?"

A. "Yes, sir."

Q. "He was your friend, wasn't he?"

A. "Yes, sir."

Q. "She knew nothing about him?"

A. "No."

Q. "She took him to the house on your recommendation?"

A. "Yes."

Q. "Did she wear her diamonds at this dinner party?"

A. "I don't remember."

Q. "You told him that she was a rich woman?"

A. "Yes."

Q. "Did you tell him that she had a great many jewels?"

A. "Yes."

Q. "Have your suspicions ever turned towards this man?"

A. "Never."

Q. "Do you know of any other man who would be as familiar with those premises, the wealth of the old lady, her jewelry, and the way to get into the premises as that man?"

A. "No, sir."

Q. "Was the man you met in the hallway this man?"

A. "No, sir."

This is a condensation of a very interesting and searching piece of the cross-examination which reveals several things. One is Lambie's qualities as a witness. Another is the very curious picture of the old lady, the book-maker and the servant-maid all sitting at dinner together. The last and most important is the fact, that a knowledge of the jewels had got out. Against the man himself there is no possible allegation. The matter was looked into by the police, and their conclusions were absolute, and were shared by those responsible for the defence. But is it to be believed that during the months which elapsed between this man acquiring this curious knowledge, and the actual crime, never once chanced to repeat to any friend, who in turn repeated it to another, the strange story of the lonely old woman and her hoard? This he would do in full innocence. It was a most natural thing to do. But for almost the first time in the case we seem to catch some glimpse of the relation between possible cause and effect, some connection between the dead woman on one side, and outsiders on the other who had the means of knowing something of her remarkable situation.

There is just one other piece of Lambie's cross-examination, this time from the Edinburgh trial, which I would desire to quote. It did not appear in America, just as the American extract already given did not appear in Edinburgh. For the first time they come out together:

Q. "Did Miss Gilchrist use to have a dog?"

A. "Yes, an Irish terrier."

Q. "What happened to it?"

A. "It got poisoned."

Q. "When was it poisoned?"

A. "I think on the 7th or 8th of September."

Q. "Was that thought to be done by some one?"

A. "I did not think it, for I thought it might have eaten something, but Miss Gilchrist thought it was poisoned by some one."

Q. "To kill the watch-dog—was that the idea?"

A. "She did not say."

The reader should be reminded that Slater did not arrive in Glasgow until the end of October of that year. His previous residences in the town were as far back as 1901 and 1905. If the dog were indeed poisoned in anticipation of the crime, he, at least, could have had nothing to do with it.

There is one other piece of evidence which may, or may not have been of importance. It is that of Miss Brown, the schoolmistress. This lady was in court, but seems to have been called by neither side for the reason that her evidence was helpful to neither the prosecution nor the defence. She deposed that on the night of the murder, about ten minutes past seven, she saw two men running away from the scene. One of these men closely corresponded to the original description of the murderer before it was modified by Barrowman. This one was of medium build, dark hair and clean shaven, with three-quarter length grey overcoat, dark tweed cap, and both hands in his pockets. Here we have the actual assassin described to the life, and had Miss Brown declared that this man was the prisoner, she would have been a formidable addition to the witnesses for prosecution. Miss Brown, however identified Oscar Slater (after the usual absurd fashion of such identifications) as the second man, whom she describes, as of "Dark glossy hair, navy blue overcoat with velvet collar, dark trousers, black boots, something in his hand which seemed clumsier than a walking stick." One would imagine that this object in his hand would naturally be his hat, since she describes the man as bare-headed. All that can be said of this incident is that if the second man was Slater, then he certainly was not the actual murderer whose dress corresponds closely to the first, and in no particular to the second. To the Northern eye, all swarthy foreigners bear a resemblance, and that there was a swarthy man, whether foreign or not, concerned in this affair would seem to be beyond question. That there should have been two confederates, one of whom had planned the crime while the other carried it out, is a perfectly feasible supposition. Miss Brown's story does not necessarily contradict that of Barrowman, as one would imagine that the second man would join the murderer at some little distance from the scene of the crime. However, as there was no cross-examination upon the story, it is difficult to know what weight to attach to it.

Let me say in conclusion that I have had no desire in anything said in this argument, to hurt the feelings or usurp the functions of anyone, whether of the police or the criminal court, who had to do with the case. It is difficult to discuss matters from a detached point of view without giving offence. I am well aware that it is easier to theorise at a distance than to work a case out in practice whether as detective or as counsel. I leave the matter now with the hope that, even after many days, some sudden flash may be sent which will throw a light upon as brutal and callous a crime as has ever been recorded in those black annals in which the criminologist finds the materials for his study. Meanwhile it is on the conscience of the authorities, and in the last resort on that of the community that this verdict obtained under the circumstances which I have indicated, shall now be reconsidered.

ARTHUR CONAN DOYLE
Windlesham,
Crowborough.

CHAPTER TWO

A DESPERATE PLEA
GETS MIXED RESULTS

Oscar Slater's conviction for the murder of Marion Gilchrist on May 6, 1909, came as a shock not only to Slater but to his lawyers, courtroom spectators, and much of the general public. The case against him was circumstantial at best, but it had been buoyed by the unchallenged outright lies of the prosecutor and the judge's clear prejudice against the menacing-looking foreigner. Yet even the fifteen-man jury couldn't reach a unanimous verdict; nine voted Slater guilty, one not guilty, and five nonproven.

Imagine, then, the commotion when on such a weak case and ambivalent conviction, Slater was sentenced to hang.

In a desperate bid to save his client's life, Oscar Slater's solicitor, Ewing Spiers, appealed to the Secretary of State in Scotland for a reconsideration of the verdict. This petition, or memorial, outlined the facts of the murder and, as Conan Doyle would do later, poked holes in the prosecution's flimsy case. When Doyle first published *The Case of Oscar Slater* in 1912, he included a copy of Spiers's memorial in the volume. In faithfulness to Sir Arthur's original intentions, we do so here as well.

The appeal, by the way, was successful, but only marginally so; Slater's death sentence was commuted to life imprisonment, a concession which, at the time, may have been small comfort to the unfortunate Oscar Slater.

UNTO THE RIGHT HONOURABLE LORD PENTLAND, HIS MAJESTY'S SECRETARY OF STATE FOR SCOTLAND
MEMORIAL ON BEHALF OF OSCAR SLATER

This Memorial is humbly presented on behalf of Oscar Slater presently a Prisoner in the Prison of Glasgow, who was, in the High Court of Justiciary at Edinburgh, on Thursday, the sixth day of May, Nineteen hundred and nine, found guilty of the charge of murdering Miss Marion Gilchrist in her house in West Princes Street, Glasgow, and sentenced to death. The Prisoner is a Jew, and was born in Germany. He is 37 years of age.

The Jury returned a verdict of "Guilty" by a majority of nine to six, and the legal advisers of the condemned man hold a very strong opinion that the verdict of the majority of the Jury was not in accordance with the evidence led, and that this evidence was quite insufficient to identify the Prisoner with the murderer, and so to establish the Prisoner's guilt. This view, they believe, is shared by the general public of all classes in Scotland, and by the Glasgow press (*vide* leading article in The Glasgow Herald of 7th May, 1909, sent herewith).

Your Memorialist has endeavoured in this paper to deal with the matter as briefly and with as little argument as possible; but in view of the fact that the trial of the Prisoner occupied four days, it is inevitable that the Memorial should extend to some length.

It is common ground that the late Miss Gilchrist, a lady of about 82 years of age, resided alone with her domestic servant, Nellie Lambie, a girl of about 21 years of age.

According to the evidence of Lambie, the latter left Miss Gilchrist alone in the house at seven o'clock on the evening of 21st December, 1908, and went to purchase an evening paper. Lambie deponed that she securely shut the house door behind her, and also the door at the close, or street entry; that she was only absent about ten minutes; that on returning about ten minutes past seven o'clock she found the close door open; that upon ascending the stair she found Mr. Adams, a gentleman who resides in the flat below, standing at Miss Gilchrist's house door; that Adams informed her that he had gone up to Miss Gilchrist's door because he had heard knocking on the floor of Miss Gilchrist's house, and had rung the bell, but that he could obtain no admittance; that the lobby was lighted by one gas jet turned half up, but giving a good light; that Lambie thereupon opened the house door with her keys; that upon the door being opened a man came through the lobby or hall of Miss Gilchrist's house, passed Lambie and Adams, went downstairs, and disappeared; and that, upon Lambie and Adams entering the house, they found Miss Gilchrist lying on the dining-room floor dead, her head having been smashed.

Upon the Wednesday following the murder (23rd December, 1908), the Glasgow Police were informed by a message girl named Mary Barrowman (about 15 years of age), that she had seen a man wearing a Donegal hat and a light coat running out of the close which leads from the street to Miss Gilchrist's house shortly after seven o'clock on the night of the murder; that the man passed her, running at top speed; that she noticed that he was dark, and clean shaven, and that his nose was twisted towards the right side. The servant Lambie had also informed the Police that a gold crescent brooch, set in diamonds, had disappeared from Miss Gilchrist's house on the night of the murder, and that this was all of Miss Gilchrist's property that she missed. These statements were published in the Glasgow newspapers on Friday, 25th December, 1908, and following upon this the witness Allan Maclean, a member of a club to which Slater belonged, informed the Police that Slater's appearance somewhat corresponded with the description advertised, and that he had been trying to sell a pawn ticket for a diamond brooch. Following up this clue, the Police went to Slater's house at 69, St. George's Road, Glasgow, on the night of Friday, 25th December, and learned that he and Miss Andrée Antoine, with whom he had been cohabiting, had left Glasgow that night with their belongings. The Police thereafter ascertained that Slater had sailed on the "Lusitania" for New York from Liverpool on Saturday, 26th December, and cabled to the Authorities at New York to detain and search him on his arrival. This was done, and the pawn ticket, which he had been trying to sell, was found upon him, but turned out to be a pawn ticket for a brooch which belonged to Miss Antoine, had never belonged to Miss Gilchrist, and had been pawned a considerable time before the murder. Proceedings, however, were instituted for Slater's extradition. The witnesses Lambie, Adams, and Barrowman gave evidence in America, purporting to identify him as the man seen leaving Miss Gilchrist's house, and Slater was (he states of his own consent) extradited, and brought back to Scotland for trial.

An advertisement was published by the Authorities in Glasgow offering a reward of £200 for information which would lead to the arrest of the murderer.

The only evidence against Slater, which might be called direct evidence, was the evidence of the persons who saw a man walk out of the lobby or hall in Miss Gilchrist's house on the night of the murder (Lambie and Adams), or leaving the close leading therefrom, or running along the street (Barrowman).

At the trials Lambie professed to identify Slater, as the man whom she had seen leaving the house, by the side of his face. It was put to her, however, and clearly proved, that when she gave evidence in New York in the extradition proceedings she stated in Court there that she did not see the man's face, and professed to identify him by his walk. When Slater's own coat, the one found in his luggage, was shown to her at the trial, she at once remarked, even before it was unrolled, that it was not like the coat the man in the lobby wore—it was the coat. It was obviously impossible that she knew it to be the same coat. Lord Guthrie referred to this in his charge to the jury as a typical example of the nature of her evidence. With regard to the positive nature of her evidence generally, it is interesting to note that her first answer in America, when asked if she saw the man, was, "One is very suspicious, if anything." She stated that, when she saw Slater in the Central Police Office at Glasgow, she recognised him in his "own coat." It was proved that he was not then wearing his own coat, but one with which he had been dressed for identification purposes.

The witness only saw the man who was leaving the house for a moment or two. Adams and she contradicted each other as to where she was when the man walked across the lobby. Adams deponed that she was by the lobby clock and walking towards the kitchen. If so, she must practically have had her back to the man. She says she was on the threshold of the door. In any event, her view was momentary.

The witness Adams, who deponed that he had a better view of the man in the house than Lambie, stated at the trial that he, standing at the threshold, saw the man's face as he approached, that their eyes met, and that the man walked slowly towards him, face to face, but Adams would not go further than to say that Slater resembled the man very much. He is superior to Lambie and Barrowman in years, education and intelligence. Your Memorialist begs to emphasise the fact that this witness had a much better view of the man than any of the other witnesses.

The witness Barrowman stated at the trial that the man ran out of the close and rushed past her at top speed, brushing against her, and that he had his hat pulled well down over his forehead. The witness is a message girl, about 15 years of age. She also stated that the man had on brown boots, a Donegal hat, and a fawn coat, and that he was dark and clean shaven, and that his nose had a twist to the right. She professed to have noticed all these things as he rushed past her at top speed. At the trial this witness stated in cross-examination (1) that she was proceeding in the opposite direction from the man, to deliver a parcel, but that she turned and went some distance after him; that she thought he was probably going to catch a tram-car; but she could not explain why she should go out of her way to turn and follow a man running for a car in a busy city like Glasgow; and (2) that, although the girl Lambie and she had occupied the same cabin on the voyage to America, which lasted about twelve days, she had not once discussed the appearance of the man, and that no one had warned her not to do so. These two statements do not impress your Memorialist as bearing the stamp of truth. This girl started the description of the twisted nose. She is the only witness who refers to it. Her view of the man's face must necessarily have been momentary. Slater's nose cannot properly be described as "twisted to the right." It has a noticeable prominence in the centre.

All of these three witnesses had, as has been said, only a momentary view of the man, and it was proved that before Barrowman professed to identify Slater in New York she was shown his photograph, and that both she and Lambie, before attempting to identify him in New York, saw him being brought into Court by a Court official, wearing a badge. In her New York evidence she first said, "He is something like the man I saw." At the trial she stated that he was the man. These facts very much reduce, if they do not altogether vitiate, the value of the evidence of these identifying witnesses.

Another witness, Mrs. Liddell, who is a married sister of the witness Adams, stated that, at five minutes to seven on the evening of the murder, she saw a dark, clean-shaven man leaning against a railing at the street entry to Miss Gilchrist's house, but that this man wore a heavy brown tweed coat and a brown cap. It is to be observed that Constable Neil, who passed the house at ten minutes to seven, saw no one there: and Lambie, who left the house promptly at seven, or, as she said in America, "perhaps a few minutes before seven," saw no one there. Further, Mrs. Liddell did not observe where the man went to; according to her he merely glided away; and although she was in Miss Gilchrist's house that night and saw the body, and would naturally be greatly concerned over the murder, she did not recollect having seen this man until the Wednesday after the murder. Even taking her evidence as absolutely true and reliable, it provides an excellent object-lesson on the difficulty and responsibility of convicting on such evidence as this, because the man she saw was obviously dressed differently from the man seen by the other three witnesses. Her evidence does not, to any appreciable extent, further the case against Slater, as she stated that she thought this man was Slater, but admitted that she might be in error.

The other witness is a girl named Annie Armour, a ticket clerk in the Subway Station at Kelvinbridge, who says that between 7.30 and 8 that evening a man, whom she identified as Slater, rushed past her office without waiting for a ticket, and seemed excited. Lord Guthrie in his charge to the jury did not refer to this witness, and your Memorialist thinks advisedly. The mere question of time is sufficient to render her evidence valueless. She is sure the incident did not happen before 7.30. According to the other witnesses, the murderer must have run from the house by at least 7.15. It was proved that it would only take a man five or six minutes to run from the scene of the tragedy to this station, either by the most direct route or by the route which Barrowman's evidence suggests he took. Then it is impossible to suppose that she could get anything like a good view, even of the side face, of a man who rushed past her in the way she described.

All the witnesses who saw the man on the night of the murder (Monday) say that he was clean shaven. It was proved that on the next day or two after the murder Slater had a short, black, stubbly moustache.

These were the only witnesses called by the Crown to identify Slater with the murder. Further circumstantial evidence, however, was led by the Crown to show that, on occasions before the day of the murder, Slater had been seen standing in or walking up and down West Princes Street—Mrs. M'Haffie, her daughters and niece, Campbell, Cunningham, Bryson, Nairn, and O'Brien and Walker (two policemen). It may be noted that Slater's house was situated about three minutes' walk from West Princes Street.

These witnesses did not all agree in their evidence. Some said that Slater was the man they had seen; others, equally or perhaps better able to judge, only said that he was very like him. The Memorialist does not propose in this paper to deal at length with this part of the evidence, except to point out that two witnesses (Nairn and Bryson) say they saw Slater in West Princes Street on the Sunday evening previous to the murder. Against this there is the evidence that Slater on this day, as usual, spent all Sunday (day and evening) in his house. Three witnesses from Paris, London, and Dublin spoke to this. Coming from different places, they had no chance to concoct a story.

At Slater's trial it was suggested that there were various circumstances tending to create an atmosphere of suspicion around him; but it is submitted that all these were capable of explanation, and in no way pointing to Slater's guilt as a murderer. Slater had written to Cameron that he could prove where he was on the evening of the murder "by five people." When this letter was written, he thought that the date of the murder was the Tuesday, the 22nd.

The evidence of his witnesses was to the effect that on the evening of the murder he was in a billiard room until 6.30 p.m, after which he went home for dinner.

It was shown that Slater dealt in diamonds. There was, however, no evidence of any dishonest dealing of any kind. The brooch said to have been missing from Miss Gilchrist's house has not been traced. There was no evidence of any kind led to show that Slater ever knew, or even heard of, Miss Gilchrist or her house, and the Memorialist would emphasise the fact that it was the missing brooch that put the Police on the track of Slater.

With reference to Slater's departure for America on 25th December, 1908, it was proved that he had formed the intention, some weeks before the murder, of going to America. Cameron, Rattman, and Aumann proved this. Slater had, in fact, tried to get the last named to take over his flat. The letter from Jacobs, of 28th December, and the card bearing the words "address till 30th December," produced by the Crown, also corroborate the evidence of this intention of leaving, which is further corroborated by the evidence of Nichols, the barber, a Crown witness.

On the morning of 21st December, 1908, Slater received two letters—one from London, stating that his wife was demanding his address, and the other from San Francisco, asking him to come over. These were spoken to by

Schmalz, his servant girl, and Miss Antoine. Further corroboration of his intention to leave is (1) on the morning of 21st December he raised a further £30 from Mr. Liddell, pawnbroker, on his brooch, and on the same day tried to sell the ticket; (2) he wrote to the Post Office for payment of the money at his credit; (3) he wired to Dent, London, to send on his watch, which was being repaired, immediately; (4) on the Monday morning he gave notice to the servant girl that she would not be required after the following Saturday (these events all happened before the murder); (5) on the Tuesday morning he redeemed a pair of binoculars from another pawnbroker whose assistant, Kempton, proved this, and who stated that he was in no way excited; (6) on the 23rd and 24th December he made inquiries at Cook's Shipping Offices regarding berths, and betrayed no signs of any excitement; on the 23rd he was, in the evening, in Johnston's billiard room, which he used to frequent; and on the 24th he spent the afternoon about Glasgow with his friend Cameron, who gave evidence; (7) on Friday morning a Mrs. Freedman and her sister arrived from London to take over his flat, so that he and Miss Antoine left on Friday night.

A rumour got abroad at the time to the effect that he booked to London and left the train at Liverpool. This rumour was published in the various newspapers, to Slater's great prejudice, but nothing of the kind was proved at the trial. The Police were evidently misled by the fact that he went by a London train, but it was proved that there were two carriages in that train for Liverpool, and also that Slater's luggage, consisting of nine boxes, was labelled to Liverpool. The Porter who labelled the luggage was called, and stated that Slater told him that he was going to Liverpool, and entered a Liverpool carriage.

The point was also raised against Slater that he used various aliases. He had been staying apart from his wife for about four years, during which time he cohabited with Miss Antoine. She stated that Slater's wife was a drunken woman, and caused him a deal of trouble. At one time he adopted the name of "George," and when he came to Glasgow on the last occasion he took the name of "Anderson." On the voyage to America he took the name of Otto Sando, because his luggage was labelled O.S. At times he called himself a dentist. There was no evidence that he really was a dentist. Miss Antoine explained that he adopted the title of dentist, as he required a designation of some sort, although he was a gambler. A great deal was published in the newspapers about a hammer that had been found in one of his boxes. This turned out to be an ordinary small domestic nail hammer, purchased on a card containing several other tools, the lot costing only 2s. 6d. He, of course, took the hammer to America with him with all the rest of his belongings.

Nothing incriminating was found in any of his boxes.

No evidence whatever was led to show how the murderer gained access to the house.

It will be conceded that identification evidence, especially in a serious charge of this kind, must be examined very carefully, and should have little weight attached to it, unless it is very clear.

To sum up, the only real evidence in the case is that of those who saw a man running away on the night of the murder; and, as has been pointed out, these witnesses had only a momentary glance at him. Adams does not positively identify the prisoner as the man. He says he closely resembles him.

Lambie's New York evidence has already been referred to, and her evidence at the trial cannot be reconciled with it.

Lambie and Barrowman both saw him in custody before trying to identify him in New York, and the latter, before identifying him, was shown his photograph.

All the other identifying witnesses called to give evidence as to his having been seen in the vicinity on days previous to the murder were taken down to the General Police Office when Slater returned from America to identify him. They were shown into one room together, and then separately taken into a room in the Police Office, where Slater was amongst about a dozen men, none of whom were like him. (Cunningham says she could see that the other men were policemen in plain clothes.) All these witnesses knew that Slater had arrived from America, and was in the room. They had all read his

description in the newspapers, or had seen his photograph. They all, therefore, looked for, and had no difficulty in pointing out, a dark, foreign-looking
man, with a somewhat peculiarly shaped nose. It is submitted that this is not
identification evidence in the proper sense at all. Had these people been able
to pick out, as their man, from amongst several others, a man whose description they only knew from what they had previously seen of him, unassisted
by description, and unassisted by a photograph, the value of their evidence
would have been entirely different.

Some Crown witnesses identified him as the man they had seen and
talked to (Shipping Clerk, Porter, &c.), but they, of course, were able to do
so. None of the identifying witnesses had ever spoken to him.

Identification evidence is a class of evidence which the law distrusts.
The most famous authority is the case of Adolf Beck. Beck was, in 1896,
sentenced to seven years penal servitude, on the evidence of ten women,
who swore positively that he was a man whom they had each met on two
occasions, and spent some time with in their own houses, and who had
defrauded them, and on the evidence of two policemen, who swore positively that Beck was the man who had been previously convicted of similar
crimes, taken along with certain circumstantial evidence—that he was
known to frequent a hotel on the notepaper of which one of the women had
received a letter. Again, in 1904, Beck was convicted of similar crimes on
similar evidence. It was subsequently demonstrated that Beck committed
none of the crimes, but that a man bearing a general similarity to him was
the criminal.

In the report issued by the Commission appointed to investigate the
matter, consisting of Lord Collins, Sir Spencer Walpole, and Sir John Edge,
the following passage occurs:—"Evidence of identity, upon personal impression, however bona fide, is of all classes of evidence the least to be relied
upon, and, unless supported by other evidence, an unsafe basis for the verdict
of a Jury."

Now, the evidence in the Beck case was infinitely more overwhelming
and consistent than in this case; and the report in the Beck case, and the

report on which it followed, make it clear that on the evidence in this case the Jury had no right to bring in a verdict of "Guilty."

A good deal was said by the learned Lord Advocate to the Jury about Slater's immoral character. It was not disputed that he was a gambler. It was also admitted that he had cohabited for about four years with Madame Antoine, who was of doubtful virtue, and who gave evidence. Yet the learned Lord Advocate addressed the Jury to the effect that the prisoner "had followed a life which descended to the very depth of human degradation, for, by the universal judgment of mankind, the man who lived upon the proceeds of prostitution has sunk to the lowest depth, and all moral sense in him had been destroyed." This he cited as proof of the disappearance of an obstacle which had previously been in his way, viz:—Whether it was conceivable that such a man as Slater could commit such an inhumanly brutal crime. The only evidence on that point was that of Cameron, Slater's friend, who, in cross-examination, said he had heard that Slater lived on the earnings of prostitution, but who did not say he knew. The Jury were distinctly told by the Lord Advocate, and by the prisoner's Counsel, and by the Judge, to banish from their minds anything they had heard regarding the man's character; but they had previously heard all about it, and the Memorialist feels strongly that they were evidently unable to do so.

Public feeling is also very strong on the point that the question of Slater's character should never have been brought before the Jury.

The Memorialist thinks it is only fair to prisoner to point out that he was all along anxious to give evidence on his own behalf. He was advised by his Counsel not to do so, but not from any knowledge of guilt. He had undergone the strain of a four days' trial. He speaks rather broken English—although quite intelligibly—with a foreign accent, and he had been in custody since January.

Apart from what has been set forth above, your Memorialist begs to draw attention to the fact that on the Crown list of witnesses is the name of a witness, Miss Agnes Brown (No. 46). This lady is 30 years of age, and a very intelligent school teacher. Your Memorialist is informed that she told the Police and Procurator-Fiscal that on the night of the murder, about ten minutes past seven o'clock, two men in company rushed along West Princes Street from the direction of Miss Gilchrist's house, and passed close to her at the corner of West Princes Street and West Cumberland Street; that one of them was dressed in a blue Melton coat with a dark velvet collar, black boots, and without a hat; that both men ran past the opening of West Cumberland Street, straight on along West Princes Street, crossed West Princes Street, and ran down Rupert Street, a street further west, and opening off the opposite side of West Princes Street. Your Memorialist understands that, in the identification proceedings before referred to, this witness pointed out Slater as the man in the Melton coat, as she thought. This witness's evidence is thus in sharp contradiction on material points to that of the message girl Barrowman (who had only a momentary glance at the man), but upon whose evidence so much weight has evidently been laid, and who says that Slater was dressed in a light coat, a Donegal hat, and brown boots, was alone, and ran down West Cumberland Street.

Your Memorialist respectfully submits that this illustrates the danger of convicting a man upon the kind of evidence given in this case. Miss Brown was in attendance at the trial, but was not called as a witness. Even on the evidence led, the votes of two more jurymen in his favour would have liberated the prisoner. In England the probability is that a conviction would never have been obtained.

Your Memorialist is authorised to state that Slater's Counsel agree that the evidence did not justify the conviction.

Your Memorialist, who has all along acted as Slater's Solicitor since he was brought back from America after the Extradition Proceedings, and who has had very many interviews with Slater, begs respectfully to state his absolute belief in Slater's innocence.

May it therefore please the Right Honourable the Secretary of State for Scotland to take this Memorial into his most favourable consideration, and

thereafter to advise his Most Gracious Majesty to exercise his royal prerogative to the effect of commuting the sentence passed upon the prisoner, or to
do otherwise as in the circumstances may seem just.

And your Memorialist will ever pray.

EWING SPIERS,
190 West George Street, Glasgow, Oscar Slater's Solicitor
Dated this seventeenth day of May, One thousand nine hundred and
nine.
Editors' note: The appeal was denied!

SLATER FINALLY GETS HIS SAY

When *The Truth About Oscar Slater* by William Park was published by Sir Arthur Conan Doyle in 1927, it came with the subtitle *With the Prisoner's Own Story*. Here now is Slater's own account of himself and the blighted days surrounding Christmas of 1908. Although Slater was finally set free on the reopening of his case in the year 1928, he was never allowed to make his own statement before open court. Even his defenders thought he made such a poor appearance they did not want him to open his mouth. This written statement, with supplementary notes by Park, was all he was ever allowed.

This excerpt is taken from the book *The Truth About Oscar Slater* by William Park. The items marked "Note" are by him.

Note.—The prisoner's story, as furnished to his law agent while in Duke Street Prison, Glasgow, in preparation for the trial at Edinburgh. This statement was taken by the late Mr. Ewing Spiers, of Messrs. Shaughnessy & Co., and was passed to the writer, authenticated by the firm, in its original form. Slater intended to give his own statement to the

Jury, but after four days' strenuous and painful ordeal, his Counsel, having regard to his broken English, deemed it prudent not to put his client in the box. The original statement of the prisoner as so taken is now presented with slight annotations to make clear the significance of the various points.

I am thirty-seven years of age. I am a Jew. I was born in Germany. I left that country because I did not wish to serve in the Army. When I came to this country I acted as a bookmaker's clerk. I stayed in Glasgow and Edinburgh. I was married seven years ago in Glasgow to May Curtis. Our marriage was unfortunate. I met Antoine about five years ago in London. I was residing at the time in Russell Square. About eighteen months later we left for Brussels, where we stayed together for about three weeks. We visited New York and stayed there for about a year. Paris was our next place of residence, two months being spent there. It was London next, spending several months in that City.

We came to Glasgow about the beginning of November last or the end of October. I stayed for some days in the Central Station Hotel, and thereafter for some time at 138 Renfrew Street, Glasgow. About the middle of November I rented a flat at 69 St. George's Road. I had it furnished on the instalment system. I paid them £16. Miss Antoine, who is a Frenchwoman, was with me there, and we had a servantmaid named Catherine Schmalz. I frequented the M.O.S.C. Club in India Street. I have also been in the Motor Club next door. For some time prior to 25th December, 1908, I had formed the ambition to go back to America, as I thought I would make more money there. I had received a letter from a friend called John De Voto in San Francisco asking me to come out. I showed this letter to my friends, Rattman and Cameron, and I frequently stated my intention of going to America with my friends. With this view I was in negotiation with a Mr. Aumann (a witness at the trial) to try to get him to take over my furnished flat. I understand that his wife did not agree with this idea and negotiations fell through. I thereafter wrote to a friend of mine in London called Freedman asking him to take over my flat, and I made up my mind to leave Glasgow immediately his wife came.

Mrs. Freedman and her sister, Elsie Hoppe, arrived at my flat on Friday, 25th December, 1908, and I gave her the keys of the house. She made no payment to me but this was to be sent on.

Note.—This evidence of Slater's, afterwards admitted by the police to be correct, destroyed the whole story laid to his charge at the trial by Superintendent Ord and the Lord Advocate that it was the publication of his name and description (that also totally wrong) which sent Slater flying out of Glasgow after the murder. Ord told the 1914 Commissioner that when Freedman called, she found Slater "packing up." What else was he to have done since he had brought the people from London who were to take over his flat, and had actually installed them?

Miss Antoine and I left Glasgow with the 9.05 p.m. train from the Central Station. I had that evening taken two tickets for Liverpool—one for myself and one for Antoine. My luggage was labelled for Liverpool at the station. I did not change trains. The carriage that I travelled in went right through to Liverpool.

Note.—This refers to a statement in the early newspaper reports, prompted by the police, that Slater took London tickets but broke his journey and went on to Liverpool. We also showed that in this statement Slater was challenged by railway officials as being in error as to the through-carriage to Liverpool, and his persistence in this led them at length to remember that it was Christmas night and that a special throughcarriage had been added.

My luggage consisted of nine boxes and a parcel. My luggage was weighed at the station, and I had to pay excess rate amounting to £1 2s. 6d. I asked for Liverpool tickets. No one challenged the tickets.

Note.—The police attempted to make out at the trial that he took tickets for London. The information from Liverpool was there were "only two tickets" handed up there; while, if he had occupied the through Liverpool carriage the guard or inspector checking the tickets would have instructed him to leave the carriage and these officials would have been produced as witnesses against him.

We sailed by the *Lusitania* for New York next day, having previously put up at the North Western Hotel, Liverpool. We took the name of Mr. and Mrs. Otto Sando from the hotel. I wrote a letter to Max Rattman (produced at the trial). I took the name of Otto Sando because my luggage was labelled "O.S.," and I did not wish to travel under the name Oscar Slater, as I did not wish my wife to have trace of me. Our servant, Catherine Schmalz, saw us off in the train from the Central Station, and it was arranged that she should remain with the Freedmans in our Glasgow flat for a day or so.

I know nothing about the murder of Miss Gilchrist. I never heard of her or her servant before the murder, and when the police stopped me at New York that was the first intimation that I ever had I was suspected. The police found a pawn-ticket in my pocket for a gold brooch set with three rows of diamonds. This brooch belonged to Miss Antoine. I had pawned it with Mr. Liddell, pawnbroker, Sauchiehall Street, about the middle of November, 1908. During the week on which I left Glasgow, I endeavoured to sell this ticket to various people but did not succeed. I remember being in Galls' Public House in the afternoon of Monday, 21st December (day of tragedy), where I met Rattman and Aumann. I tried to sell the pawn-ticket then. I went alone also that afternoon to Miller's public-house in Cambridge Street, to try to sell the ticket. I remember that evening later I was with Rattman and Aumann in Johnstone's billiard room, and I remember shortly after 6 p.m. sending a telegram from Central Station Telegraph Office to Dent, London, for my watch, which was under repair. If I said in some of my telegrams to him that I was going to the Continent this was simply to hurry him up.

My recollection is that I was in Miller's public-house that evening shortly before seven o'clock and went straight home for dinner, arriving there at seven o'clock [the moment of the tragedy], but I may be wrong in this [it is to be remembered Slater was here speaking at a date two months after events] and may have come from Johnstone's billiard rooms, leaving it about 6.30 p.m. and arriving home at 7 o'clock. After dinner I may have left my house between seven and eight o'clock. I cannot remember definitely where I spent the remainder of the evening.

Note.—It is to be recollected that the witness McBrayne, unheard at the trial, found Slater at the foot of his stairway at 8.15 p.m.

I am aware that the witness Henderson has said that on the night of the murder about a quarter to ten I called at his Club, the Motor Club, and asked for the loan of money. I am almost sure I did not do so that night. As a matter of fact I had that very day obtained from Mr. Liddell, pawnbroker, a further allowance of £30 on the brooch. I had no bills to pay. I remember borrowing some money from Beveridge and I am quite sure that it was the same night that I borrowed the money from Beveridge that I asked Henderson for the money. I understand Beveridge states that I borrowed from him on the Saturday night previous to the night of the murder. This is likely to be right. I did not go back immediately to the M.O.S.C. Club after talking to Henderson. I cannot remember anything more as to how I spent the Monday evening. I had no notice until I reached America that I would ever be called upon to explain, and to me that night is just like any other might.

Note.—Slater did not ascertain the date of the murder until sometime after his arrest at New York. It would probably be almost a month before he was asked to say where he had been on the night of the tragedy.

I may say that I ordered Christmas cards from More, Sauchiehall Street, with my name, Oscar Slater, on them, on the 19th December [this, two days before the murder: an act which makes ridiculous the police story of prior watching of Miss Gilchrist's house and flight so soon as the crime was over].

During the rest of the week after the Monday I went about just as usual. I frequented my usual billiard rooms, the Crown billiard rooms and the Johnstone's billiard rooms. I called at my usual barbers, Charing Cross, and was shaved. In this connection I may explain that I had a short black moustache. When I left Glasgow I had been letting it grow for about two weeks. I spent Thursday afternoon with my friend, Cameron, about the city. I posted a Bank of England £5 note to my people in Germany that afternoon in a registered envelope at Hope Street Post Office.

Regarding the hammer found in my box I purchased it from Messrs. Hepburn & Marshall, Charing Cross. I wanted a hammer to fix things up when I took possession of my flat, but instead of buying a hammer alone, I saw a card with hammers and other tools on it and I bought the lot for 2s. 6d. I took it with us to America as part of my belongings. I think it was in a box in the hold during the voyage.

I did not cut any holes in my waterproof. These may have been mud-stains on the waterproof as it got frequently splashed with mud. I know of no other stains.

Note.—The Crown cut the holes to examine some stains on the coat for blood. None found.

The hammer was never washed so far as I am aware.

It is not true that on the night of the murder I rushed through Kelvin-bridge Subway or that I ran along West Princes Street. I was in neither of those places that night.

Note.—McBrayne corroborated, but he was ignored.

I never loitered about West Princes Street. I never inquired at any house there for anybody called Anderson. I never stood in that street during the day about one o'clock. I usually had lunch at 1 p.m. in my house.

It is not the case that on the Sunday evening before the murder I was loitering about on the street. I was in the house on the whole of that Sunday and dined on that evening with Antoine and a man named Reid, who did not leave the house till about 10 o'clock.

Note.—This is in denial of a statement by two witnesses, Bryson and Grant, who told the Jury they saw a man like Slater in West Princes Street. Their identification was far from satisfactory. One said that at a distance of thirteen yards he knew him by his "back." The man spoken of as Reid corroborated Slater at the trial that he had dined with the prisoner at his house.

I am informed that Rattman says that a few nights after the murder he referred to it, and that I had said I had not heard of it. This must be a mistake. I remember we were standing near my house about midnight on one occasion and what I certainly meant was that I had not known that the scene of the murder was so near at hand. We then went to have a look at the street where it took place.

The witnesses who tried to identify me (Lambie and Barrowman) in America in the American Court, were standing at the end of a corridor, and I was brought along the corridor between a marshall, 6 ft. 2 ins. in height, and another official. One of these officials had on a badge. These witnesses could not help knowing that I was in charge of these men.

[Some other minor items not included.]

NO. 2

Humbly showeth,

That the Petitioner has charged Oscar Slater alias Otto Sando, alias Anderson, sometimes of 69 St. George's Road, Glasgow, *with the crime of murder of Miss Marion Gilchrist,* in her house at 15 Queen's Terrace, West Princes Street, Glasgow, on 21st December, 1908.

That it appears that said Oscar Slater, alias Otto Sando, alias Anderson, was on said date, and for some time before and some time thereafter in a house at 69 St. George's Road, aforesaid, taken by him in name of "A. Anderson," and *that he has since absconded.*

That it seems necessary that a search be made of the house, clothing, papers and repositories therein, and the petitioner therefore craves warrant to officers of law to search the said house where the said Oscar Slater, alias Otto Sando, alias Anderson, then resided, and all papers, clothing and repositories therein.

May it therefore please your Lordship to grant warrant to search for and secure for the purpose of precognition all articles, papers, clothing or documents found therein, importing guilt or participation in the crime foresaid.

According to Justice,

(SGD.) JAMES N. HART, P.F.
Glasgow,
2nd January, 1909.

The Sheriff Substitute grants warrant as craved.

(SGD.) A. T. GLEGG

Note.—This document shows that the house vacated by Slater was searched for all articles "importing guilt." None was found, which converts the document into another argument in favour of the prisoner's innocence.

NO. 3

MINNIE HEPBURN OR HAMILTON

Statement of evidence given to Slater's agent in May, 1909, and re-confirmed at date of publication.

I am twenty-nine years of age. Up to a short time ago I had a restaurant at 415 Argyle Street. At that time I was staying at my present address.

I have a friend named Mrs. Roger, who stays in Argyle Street, Mary-hill, and I am in the habit of visiting her. She is a great friend of mine.

I remember the evening of 21st December, 1908, I had been up at Mrs. Roger's that evening. I had taken the car there, but, as I am fond of walking, I walked back to my restaurant in Argyle Street.

I left Mrs. Roger's house some time after six o'clock, not later than 6.30 anyway. I cannot remember what street I took after leaving New City Road, but after leaving Great Western Road, I went through Melrose Street, Queen's Terrace and into West Princes Street.

So soon as I got into West Princes Street I crossed to the opposite side of the road. I was proceeding down West Princes Street when a man came running down so quickly that he knocked me down. I was knocked right off the pavement. I saw him as he was coming down the steps. He was a man of about medium height, slimly built, with a Donegal hat on and a light waterproof, brown leggings and brown boots. He had a fair moustache, and it was pretty long at the points. It was a heavy moustache.

The waterproof had a wide sack back and came down to the top of his leggings. So far as I could see there was no split in the back of the water-proof.

So far as I could see the man had a thin face. The Donegal hat was well pulled down over his eyes. He had both hands in his pockets.

I was surprised at the time, as the man did not offer to apologise to me nor help me up, but ran on at full speed towards St. George's Road. I got up and looked after him as he ran away. I did not see anybody else in the street at the time.

I arrived at my shop in Argyle Street about a quarter to eight. I think the incident I refer to would happen about 7.15 p.m.

I thought nothing more of it at the time, nor did I connect this man in any way with the murder until the day of Miss Gilchrist's funeral. I think on that day there was a photo of Miss Gilchrist's house in the newspaper. Whenever I saw the photo of the house I remarked to the servant in the house that it was there I was knocked down by the man. I had not mentioned to anyone that I had been knocked down in West Princes Street.

When I saw the photo of the house and with what I read in the newspaper about when the murder took place, I at once thought that this man might have had something to do with it.

I recognised the house at once. I have been in West Princes Street several times since, and I have recognised Miss Gilchrist's close as the place out of which the man came. I did not see any other person in the street at the time.

I did not know about the murder until next morning. I also mentioned the incident to my husband when I saw the photograph of Miss Gilchrist's house.

When Slater was brought from America I wanted to go to the Shaughnessy's office and tell my story, but my husband did not want me to be mixed up with it and persuaded me not to go.

I have not told my husband about coming here to-day. I happened to be up the same stair on other business, and I thought I would come in and tell what I had seen.

I have seen a photo of Slater in the newspaper and he is certainly not the man I saw running away that night.

NO. 4

EMPIRE NEWS EXTRACT

How the mistaken brooch clue disappeared from the case and a new originating clue was substituted to explain the arrest.

The following extract from a well-informed article in the *Empire News* draws attention to one point of the case which is of supreme importance, namely, the strange way in which when the original brooch clue broke down utterly, the cause of arrest was suddenly shifted on to quite another matter, and the Jury was so handled that it quite lost sight of the fact that the second reason had been substituted for the first:—

It is one of the new points against the police (and this is absolutely fresh to it) that the Jury was entirely misled at the trial as to the nature of the originating cause of the arrest of Slater, and that the Crown presented to the Court an absolutely new case, one that did not exist in reality, and was inconsistent to the known facts concerning his arrest.

This was achieved in the following manner before the Court. As little as possible, apparently, was said about the brooch clue. It only came out at the trial, furtively, and without clear and distinct reference to it having been the originating cause of Slater's arrest.

On the other hand, Superintendent Ord, as chief of the police, stated to the Jury that one Allan McLean reported to him that he had observed in the newspapers a description of the murderer, as provided by an eye-witness who had seen the culprit run along the street, and that he thought this description agreed with the man whom he knew, Slater.

Founding upon that statement, the Lord Advocate told the Jury that the description furnished by that eye-witness, Barrowman, had been so accurate it had enabled the police to trace the prisoner.

TWO DIFFERENT STORIES

McLean said to the police:—

I noticed that after the murder of Miss Gilchrist on 21st December he [Slater] did not return to the club, and on hearing that he had been offering a pawn-ticket for a valuable diamond brooch, which was alleged to have been pledged for £50 on the day of the murder, I, on Friday, 25th December, went to the detective department, Central Police Office, and reported the matter.

Nothing there about the resemblance to a description he had read in the papers between it and Slater.

Before the 1914 Commissioner, who afterwards inquired into the case, here is what McLean said on the question of what made him report Slater to the police:—

It was not so much his absence from the club that directed my suspicion towards him *as his offering the pawn-ticket for sale.*

Here is what Ord said to the Jury:—

About 6.10 p.m. on 25th December the witness Allan McLean called at the Central Police Office. He gave me information where a man of the description (published that day in the paper) was to be found. *He said that in consequence of the description having appeared in the newspapers, he had called to give me information about the man.*

The Jury got a new story altogether. They believed that Slater was arrested because in appearance he was like the man who ran out of the house of the victim. The truth was he was arrested because he had a pawn-ticket for a diamond brooch, which was his own property.

[The Glasgow police never reopened the case of Marion Gilchrist. Too many of the principals were dead by the time Slater was released some twenty years after the trial.]

SELECTED BIBLIOGRAPHY

Booth, Martin. *The Doctor and the Detective: A Biography of Sir Arthur Conan Doyle.* New York: St. Martin's Minotaur, 1997.

Costello, Peter. *The Real World of Sherlock Holmes: The True Crimes Investigated by Sir Arthur Conan Doyle.* New York: Carroll & Graf Publishers, 1991.

Lellenberg, Jon L., ed. *The Quest for Sir Arthur Conan Doyle: Thirteen Biographers in Search of a Life.* Carbondale and Edwardsville: Southern Illinois University Press, 1987.

Nordon, Pierre. *Conan Doyle: A Biography.* New York: Holt, Rinehart and Winston, 1967.

Park, William. *The Truth About Oscar Slater: With the Prisoner's Own Story.* London: The Psychic Press, 1927.

Roughead, William. *Classic Crimes.* London: Cassell, 1951.

Stashower, Daniel. *Teller of Tales: The Life of Arthur Conan Doyle.* New York: Henry Holt and Company, 1999.

Toughill, Thomas. *Oscar Slater: The Mystery Solved.* London: Canongate, 1993.

Watson, Eric Russell. *Adolf Beck, 1841–1909*. Edinburgh: W. Hodge, 1924.

Whittington-Egan, Richard and Molly., ed., *The Story of Mr. George Edalji*. London: Grey House Books, 1985.